REVERED WISDOM:

JUDAISM

REVERED WISDOM

JUDAISM

STERLING INNOVATION
An imprint of Sterling Publishing Co., Inc.

New York / London
www.sterlingpublishing.com

STERLING, the Sterling logo, STERLING INNOVATION,
and the Sterling Innovation logo are registered trademarks of
Sterling Publishing Co., Inc.

10 9 8 7 6 5 4 3 2 1

The text in this book is abridged versions of *The Makers and Teachers of
Judaism: From the Fall of Jerusalem to the Death of Herod the Great* by Charles
Foster Kent PhD, originally published in 1911 and *Jewish Literature and
Other Essays* by Gustav Karpeles, originally published in 1895.

Published by Sterling Publishing Co., Inc.
387 Park Avenue South, New York, NY 10016

Distributed in Canada by Sterling Publishing
c/o Canadian Manda Group, 165 Dufferin Street
Toronto, Ontario, Canada M6K 3H6

Distributed in the United Kingdom by GMC Distribution Services
Castle Place, 166 High Street, Lewes, East Sussex, England BN7 1XU

Distributed in Australia by Capricorn Link (Australia) Pty. Ltd.
P.O. Box 704, Windsor, NSW 2756, Australia

Printed in Singapore

Design by Barbara Balch

Sterling ISBN 978-1-4027-7042-5

For information about custom editions, special sales, premium and
corporate purchases, please contact Sterling Special Sales Department
at 800-805-5489 or specialsales@sterlingpublishing.com.

CONTENTS

....

Preface to Part I • 8

PART I:

THE MAKERS AND TEACHERS

OF JUDAISM • *13*

SECTION I: THE EXILE AND REVIVAL OF THE
JUDEAN COMMUNITY • *15*

1 : The Jews in Palestine and Egypt • *17*

2 : Ezekiel's Message to His Scattered
Countrymen • *30*

3 : The Closing Years of the Babylonian Rule • *39*

4 : The Rebuilding of the Temple • *52*

5 : Zechariah's Visions and Encouraging
Addresses • *60*

6 : Israel's Training and Destiny • *68*

7 : Conditions and Problems Within the Judean
Community • *76*

8 : The Problem and Teachings of the Book
of Job • *82*

9: The Training and Mission of the True
Servant of Jehovah · *93*

10: Nehemiah's Work in Rebuilding the Walls
of Jerusalem · *101*

11: Nehemiah's Social and Religious Reforms · *110*

12: Traditional Account of the Adoption of the
Priestly Law · *116*

13: The Jewish State during the Last Century
of Persian Rule · *124*

SECTION II: THE GREEK AND
MACCABEAN AGE · *135*

14: The Jews under Their Greek Rulers · *137*

15: The Wise and Their Teachings · *147*

16: The Different Currents of Thought in
Judaism during the Greek Period · *160*

17: The Teachings of Jesus, the Son of Sirach · *168*

18: The Causes of the Maccabean Struggle · *177*

19: The Effect of Persecution upon the Jews · *186*

20: The Victories That Gave the Jews Religious
Liberty · *192*

21: The Long Contest for Political
Independence · *200*

22: Peace and Prosperity under Simon • *209*

23: The Rule of John Hyrcanus and Aristobulus • *215*

24: The Pharisees, Sadducees, and Essenes • *220*

25: The Life and Faith of the Jews of the
Dispersion • *226*

26: The Decline of the Maccabean Kingdom • *235*

SECTION III: THE RULE OF ROME • *243*

27: The Rise of the Herodian House • *245*

28: Herod's Policy and Reign • *252*

29: Herod's Temple • *259*

30: The Messianic Hopes and the Religious
Beliefs of Judaism • *265*

Preface to Part II • *274*

PART II:
JEWISH LITERATURE • *277*

31: A Glance at Jewish Literature • *279*

32: The Talmud • *317*

Index • *334*

The period represented by this volume is in many ways the most complex and confusing in Israel's history. The record is not that of the life of a nation but of the scattered remnants of a race. It was inevitable that under the influence of their varied environment, the survivors of the Jewish race should develop very different beliefs and characteristics. The result is that many different currents of thought and shades of belief are reflected in the literature of this period; some of it is dross, but much of it is purest gold. While the period following the destruction of Jerusalem was a reflective and a retrospective age in which the teaching of the earlier priests and prophets gained wide acceptance, it was also a creative era. Fully half of the literature of the Old Testament and all of the important writings of the Apocrypha come from these tragic five centuries. Although the historical records are by no means complete, the great crises in Israel's life are illuminated by such remarkable historical writings as the memoirs of Nehemiah, the first book of Maccabees, and the detailed histories of Josephus. The majority of the writings, however, reveal above all the soul of the race. Out of its anguish and suffering came the immortal poems found in Isaiah 40–66, the book of Job, and the Psalter. Instead of the distinctly nationalistic point of view, which characterizes practically all of the writings of the pre-exilic period, the interest becomes individual and the outlook universal. During these centuries Israel's prophets, priests, and sages became not merely teachers of the nation but of humanity. Conspicuous among the great teachers of his day stands the noble sage, Jesus the son of Sirach, who gleaned out and presented in effective form that which was most vital in the earlier teaching of his race. In his broad, simple faith in God and man, in his emphasis on deeds and character, as well as ceremonial, and in his practical philosophy of life he was a worthy forerunner of the Great Teacher whose name he bore. This period represents the culmination and fruition of the divine influences at work in Israel's early history. It was during this period that Judaism was born and attained its full development, Israel accepted the absolute rule of the written law, and the scribes succeeded the earlier prophets and sages. Out of the heat and conflict of the Maccabean struggle the parties of the Pharisees and Sadducees sprang into existence and won their commanding place in the life of Judaism. Hence this period is the natural historical introduction to the study of the birth and early development of Christianity. It is also the link that binds the revelation found in the Old Testament to that of the New. The volume of literature coming from this period is so vast that it has been necessary to abridge it at many points in order to utilize that which is most valuable. This has been done by leaving out those passages which are of secondary origin or value, and by preserving at the same time the language and logical thought of the original writers. In the verbose and voluminous writings of Josephus the resulting text is in most cases far clearer and more useful; for the repetitious clauses found in the original often obscure the real thought of the writer. No apology or explanation is required for the use of such apocryphal writings as I Maccabees, Ben Sira, the Wisdom of Solomon, or Josephus's histories, for these are required to bridge the two centuries which intervene between the latest writings of the Old Testament and the earliest writings of the New. They make it possible to study biblical history as an unbroken unit from the days of Moses to the close of the first Christian century, and thus concretely to emphasize the significant but often the forgotten fact that God was revealing himself unceasingly through the life of his people, and that the Bible which records that revelation consists not of two disconnected parts but is one book.

THE MAKERS AND TEACHERS OF JUDAISM

SECTION I

THE EXILE AND REVIVAL OF THE JUDEAN COMMUNITY

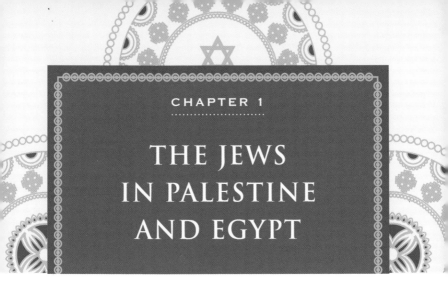

CHAPTER 1

THE JEWS IN PALESTINE AND EGYPT

The destruction of Jerusalem in 586 B.C. resulted in a mighty transformation of the life and thought of Israel. It marked the final overthrow of the old Hebrew kingdoms and the gradual rise of that new and important factor in human history known as Judaism. For more than three centuries the Jews who survived the great catastrophe were helpless under the rule of the great world powers that in succession conquered southwestern Asia. For the great majority of the Jewish race it represented the beginning of that long exile that has continued until the present. Scattered from the desert of Sahara to the distant land of China, and from the Black Sea to the Indian Ocean, the different groups of exiles quickly began to adapt themselves to their changed surroundings and to absorb the new knowledge and the powerful influences that gradually transformed their beliefs and ideals. While their vision was vastly broadened by this contact, the danger and horror of being completely engulfed in the great heathen world bound the faithful more closely together, and in time made Judaism a solid, unbreakable rock that has withstood the assaults and the disintegrating forces of the ages. At first the survivors of the great catastrophe were stunned by the blow that had shattered their nation. They lived only in their memories of the past and in their hopes for the future. At last, in the long period of misery and enforced meditation, they began not only to accept but also to apply the eternal principles proclaimed by their earlier prophets. Thus amid these entirely new conditions they gained a broader and deeper faith and were still further trained for the divine task of teaching mankind.

The Book of Lamentations After describing the destruction of the little kingdom established at Mizpah under Gedaliah, the Hebrew historical records suddenly become silent. This silence is due to the fact that there was little of external interest to record. The real history of this tragic half-century is the record of the anguish and doubts and hopes in the hearts of the scattered remnants of the race. The little book of Lamentations expresses dramatically and pathetically the thoughts of the people as they meditated upon the series of calamities that gathered about the great catastrophe of 586 B.C. Like the ancient Torah, or five books of the Law, it contains a quintet of poems. These are very similar in theme and form to many of the psalms of the Psalter. In the first four the characteristic five-beat measure by which the deep emotions, especially that of sorrow, were expressed is consistently employed. Each of these four is also an acrostic; that is, each succeeding line or group of lines begins with a succeeding letter of the Hebrew alphabet. This acrostic form was probably adopted in order to aid the memory, which suggests that from the first these poems were written to be used in public. Even so the Jews of Jerusalem today chant them on each of their Sabbaths beside the foundation walls of the great platform on which once stood their ruined temple. Although the artificial character of these poems tends to check the free expression of thought and feeling, it is possible to trace in them a logical progress and to feel the influence of the strong emotions that inspired them.

Authorship and Date of the Book In theme and literary form these poems are so strikingly similar to Jeremiah's later sermons that it was almost inevitable that tradition should attribute them to the great prophet of Judah's decline. This tradition, to which is due the position of the book of Lamentations in the Greek and English Bibles, cannot be traced earlier than the Greek period. The evidence within the poems themselves strongly indicates that they were not written by Jeremiah. It is almost inconceivable that he would subject his poetic genius to the rigid limitations of the acrostic structure. Moreover, he would never have spoken of the weak Zedekiah, whose vacillating policy he condemned, in the terms of high esteem that appear in Lamentations 4:20. These poems also reflect the popular interpretation of the great national calamity, rather than Jeremiah's searching analysis of fundamental causes. A careful study of Lamentations shows that chapters 2 and 4 were probably written by one who was powerfully influenced by Ezekiel's thought. They both follow in their acrostic structure an unusual order of the Hebrew alphabet, differing in this respect from chapters 1 and 3. They have so many close points of contact with each other that it is safe to say that they are both from the same author. They reveal an intimate familiarity with events immediately following the destruction of Jerusalem and were probably written between 580 and 561 B.C., when Jehoiachin was liberated. Chapters 1 and 3 follow the regular order of the Hebrew alphabet and apparently represent the work of a later author or authors. Chapter 1 is full of pathos and religious feeling and is closely parallel in thought to such psalms as 42 and 137. Chapter 3 is a poetic monologue describing the fate and voicing the contrition of the righteous within the Judean community. Chapter 5, on the contrary, is in the three-beat measure and lacks the acrostic structure of the preceding chapters. Its style and point of view are so different from those of the preceding chapters that it must be the work of another author, who probably lived in the Persian period.

Its Real Character The purpose of the book of Lamentations was evidently (1) to give appropriate expression to the feelings of the Jews who survived the destruction of Jerusalem in 586 B.C.; (2) to drive home the great lessons taught by their past history, and thus to arouse true repentance; and (3) to kindle in turn hopes regarding their future. Through them Jeremiah and Ezekiel live and speak again, but from the point of view of the people. These tragic poems also throw contemporary light upon the horrors of the final siege and capture of Jerusalem and upon the fate of those who survived.

Numbers and Fortunes of the Jews Who Remained in Palestine The Jews actually carried into captivity constituted only a small part of the total population of Judah. The peasants and the inhabitants of the towns outside Jerusalem remained undisturbed, except as some of them were doubtless drafted into the army that under Zedekiah undertook to defend Jerusalem against the Chaldeans. From the later record of Nehemiah's work the names of many of these towns can be determined. In the north were Jericho, Geba, Mizpah, Anathoth, and Kirjath-jearim; in the center, Netophah and Bethlehem; and in the south, Tekoa, Keilah, and Bethzur. The lot of these, who are later known as the people of the land, was pitiable indeed. There are many references in Lamentations and Ezekiel to the persecutions to which they were subjected by their malignant foes, the Moabites and Ammonites to the east and the Philistines to the west. Even more cruel and aggressive were the Edomites, who had suffered many wrongs at the hands of the Hebrews. It was probably about this time that this half-nomadic people began to be driven northward by the advance of the Nabateans, an Arab people who came from the south. Dislodged from their homes, the Edomites took advantage of the weakness of the Jews and seized southern Judah, including the ancient capital Hebron. The doom that Ezekiel pronounces upon the Edomites in 25:12–14 is because of the revenge that they wreaked upon the Jews at this time. It is significant that Ezekiel's sermons in the period immediately following the fall of Jerusalem contain dire predictions of divine vengeance upon all these foes. After the overthrow of Gedaliah's kingdom, the Jews who remained in Palestine appear to have been left wholly without defenses or defenders. Ezekiel, in 33:23–29, speaks of those who inhabit the waste places in the land of Israel, who live in the strongholds and the caves. Some of them appear to have turned into robbers. Foreign settlers came in from every side and in time intermarried with the natives and led them into idolatry. Ezekiel sternly condemns their immorality and apostasy.

From the references in Jeremiah 41:5 and Ezra 3:3 it is clear that even during this reign of terror many of the people continued to offer sacrifices to Jehovah at the great altar cut in native rock that stood before the ruins of their temple in Jerusalem. Priests were also doubtless found in the land to conduct these services. The ancient feasts, however, with their joyous merrymaking and the resulting sense of divine favor, were no longer observed. Instead, the people celebrated in sackcloth and ashes the fasts commemorating the successive stages in the destruction of their city (Zech. 7:3–7). While their lot was pitiable and their character seemingly unpromising, these people of the land were important factors in the reestablishment of the Judean community.

Fortunes of the Jews in Egypt The narrative in Jeremiah states definitely that the large proportion of those who had rallied about Gedaliah after his death found a temporary asylum on the eastern borders of Egypt. Here they were beyond the reach of Chaldean armies and within the territory of the one nation that offered a friendly asylum to the Jewish refugees. Most of this later group of exiles settled at the towns of Tahpanhes and Migdol. The latter means "tower" and is probably to be identified with an eastern outpost, the chief station on the great highway that ran along the southeastern shore of the Mediterranean directly to Palestine and Syria.

The excavations of the Egypt Exploration Fund at Tahpanhes, which was the Daphnae of Herodotus, have thrown much light upon the home of this Jewish community. The town was situated in a sandy desert to the south of a marshy lake. It lay midway between the cultivated delta on the west and what is now the Suez Canal on the east. Past it ran the main highway to Palestine. Its founder, Psamtik I, the great-grandfather of Hophra, had built here a fort to guard the highway. Herodotus states that he also stationed guards here, and that until late in the Persian period it was defended by garrisons whose duty was to repel

Asiatic invasions. Here the Ionian and Carian mercenaries, who were at this time the chief defense of the Egyptian king, were given permanent homes. By virtue of its mixed population and its geographical position, Tahpanhes was a great meeting place of Eastern and Western civilizations. Here native Egyptians, Greek mercenaries, Phoenician and Babylonian traders, and Jewish refugees met on common ground and lived side by side. It corresponded in these respects to the modern Port Said.

Probably in remembrance of the Jewish colony that once lived here, the ruins of the fort still bear an Arab name that means "the palace of the Jew's daughter." The term "palace" is not altogether inappropriate, for apparently the fort was occasionally used as a royal residence. Many wine jars bearing the seals of Psamtik, Hophra, and Amasis have been found in the ruins. In the northwestern part of these ruins has been uncovered a great open-air platform of brickwork, referred to in Jeremiah 43:8–10. It was the place of common meeting found in connection with every Egyptian palace or private home. When Amasis came to the throne of Egypt in 564 B.C. he withdrew the privileges granted by his predecessors to foreigners. The Greek colonists were transferred to Naukratis, and Tahpanhes lost most of its former glory. About this time, if not before, the great majority of the Jewish refugees who had settled in these frontier towns probably returned to Palestine to find homes in its partially depopulated towns.

Ezekiel from distant Babylon appears to have regarded the Jews in Egypt with considerable hope (Ezek. 29:21).

But Jeremiah, who knew them better, was keenly alive to their faults. In their despair and rage many of them evidently rejected the teachings of the prophets and became devotees of the Aramean goddess, the Queen of Heaven, mentioned in the recently discovered Aramean inscription of Zakar, king of Hazrak. Jeremiah's closing words to them, therefore, are denunciations and predictions that they should suffer even in the land of Egypt, at the hand of Nebuchadrezzar, the same fate that had overtaken their fellow countrymen at Jerusalem. Both Jeremiah and Ezekiel (Ezek. 30) predicted that Nebuchadrezzar would invade and conquer Egypt. In 568 B.C. his army actually did appear on the borders of Egypt, but how far he succeeded in conquering the land is unknown. The complete conquest of Egypt certainly did not come until the Persian period under the leadership of the cruel Cambyses.

The Jewish Colony at Elephantine Jeremiah and Ezekiel also refer to the Jewish colonists at Memphis and at Pathros, which is the biblical designation of upper Egypt. Many of the colonists who had settled there had doubtless fled before the conquests of Jerusalem. The presence of a great number of Jews in Egypt at a later period indicates that even at this early date more exiles were probably to be found in Egypt than in Babylon. Recent discoveries on the island of Elephantine in the upper Nile, opposite the modern Assuan, have thrown new light upon the life of these Jewish colonists. These records consist of a series of beautifully preserved legal documents written in Aramaic on papyrus and definitely dated between the years 471 and 411 B.C. They include contracts between the Jews residing on the island of Elephantine regarding the transfer of property and other legal transactions. They contain many familiar Jewish names, such as Zadok, Isaiah, Hosea, Nathan, Ethan, Zechariah, Shallum, Uriah, and Shemaiah. They indicate that by the earlier part of the Persian period a large and wealthy colony of Jewish traders and bankers was established on this island. They appear to have lived in a community by themselves, but in the heart of the city, side by side with Egyptians, Persians, Babylonians, Phoenicians, and Greeks, whose property in some cases joined their own. The Jews had their own court, which ranked equally with the Persian and Egyptian law courts. Even native Egyptians, who had cases against the Jews, appeared before it. The names of Arameans and Arabs also appear in its lists of witnesses. From these contemporary documents it is clear that the Jews of upper Egypt enjoyed great privileges and entered freely into the life of the land. Ordinarily they married members of their own race, but the marriage of a Jewess with a foreigner is also reported. He appears, however, to have been a proselyte to Judaism. Another Jewess married an Egyptian and took oath by the Egyptian goddess Sati, suggesting that she had nominally at least adopted the religion of her husband. One Hebrew also bears the suggestive name of Hosea, the son of Petikhnum (an Egyptian name meaning "gift of the god Khnum").

The Temple of Yahu at Elephantine These Aramaic legal documents also contain many references to Yahu (the older form of Yahweh or Jehovah), the god worshipped by the Jews, and to Yahu's temple situated on King's Street, one of the main thoroughfares of the city. These references have been signally confirmed by a most remarkable letter recently discovered by the Germans at this site. It was written in November of the year 408 B.C. by the members of the Jewish colony at Elephantine to Bagohi (the Bagoas of Josephus), the Persian governor of Judah. It states, among other things, that "Already in the days of the kings of Egypt our fathers had built this temple in the fortress of Elephantine. And when Cambyses (529–522 B.C.) entered Egypt he found this temple built, and, though the temple of the gods of Egypt were all at that time overthrown, no one injured anything in this temple." It further states that recently (in the year 411 B.C.), in the absence of the Persian governor in Egypt, the foreigners in Elephantine had stirred up a certain minor official to instruct his son, who was commander of a neighboring fortress, to destroy the Jewish temple.

The Aramaic letter was intended to be sent, together with rich gifts, to influence the powerful Persian governor of Judah, Bagohi, to issue an order permitting the Jews to rebuild their temple. From this letter we learn that the temple of the god Yahu was built of hewn stone with pillars of stone in front, probably similar to those in the Egyptian temples, and had seven great gates built of hewn stone and provided with doors and bronze hinges. Its roof was wholly of cedar wood, probably brought from the distant Lebanon, and its walls appear to have been ceiled or adorned with stucco, as were those of Solomon's temple. It was also equipped with bowls of gold and silver and the other paraphernalia of sacrifice. Here were regularly offered cereal offerings, burnt offerings, and frankincense. The petitioners also promised that, if the Persian officials would grant their request, "we will also offer cereal-offerings and frankincense and burnt-offerings on the altar in your name, and we will pray to God in your name, we and our wives and all the Jews who are here, if you do thus until the temple is built. And you shall have a portion before the God Yahu, the God of Heaven, from every one who offers to him burnt-offerings and sacrifices."

Historical students have long been familiar with the fact that late in the Greek period the Jews of Egypt built a temple to Jehovah at Leontopolis, in the delta, but these recent discoveries open an entirely new chapter in Jewish history. They indicate that probably within a generation after the destruction of the Jerusalem temple in 586 B.C., the Jewish colonists in Egypt built for themselves far up the Nile, and possibly at other points in this land of their exile, a temple or temples to Jehovah; that they remained loyal to God and the institutions of their race; and that in the midst of cosmopolitan Egypt they preserved intact their racial unity. In the light of these discoveries it is also clear that because of their character and numbers and nearness to

Palestine the Jews of Egypt, even at this early period, were a far more important factor in the life and development of Judaism than they have hitherto been considered. These discoveries also afford definite grounds for the hope that from this unexpected quarter much more valuable material will come to illumine this otherwise dark period of post-exilic Jewish history.

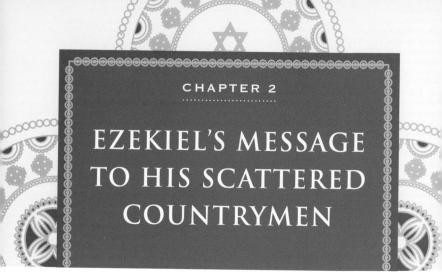

CHAPTER 2

EZEKIEL'S MESSAGE TO HIS SCATTERED COUNTRYMEN

From the references in the contemporary writers it is possible to gain a reasonably definite idea regarding the environment of the Jewish exiles in Babylon. Ezekiel describes the site as "a land of traffic, a city of merchants, a fruitful soil, and beside many waters," where the colony like a willow was transplanted [17:5]. The Kabaru Canal (the River Chebar of Ezekiel) ran southeast from Babylon to Nippur through a rich alluvial plain intersected by numerous canals. Beside it lived a dense agricultural population. On the tells, or artificial mounds made by the ruins of earlier Babylonian cities, were built the peasant villages. Ezekiel speaks of preaching to the Jewish colony of Tel-Abib (Storm Hill), and the lists of those who later returned to Judah contain references to those who came from Tel-Melah (Salt Hill) and Tel-Harsha (Forest Hill).

Their Condition and Occupations It is probable that these mounds were not far from each other and that the adjacent fields were cultivated by the Jewish colonists. Thus they were able, under even more favorable conditions than in Judah, to continue in their old occupations and to build houses and rear families as Jeremiah had advised (Jer. 29). In Babylonia, as at Elephantine, so long as they paid the imperial tax and refrained from open violence they were probably allowed to rule themselves in accordance with their own laws. The elders of the different families directed the affairs of the community and acted as judges, except in the case of capital offenses, which were punished in the name of Nebuchadrezzar (Jer. 29:22). Thus for a long time the exiles constituted a little Judah within the heart of the Babylonian empire, maintaining their racial integrity even more completely than the Jews resident in Egypt.

Babylonia was the scene of intense commercial activity. The opportunities and allurements of the far-reaching traffic that passed up and down the great rivers and across the neighboring deserts were eventually too strong for the Jews to resist. Hence in Babylonia, as in Egypt, they gradually abandoned their inherited agricultural habits and were transformed into a nation of traders. In the recently discovered records of the transactions of the famous Babylonian banking house that flourished during the earlier part of the Persian period, under the direction of succeeding generations of the Murashu family, are found many familiar Jewish names. These indicate that within a century after the fall of

Jerusalem many sons of the exiles had already won a prominent place in the commercial life of that great metropolis.

Their Religious Life With this transformation in their occupation came a great temptation to forget their race and to lose sight of its ideals. The temptation was all the greater because their capital city and temple were in ruins and the belief was widely held that Jehovah had forsaken his land and people and retired to his "mount in the uttermost parts of the north" (Isa. 14:13; Ezek. 1:4). Their actual experiences had proved so fundamentally different from their hopes that there was undoubtedly in the minds of many a dread doubt as to whether Jehovah was able to fulfill his promises. False prophets were also present to mislead the people (Jer. 39:21–23; Ezek. 13:1–7, 14:8–10). There is also no indication that the Jews of Babylon ever attempted to build a temple to Jehovah in the land of their captivity. Hence there were no ancient festivals, public or private sacrifices, or impressive ceremonials to kindle their religious feelings and to keep alive their national faith. Instead, the imposing religion of the Babylonians, with its rich temples, its many festivals, its prosperous and powerful priesthood, and its elaborate rituals must have profoundly impressed them and led them to draw unfavorable comparisons between it and the simple services of their pre-exilic temple. Nevertheless, in spite of these temptations, there were many who proved themselves loyal to Jehovah. Prayer and fasting and Sabbath observance took the place of sacrificial rites. A strong emphasis is laid by Ezekiel on the Sabbath (Ezek. 20:12–31, 22:26, 23:38). From this time on it became one of the most important and characteristic institutions of Judaism. Under the influence of the new situation it lost much of its original, philanthropic, and social character and became instead a ceremonial institution. In faithfully observing it the exiles felt that even in captivity they were paying homage to their divine King. The more it took the place of the ancient feasts and sacrifices, the more they forgot that the Sabbath was God's gift to toiling man rather than man's gift to God. From the Babylonian exile, also, probably dates that custom of assembling on the Sabbath to read the ancient scriptures, which represents the genesis of the later synagogue and its service.

The Prophecies of Ezekiel The priest-prophet Ezekiel was the interpreter, pastor, and guide of the Babylonian exiles. He met their problems and proposed the solutions that became the foundation principles of later Judaism. His prophecies fall naturally into four distinct groups: (1) Chapters 1–24, which recount his call and deal with the issues at stake in the different Judean communities in the critical years between the first and second captivities. They represent the prophet's work between the years 592 and 586 B.C. (2) Chapters 25–32 include seven oracles regarding Ammon, Moab, Edom, Philistia, Tyre, and Egypt, the nations that had taken part in the destruction of Jerusalem or else, like Egypt, had lured Judah to its ruin. The complete destruction of these foes is predicted, and chapter 32 concludes with a weird picture of their fate, condemned by Jehovah to dwell in Sheol, the abode of the shades. (3) Chapters 33–39 contain messages of comfort and promise to Ezekiel's fellow exiles in Babylonia and in the distant lands of the dispersion. They are dated between the years 586 and 570 B.C. (4) Chapters 40–48 present Ezekiel's plan for the restored temple and service and for the redistribution of the territory of Canaan, and his belief that Judah's fertility would be miraculously increased. This plan is definitely dated in the year 572 B.C., two years before the prophet's death.

The Resurrection of the Dead Nation Ezekiel dealt with the problems of his fellow exiles concretely and from a point of view that they could readily understand. He fully realized that if the faith of the people was to be saved in this crisis, a definite hope, expressed in objective imagery, must be set before them. With the same inspired insight that had prompted Jeremiah to purchase his family estate in the hour of Jerusalem's downfall, Ezekiel saw that Jehovah would yet restore his people, if they would but respond to the demands of this crisis. His message was, therefore, one of hope and promise. In the memorable chapter in which he pictures a valley filled with dry bones, he aimed to inspire their faith by declaring that Jehovah was not only able but would surely gather together the dismembered parts of the nation and impart to it new life and activity. The prophet was clearly speaking of national rather than of individual resurrection. Like Jeremiah, he anticipated that the tribes of the north and south would again be united, as in the days of David, and that over them a scion of the Davidic house would rule as Jehovah's representative. He also assured them that Jehovah would come again to dwell in the midst of his purified and restored people.

The Divine Shepherd In its thirty-fourth chapter Ezekiel deals with the same theme under a different figure. First he traces the cause of the exile to the inefficiency and greed and oppression of the earlier shepherds, the rulers like Jehoiakim, who had scattered rather than gathered and led the people entrusted to them. Now Jehovah himself, the great Shepherd of the People, will arise and gather his flock, and lead them back to their home and give them a rich pasture. Over them he will appoint a descendant of David, but this prince shall be shorn of his ancient kingly power.

Ezekiel also presents in his characteristic symbolic form the promise that Jehovah will now fulfill the popular hopes and destroy the wicked foes who have preyed upon his people, and thus vindicate his divine rulership of the world. In one passage Judah's worst foes, the Edomites, represent aggressive heathendom. Again, in a still more impressive picture, suggested by an experience in his own childhood when the dread Scythians swept down from the north, he portrays the advance of the mysterious foes from the distant north under the leadership of Gog (38, 39). When they are already in the land of Palestine, the prophet declares, Jehovah will terrify them with an earthquake, so that in panic they shall slay each other, as did the Midianites in the days of Gideon, until they shall all fall victims of Jehovah's judgment. Ezekiel thus revived in the changed conditions of the exile that popular conception of the day of Jehovah that the earlier prophets had refused to countenance. It was the prophet's graphic way of declaring that Jehovah would prepare the way for the return of his people, if they would but respond when the opportune moment should arrive. Later Judaism, however, and especially the apocalyptic writers, interpreted literally and developed still further this picture of Jehovah's great judgment day until it became a prominent teaching of later Jewish and Christian thought.

Similarly Ezekiel declared that the barren lands of Judah would be miraculously transformed and rendered capable of supporting the great numbers of the exiles who should return. In this respect Ezekiel became the father of the later priestly school to which belongs the author of the book of Chronicles, in whose thought the events of Israel's history came to pass, not through man's earnest effort and in accordance with the established laws of the universe, but through special divine interposition. It is difficult to determine whether Ezekiel himself was simply endeavoring to state dramatically that Jehovah would fully anticipate the needs of his people, or whether he did actually anticipate a series of prodigious miracles.

Ezekiel's Plan of the Restored Temple Ezekiel, being a true prophet, fully realized that the fundamental question regarding the future of his race was not whether they would be restored to their home but whether or not they would guard against the mistakes and sins of the past and live in accord with Jehovah's just demands. The solution of this question that he proposes reveals his priestly training. With infinite pains and details he develops the plan of a restored temple and ritual. The details were doubtless in part suggested by his remembrance of the temple at Jerusalem and in part taken from the great temples of Babylon. By means of this elaborate picture he declared his firm conviction that his race would surely be restored. His chief purpose, however, was to impress upon the minds of his people the transcendent holiness of Jehovah and the necessity that he be worshipped by a holy people. The entire plan of the temple, of the ritual, and even of the allotment of the territory of Canaan was intended to enforce this idea. His plan, if adopted, was calculated to deliver the people from the temptations and mistakes of the past. With this end in view Jehovah's sacred abode was guarded with massive double walls and huge gateways. Only the priests were allowed to enter the inner court, and a sharp distinction was made between the priests who were the descendants of Zadok and the Levites whose fathers had ministered at the many sanctuaries scattered throughout the land of Israel. The territory immediately adjacent to the temple was assigned to the priests and Levites, and its sanctity was further guarded on the east and west by the domains of the prince. His chief function was not to rule, as had the selfish and inefficient tyrants who had preceded him, but to provide the animals and the material requisite for the temple service. The territory on the north and the south of the temple was assigned to the different tribes of Israel.

No political or social problems clouded the prophet's vision. The entire energies of priest, Levite, prince, and people were to be devoted to the worship of the Holy One, whose restored and glorified sanctuary stood in their midst. Thus it was that Ezekiel reversed the ideals of the pre-exilic Hebrew state and presented the program that with many modifications was adopted in principle at least by the post-exilic Judean community. In place of the monarchy appeared the hierarchy; instead of the king the high priest became both the religious and the civil head of the nation. Soon the Davidic royal line disappeared entirely, and the interests of the people centered more and more about the temple and its ritual. Although Ezekiel's vision was not and could not be fully realized, except by a series of miracles, this devoted priest-prophet of the exile was in a large sense the father of Judaism.

CHAPTER 3

THE CLOSING YEARS OF THE BABYLONIAN RULE

The destruction of Jerusalem transformed the Jewish peasants of Palestine into a literary race. Before the final destruction of Jerusalem they had lived together in a small territory where communication was easy and the need for written records was slight. The exile separated friends and members of the same families, and scattered them throughout the then known world. The only means of communicating with each other in most cases was by writing, and this necessity inevitably developed the literary arts. The exiles in Babylonia and Egypt were also in close contact with the two most active literary peoples of the ancient world. In countries where almost every public or private act was recorded in written form, and where the literature of the past was carefully preserved and widely transcribed, it was inevitable that the Jews should be powerfully influenced by these examples. Furthermore, the teachers of the race, prophets and priests alike, prevented by the destruction of the temple from employing their former oral and symbolic methods of instruction, resorted, as did the priest Ezekiel, to the pen. Thus the religious thought and devotion of the race began to find expression in its literature.

The incentives to collect the earlier writings of the priests and prophets were also exceedingly strong, for the experiences and institutions of their past, together with their hopes for the future, were the two main forces that now held together the Jewish race. Fortunately, the more intelligent leaders realized, even before 586 B.C., that the final catastrophe was practically certain, and therefore prepared for it in advance. The decade between the first and second captivities also gave them an opportunity to collect the more important writings of their earlier prophetic and priestly teachers, while the Judean state was still intact and while these earlier writings could be readily consulted.

The Literary Activity of the Babylonian Period The literary work of this period took three distinct forms. First was the collection, compilation, and editing of earlier historical writings. It was probably during this period that the narratives of Judges, Samuel, and Kings, which carried the history down into the exile itself, received their final revision. Second, earlier writings were revised or supplemented so as to adapt them to the new and different conditions. Thus the sermons of the pre-exilic prophets, for example, those of Amos and Isaiah, were then revised and supplemented at many points. These earlier prophets had predicted doom and destruction for their nation, but now that their predictions had been realized what was needed was a message of comfort and promise. The fulfilment of their earlier predictions had established their authority in the minds of the people. The purpose of the later editors was evidently to put in the mouths of these earlier prophets what they probably would have said had they been present to speak at the later day to their discouraged and disconsolate countrymen. Studied in the light of these two fundamentally different points of view, the glaring inconsistencies that appear in the prophetic books are fully explained and the consistency of the earlier prophets vindicated.

The third form of literary activity is represented by the writings of Ezekiel. With the authority of a prophet, he dealt directly with the problem of his day, and the greater part of his book consists of the records of his prophetic addresses or of epistles that he sent to his scattered fellow countrymen, even as Jeremiah wrote from Judah a letter to the distant exiles in Babylon. His new constitution for the restored Jewish state was also based on earlier customs and laws, but was adapted to the new needs of the changed situation. He was not the only one to undertake this task. Other priests gathered earlier groups of oral laws and put in written form the customs and traditions of the pre-exilic temple. At the same time they modified these earlier customs so as to correct the evils that past experience had revealed.

The Holiness Code The chief product of the literary activity of the earlier part of the exile is the collection of laws found in the seventeenth to the twenty-sixth chapters of Leviticus. Because of its strong emphasis on the holiness of Jehovah and on the necessity that he be worshipped by a people both ceremonially and morally holy, it is now commonly designated as the Holiness Code. In theme, in point of view, in purpose, and in literary form it has many close points of contact with the writings of Ezekiel. In its original unity it evidently came from the period and circle of thought in which the great priest-prophet lived. His sermons, however, suggest that he was acquainted with its main teachings. In distinguishing sharply between the Jerusalem priests and the ministering Levites, and in prohibiting the marriage of a priest with a widow, Ezekiel shows that his work represented a slightly later stage in the development of Israel's religious standards. The most probable date, therefore, for the Holiness Code is the decade between the first and second captivity (597–586 B.C.).

Like every ancient law book the Holiness Code contains many laws and regulations that evidently come from a much earlier period in Israel's history. Some of its enactments are very similar to those of the primitive codes of Exodus 21–23. In spirit it is closely related to the book of Deuteronomy. It also reproduces many of the laws found in this earlier code. Both codes represent the fruitage of the teaching of the pre-exilic prophets and priests. Each contains ceremonial, civil, and moral laws, but the emphasis on ritual is more pronounced in the Holiness Code. It consists of ten or eleven distinct groups of laws. In Leviticus 18 and 19 are found certain short decalogues. They probably represent the united efforts of the Judean prophets and priests during the Assyrian period to inculcate the true principles of justice, service, and worship in the minds of the people. Some of the laws in these earlier decalogues are the noblest examples of Old Testament legislation:

DUTIES TO OTHERS

Kindness to the needy

   I. Thou shalt not wholly reap the corners of thy fields.
  II. Thou shalt not gather the gleanings of thy harvest.
 III. Thou shalt not glean thy vineyard.
  IV. Thou shalt not gather the fallen fruit of thy vineyard.
   V. Thou shalt leave them for the poor and the resident alien.

Honesty in business relations

  VI Ye shall not steal.
 VII. Ye shall do no injustice, in measures of length, weight, or quantity.
VIII. Ye shall not deal falsely with one another.
  IX. Ye shall not lie to one another.
   X. Ye shall not swear falsely by my name.

JUSTICE TO ALL MEN

Toward dependents

I. Thou shalt not oppress thy neighbor.

II. Thou shalt not rob thy neighbor.

III. The wages of a hired servant shall not remain with thee all night until the morning.

IV. Thou shalt not curse the deaf.

V. Thou shalt not put a stumbling block before the blind.

Toward equals

VI. Thou shalt not do injustice in rendering a judicial decision.

VII. Thou shalt not show partiality to the poor.

VIII. Thou shalt not have undue consideration for the powerful.

IX. Thou shalt not go about as a tale bearer among thy people.

X. Thou shalt not seek the blood of thy neighbor [by bearing false testimony in court].

ATTITUDE TOWARD OTHERS

In the heart

I. Thou shalt not hate thy fellow countryman in thy heart.

II. Thou shalt warn thy neighbor and not incur sin on his account.

III. Thou shalt not take vengeance.

IV. Thou shalt not bear a grudge against the
    members of thy race.

V. Thou shalt love thy neighbor as thyself.

The Liberation of Jehoiachin and the Hopes of the Jews

The liberation of Jehoiachin, the grandson of Josiah, from
the Babylonian prison where he had been confined since the
first capture of Jerusalem was the one event in the Babylonian
period deemed worthy of record by the biblical historians.
The occasion was the accession of Nebuchadrezzar's son
Evil-merodach (Babylonian: Amil-Marduk). The act possessed little political importance, for the Jews were helpless
in the hands of their Babylonian masters, but it evidently
aroused the hopes of the exiles, and especially the type of
hope that centered in the house of David.

Ezekiel, in his ideal program, assigned to the Davidic
prince only minor duties in connection with the temple and
transferred the chief authority to the high priest and his
attendants. But it is evident that Ezekiel did not fully voice
the hopes of the majority of the exiles. The late passage in
II Samuel 7:16, which contains the promise to David:

> *Thy house and kingdom shall always stand firm*
> *   before me,*
> *Thy throne shall be established forever*

expresses the prevailing belief in the days immediately
preceding the exile. The national hopes that looked to
the descendants of the house of David for fulfilment were

inevitably modified, however, by the experiences of the exile and strengthened by the liberation of Jehoiachin. The rule of such kings as Manasseh and Jehoiakim had revealed the overwhelming evils that unworthy rulers, even though of the house of David, could bring upon their subjects. Josiah's reign, on the other hand, established new and higher standards. The noble ethical and social ideals of Amos, Hosea, and Isaiah had not wholly failed to awaken a response.

All of these varied influences are traceable in the two prophecies found in Isaiah 9:1–7 and 11:1–10. Embodying as they do many of the social principles for which Isaiah contended, it was natural that these anonymous writings should afterward be attributed to that great statesman-prophet. Jehovah, however, was the one supreme king whom Isaiah acknowledged, and it was difficult to find in his strenuous life a logical or historical setting for these kingly oracles. They also imply that the royal house of Judah had been struck down, and that the new king is to rise out of a background of gloom and is to inaugurate an entirely new era. The character and rule of this king of popular hopes reflect many of the traits of David and Josiah, but his aims and methods are in accord with the moral and social standards of the great pre-exilic prophets. They portray a temporal ruler, but the spirit that actuates him and the principles that guide him are noble and unselfish. As subsequent history clearly shows, the prophet or prophets who painted these portraits apparently hoped that a son or grandson of Jehoiachin would realize them. It is exceedingly probable in the light of the later predictions of Haggai and Zechariah that these prophecies were written not long after the birth of Zerubbabel. The kingdom over which he was to rule and to which he was to bring perfect justice and peace was the prophetic counterpart of Ezekiel's priestly plan of the restored and redeemed community. The ethical ideals thus concretely set forth were never fully realized in Israel's troubled history, but they remain as valid and commanding today as they were far back in the Babylonian period. The abolition of all the insignia of war, the high sense of official responsibility, the protection of the weak by the strong, and the reign of perfect peace and harmony throughout all the earth are the goals for which all earnest, consecrated souls in every age and race are striving. It is natural and proper that the Christian church should see in Jesus the fullest and truest realization of these ancient kingly ideals.

The Rule of Nabonidus The successors of Nebuchadrezzar proved weak and inefficient. His dissolute son, Amil-Marduk, was soon murdered by his brother-in-law Nergalsharuzur (Gk.: Neriglissar). This ruler is probably the Nergal-sharezer of Jeremiah 39:3 who directed the final capture and destruction of Jerusalem in 586 B.C. After reigning four years he died, leaving the Babylonian empire to his young son, who soon fell a victim to a conspiracy of his nobles. They placed on the throne a certain Nabuna'id, who is known to the Greek historians as Nabonidus. He appeared to be more interested in excavating ancient ruins and in rebuilding old temples than in ruling his subjects. By his arbitrary religious policy and his neglect of the popular gods of the Babylonians, he completely alienated the loyalty of his people. During the latter part of his reign, which extended from 555 to 538 B.C., he left the government largely in charge of his son Belsharuzur, the Belshazzar of the story in Daniel.

Rise and Conquests of Cyrus While the Babylonian empire was sinking into decay, the Median kingdom on the north and east experienced a sweeping revolution. Its cause was the discontent of the older Median population under the rule of the more barbarous Umman-Manda. These later Scythian conquerors had, under their king Cyaxares, broken the power of Assyria and fallen heir to its eastern territory. The older elements found a leader in Cyrus, the king of Anshan, a little state among the mountains of Elam, northeast of Babylonia. From contemporary inscriptions it appears that the followers of Astyages, who succeeded Cyaxares to the Median throne, rebelled against their king and delivered him over into the hands of Cyrus. As soon as Cyrus became master of the Median empire, he proved an able commander, a skillful politician, and a wise statesman. Recognizing that he could hold in control the diverse and turbulent elements in his heterogeneous kingdom only as he kept them actively occupied, he at once entered upon a series of campaigns that in the end left him undisputed master of southwestern Asia. In 547 B.C., two years after he became king of Media, he crossed the Tigris and conquered Mesopotamia, which had been held for a time by the Babylonians. Apparently he did not assume the title king of Persia until 546. Appreciating the great strength of Babylon, he did not at first attempt its capture, but began at once by intrigue to pave the way for its ultimate overthrow. In 545 he set out on a western campaign against Croesus, the king of Lydia, the ancient rival of Media. After a quick and energetic campaign, Sardis, the rich Lydian capital, was captured, and Cyrus was free to advance against the opulent Greek colonies that lay along the eastern shores of the Aegean. These in rapid succession fell into his hands, so that by 538 B.C. he was in a position to advance with a large victorious army against the mistress of the lower Euphrates.

His Capture of Babylon The campaigns of Cyrus were naturally watched with keen interest by the Jewish exiles in Babylonia. The songs in Isaiah 14, 15, and 21:1–10 and in Jeremiah 51:29–31 voice their joyous expectation of Babylon's impending humiliation. In a contemporary inscription Cyrus has given a vivid account of the fall of the capital. Early in October of the year 538 B.C. he assembled a large army on the northern borders of Babylonia. Here a battle was fought in which the Babylonians were completely defeated. The town of Sippar quickly surrendered to Cyrus's general, and two days later the Persian army entered Babylon. The record states that the gates of the mighty city were opened by its inhabitants, and Cyrus and his followers were welcomed as deliverers. King Nabonidus was captured and banished to the distant province of Carmania, north-east of the Persian Gulf. In the words of Cyrus: "Peace he gave the town; peace he proclaimed to all the Babylonians." In the eyes of the conquered, he figured as the champion of their gods, whose images he restored to the capital city. The temples as well as the walls of Babylon were rebuilt, and the king publicly proclaimed himself a devoted worshipper of Marduk and Nebo, the chief gods of the Babylonians. Thus from the first the policy of Cyrus in treating conquered peoples was fundamentally different from that of the Babylonians and Assyrians. They had sought to establish their power by crushing the conquered rather than by furthering their well-being, but Cyrus, by his many acts of clemency, aimed to secure and hold their loyalty.

His Treatment of Conquered Peoples Cyrus showed the same wisdom in his treatment of the many petty peoples who had been ground down under the harsh rule of Babylon. In one of his inscriptions he declares: "The gods whose sanctuaries from of old had lain in ruins I brought back again to their dwelling-places and caused them to reside there forever. All of the citizens of these lands I assembled and I restored them to their homes" (Cyrus Cylinder 31, 32). In the light of this statement it is clear that the Jews, in common with other captive peoples, were given full permission to return to their homes and to rebuild their ruined temple. The decree of Cyrus recorded in the Aramaic document preserved in Ezra 6:3–5 is apparently the Jewish version of the general decree that he issued. It is also possible that he aided the vassal peoples in rebuilding their sanctuaries, for such action was in perfect accord with his wise policy. He also entrusted the rulership of different kingdoms as far as possible to native princes. In the Greek book of I Esdras has been preserved a list (which has fallen out of the biblical book of Ezra) of those who availed themselves of Cyrus's permission to return to Palestine. It includes simply the priest Jeshua, or Joshua, the lineal heir of the early Jerusalem priestly line of Zadok, and Zerubbabel, a descendant of the Judean royal family. They doubtless took with them their immediate followers and were probably accompanied by a few exiles whose loyalty impelled them to leave the attractive opportunities in Babylon to face the dangers of the long journey and the greater perils in Palestine.

From Jeremiah 41:5 and Haggai 2:14 it appears that a rude altar had been built on the sacred rock at Jerusalem and that religious services were held on the site of the ruined temple soon after its destruction in 586 B.C. With the gifts brought back by Zerubbabel and his followers, daily sacrifices were probably instituted on the restored altar under the direction of the priest Joshua (cf. Hag. 2:10–14). In the light, however, of the oldest records it is clear that the revival of the Judean community in Palestine was gradual and at first far from glorious. The Jews were a broken-hearted, poverty-stricken, persecuted people, still crushed by the great calamity that had overtaken their nation. The general return of the exiles was only a dream of the future, and, despite the general permission of Cyrus, the temple at Jerusalem still lay in ruins.

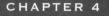
THE REBUILDING OF THE TEMPLE

The books of Ezra and Nehemiah are the chief sources of information regarding Jewish history during the Persian period. They fall into nine general divisions: (1) the return of the Babylonian exiles and the revival of the Judean community, Ezra 1–4; (2) the rebuilding of the temple, 5–6; (3) Ezra's expedition and the priestly reformation, 8–10, and Nehemiah 8–10; (4) Nehemiah's work in rebuilding the walls, Nehemiah 1:1–7:5; (5) census of the Judean community, 7:6–69; (6) measures to secure the repopulation of Jerusalem, 11; (7) genealogy of the priests and Levites, 12:1–26; (8) dedication of the walls, 12:27–43; and (9) Nehemiah's later reform measures, 12:44–13:31. It is evident that Ezra and Nehemiah were originally one book and that they come from the same author as I and II Chronicles. This important fact is demonstrated by the presence of the same marked characteristics of thought and literary style in both of these books. The closing verses of II Chronicles are also repeated verbatim at the beginning of Ezra.

Throughout these books the interest is religious and ceremonial rather than civil and national. They constitute in reality a history of the Jerusalem temple and its institutions. The whole may properly be designated as the "Ecclesiastical History of Jerusalem." It traces the history of Jerusalem and the southern kingdom from the earliest times to the close of the Persian period. Its author, who is commonly known as the Chronicler, evidently lived during the earlier part or middle of the Greek period. Certain characteristics of his literary style and point of view indicate that he wrote around 250 B.C. His peculiarities and methods of writing are clearly revealed by a comparison of the older parallel history of Samuel and Kings with the books of Chronicles. In general he lacks the historical spirit and perspective of the earlier prophetic historians. He also freely recasts his record of earlier events in order to bring it into accord with the traditions current in his own day. Above all he aimed to establish the authority and prestige of the Jerusalem temple, and to prove that Jehovah "was not with Israel" (II Chron. 25:7), which was represented in his day by the hated Samaritans. The hatred engendered by the Samaritan feud explains many of the peculiarities of the Chronicler. He was, in fact, an apologist rather than a historian. Thus post-exilic institutions, as, for example, the temple song service with its guilds of singers, are projected backward even to the days of David, and the events of early Hebrew history are constantly glorified. The numbers found in the earlier prophetic sources are magnified, and at every point it is easy to recognize the influence of the Chronicler's familiarity with the splendor and magnificence of the great Persian and Greek empires, and of his desire to inspire his fellow Jews with national pride and with loyalty to their religious institutions.

The Chronicler's Conception of the Restoration Fortunately the Chronicler did not depend entirely upon traditions current in his day, or upon his own conceptions of the early history, but quoted freely from earlier sources. As a result a large portion of the prophetic history of Samuel and Kings is reproduced verbatim in I and II Chronicles. For the Persian period, regarding which he is our chief authority, he apparently quoted from three or four documents. In Ezra 4:7–23 is found a brief description in Aramaic of the opposition of Judah's neighbors to the rebuilding of the walls, probably in the days of Nehemiah. In Ezra 5 and 6 there is another long quotation from an Aramaic document that describes a similar attempt to put a stop to the rebuilding of the temple in the days of Haggai and Zechariah. The Chronicler evidently believed that the second temple was rebuilt not by the people of the land to whom Haggai and Zechariah spoke, but by Jewish exiles who on the accession of Cyrus had returned in great numbers from Babylon. He assumed that Judah had been depopulated during the Babylonian exile, and that the only people left in Palestine were the heathen and the hated Samaritans. He also pictures the return of the exiles not as that of a handful of courageous patriots, but of a vast company laden with rich gifts and guarded by Persian soldiers.

A careful examination of Ezra 2, which purports to contain the list of the 42,360 exiles who returned immediately after 538 B.C., quickly demonstrates that, like its duplicate in Nehemiah 7:6–69, its historical basis, if it has any outside the fertile imagination of the Chronicler, is a census of the Judean community. This census was taken not at the beginning of the Persian period, but rather at the end. Thus in the list of the leaders appear the names not only of Joshua and Zerubbabel, but also of Nehemiah and Ezra (Azariah). Certain leaders, such as Mordecai and Bigvai, bear Persian names that clearly imply they lived far down in the Persian period. The family of the high priest Joshua already numbers 993. In this census are also included the inhabitants of many towns outside Jerusalem—for example, Jericho, Gibeon, and Bethlehem. Moreover, certain towns are mentioned, such as Lud and Ono, which were not added to the Judean community until the latter part of the Persian period. In view of these facts and the unmistakable implications in the sermons of Haggai and Zechariah that in their day there had been no general return of their kinsmen from Babylon, the prevailing popular interpretation of this period of Israel's history is clearly untenable and misleading. If there was a general return of exiles from Babylon, it certainly did not come until after the walls had been rebuilt under the inspiring leadership of Nehemiah. The Jews to whom Haggai and Zechariah preached and who rebuilt the second temple were the people of the land who had survived the destruction of Jerusalem, or else had returned from their temporary refuge on the borders of the land of Egypt.

Convulsions in the Persian Empire After a brilliant and successful reign Cyrus died in 529 B.C., leaving his vast empire to his son Cambyses. The new king lacked the wisdom and statesmanship of his father, but inherited his love of conquest. Most of his short reign was devoted to the conquest of Egypt. From their hilltops the Jews doubtless witnessed the march of the great armies of Persia and were forced to contribute to their support. It was a period of change and transition, when old empires went down in ruin and new forces gained the ascendancy.

On his return from Egypt, Cambyses, finding a pretender contending for the throne, committed suicide, thus leaving the empire without any legitimate head. During this crisis, in the autumn of 521 B.C., a Persian noble, Darius, was raised to the kingship by conspirators who had slain the pretender. Darius claimed relationship with the Persian royal family and strengthened his position by marrying Atossa, the daughter of Cyrus. The beginning of his reign was signalized by a series of revolts throughout the whole extent of the empire. In Susiana a certain Athrina proclaimed himself king. In Babylonia a native prince rallied his countrymen and assumed the title of Nebuchadrezzar III. The Median revolt was led by a certain Pharaortes, while among the Persians themselves a pretender who claimed to be a son of Cyrus gained a wide following. Fortunately for Darius there was no concerted action among the leaders of these different rebellions, so he was able to subdue them in succession, but to the ordinary onlooker the task seemed well-nigh impossible. Not until the spring of 519 did Darius fully become master of the situation.

Haggai's Effective Addresses It was in the autumn of 520 B.C., when the rebellions in the Persian Empire were at their height, that Haggai made his stirring appeal to the members of the Judean community. From the references in his addresses and in those of his contemporary, Zechariah, it is evident that he and his hearers were profoundly influenced by these great world movements. The situation seemed to give promise not only of deliverance from Persian rule, but an opportunity at last to realize the national hopes of the Jewish race. Haggai's message was simple, direct, and practical. According to the beliefs universally accepted in his day his logic was unanswerable. On the one hand Jehovah, through poor crops and hard times, had plainly showed his displeasure with his people in Judah. The reason was obvious: although they had built comfortable houses for themselves, Jehovah's temple still lay in ruins. If they would win his favor, it was plainly their duty to arise and rebuild his sanctuary. The upheavals in the Persian Empire also gave promise that, if they were true to their divine King, he would at last fulfill the predictions voiced by their earlier prophets.

The words of Haggai, uttered in September 520, met with an immediate response. Work was begun on the temple in October of the same year. When the energy and enthusiasm of the builders began to wane, the prophet appeared before them again in November 520 with the declaration that Jehovah was about to overthrow the great world powers and to destroy the chariots, horses, and riders of their Persian masters, "each by the sword of his brother." He also voiced the popular expectations that centered in Zerubbabel, who had already been appointed governor of Judah. The prophet declared boldly that this scion of the house of David would be Jehovah's seal ring, the earthly representative of the divine power that was about to work great revolutions in the history of the world. During the same period Zechariah also uttered his messages of encouragement and spurred the people on to continued efforts.

The Attempt to Stop the Rebuilding of the Temple The Aramaic document preserved in Ezra 5 and 6 describes in detail an attempt of the Persian governor, who ruled over the province west of the Euphrates, to put a stop to the temple building. The narrative, the letter, and the decrees it contains reveal at many points their Jewish origin. While the tradition may be comparatively late, its circumstantial character favors the conclusion that it preserves the memory of a definite historical event. The action of the Jews in rebuilding their temple was in perfect accord with the policy of Cyrus and also of Darius, as is shown by contemporary inscriptions. The attempt, therefore, to stop the building of the temple failed, and in 516 B.C., four years after the work was begun, it was completed.

The Significance of the Restoration of the Temple The rebuilding of the Jerusalem temple appears to have been of immediate significance chiefly to the Jews of Palestine. The Jews of Egypt, or at least those of Elephantine, had their own temple. From Zechariah 6:9 11 it is evident that the Jewish exiles in Babylon sent certain gifts to the Jerusalem temple, but the hundreds of miles of desert that intervened made communication exceedingly difficult, so that except at rare intervals there was apparently little interchange between Babylonia and Palestine. For all Jews, however, the rebuilding of the temple meant that at last they had a common rallying place and that Jehovah was again being worshipped by his own people at his traditional place of abode. In a sense it bridged the seventy years that had intervened since the destruction of the pre-exilic Hebrew state, and made it possible to revive the ancient religious customs. In time it attracted from the lands of the dispersion patriotic Jews whose interest was fixed upon the ceremonial side of their religious life. It also furnished a center about which gradually grew up a hierarchy with an increasingly elaborate ritual, and a body of laws that ultimately became the characteristic features of Judaism.

CHAPTER 5

ZECHARIAH'S VISIONS AND ENCOURAGING ADDRESSES

Haggai's contemporary, the prophet Zechariah, was evidently a priest. In the genealogy of Nehemiah 12:4, it is stated that he belonged to the priestly family of Iddo. This conclusion is confirmed by the character of his prophecies. Like the priest-prophet Ezekiel he is exceedingly fond of apocalyptic symbolism. He is also deeply interested in the priesthood and in its ceremonial purity. Furthermore, it is exceedingly probable that he was a descendant of one of the many priests carried as exiles to Babylon. This is shown by his keen interest in and exact knowledge of the great political movements that were then shaking the Persian Empire. His conception of Jehovah is also strongly influenced by the analogies drawn from the Persian court. In his thought Israel's God is a transcendental ruler, who communicates with his subjects not directly, but through angelic messengers, and who, like the Persian kings, is dependent for information regarding his great kingdom upon the reports of the different members of his heavenly court. Thus Zechariah marks a wide departure from the simple theology of the pre-exilic prophets who thought of Jehovah as dwelling in the midst of his people and communicating directly with all who turned to him in faith.

The Book of Zechariah The book that records the prophet's sermons contains four distinct divisions: (1) an exhortation addressed to the people in December 520, three months after Haggai first appealed to them to rise and rebuild the temple, Zechariah 1:1–8; (2) symbolic visions dealing with the problems in the Judean community, 1:7–6:8; (3) practical counsel, exhortations, and promises, 6:9–8:23; and (4) a later appendix coming from a prophet who probably lived during the earlier part of the Maccabean period, 9–14. All of Zechariah's recorded sermons probably date from the three or four years between 520 and 516 B.C. during which the temple was being rebuilt. They throw a remarkably clear light upon an exceedingly critical and significant period in the life of the Jews of Palestine. They are also in many ways the best Old Testament source for the study of the unfolding of Israel's messianic hopes.

Problems and Hopes of the Judean Community Four or five practical problems confronted and disturbed the temple builders. First, would Jerusalem and the temple, still without walls, be protected from the attack of the hostile foes that encircled them? A second and larger question was, what was to be the outcome of the great tempest through which the Persian Empire was passing, and did it mean for the Jews deliverance from the powerful conquerors who for centuries had oppressed and crushed them? Third, would the necessarily modest service of the restored temple, already sadly polluted by heathen hands, be acceptable to Jehovah? Fourth, what were the relations and the respective duties of Zerubbabel and Joshua, the civil and religious authorities in the community? It was also inevitable that at this time the hope of securing their independence under the leadership of Zerubbabel should come prominently to the front. To each of these problems Zechariah addressed himself, and his book records his convictions and public utterances.

Zechariah's Assurances of Jehovah's Care In his initial vision concerning the angelic horsemen he recognizes that the storms that have swept over the Persian Empire are beginning to subside, but he tells his fellow laborers that, if they persist, Jehovah's temple shall be rebuilt, the lands about Jerusalem shall again be sold to eager buyers, and the cities of Judah shall enjoy their former prosperity, for "Jehovah will surely comfort Zion." In the vision of the four horns and the four smiths whose mission it is to smite the horns, he assures the people that Jehovah in his good time and way will overthrow the nations that now wrong and oppress them. Although there is no promise that Jerusalem will be surrounded by walls, he declares that it shall enjoy a prosperity and a growth that no walls can confine; that Jehovah himself will be its protection, as well as its glory; that he will gather the scattered exiles; and that they, together with the nations that shall acknowledge Jehovah's rule, shall yet come streaming back to Judah.

In his next vision the prophet graphically presents a scene in Jehovah's court. Joshua the priest, representing the ceremonial service of the polluted temple, is charged by the adversary with uncleanness. Here for the first time in Hebrew literature we catch a glimpse of Satan, who is regarded not as hostile to God but as the prosecuting attorney of heaven. As in the prologue of the book of Job, he is an accredited member of the divine hierarchy. His task is to search out and report to Jehovah the misdeeds of men. In Zechariah's vision, however, the divine judge acquits Joshua of the charge and causes him to be clad with clean garments, thus proclaiming the divine approval of the modest yet devoted service of the Judean community.

Preparations for the Crowning of Zerubbabel Regarding Zerubbabel, Zechariah declares, in highly figurative language, that he shall yet be crowned and rule over a happy and prosperous people. He is spoken of as Jehovah's servant, the Branch. The term is probably original with Zechariah, although it is again used in the supplementary passages in Jeremiah 23:5 and 33:15. The word is akin to the term "shoot of the house of Jesse" used in Isaiah 11 to describe a certain scion of the house of David, who in all probability was the young Zerubbabel. Zechariah's figure describes the prince as an offshoot of the same royal tree. The obscure passage seems to mean that upon the stone, with its seven facets, which was to be set in the crown prepared for the head of Zerubbabel, Jehovah himself would engrave a fitting title.

In Zechariah's fifth vision he defined the relations between the civil and priestly authorities. The golden candlestick represented the temple and its service. The two olive trees beside it stood for Zerubbabel, the civil ruler, and for Joshua, the high priest. The duty of each was to contribute his part toward the support of the temple service. They were both Jehovah's Messiahs, that is, men anointed as a symbol of the task that each was to perform.

In this connection Zechariah declared that Jehovah would remove all obstacles from before Zerubbabel, and that he who had begun the work should live to see its completion. In an address recorded in the latter part of the sixth chapter of his prophecy (intentionally revised by a later scribe), Zechariah threw aside all symbolism and gave directions to make a crown for the head of Zerubbabel from the silver and gold that had been brought as a gift by a deputation from the Jews of Babylon. He also plainly predicted that this descendant of David should sit on the throne of Judah and that Joshua the priest should be his minister like the priests in the pre-exilic kingdom.

Disappointment of These Patriotic Hopes With Zechariah's prediction that Zerubbabel should reign on the throne of Judah the descendants of the house of David suddenly and forever disappear from Old Testament history. Whether the Jews made the attempt to shake off the yoke of Persia or whether Zerubbabel was quietly set aside cannot be determined. Contemporary history states that within at least six months after Zechariah voiced the patriotic hopes of his people the authority of Darius was fully established throughout the empire. He at once began thoroughly to organize the vast realm. Post roads bound together the distant provinces, and satraps, appointed largely from the ranks of the royal family, unified the whole empire and held it under firm control. As a rule Persian governors were substituted for the native princes. With the institution of this policy Zerubbabel may well have been quietly set aside. The event evidently made a profound impression upon the messianic expectations of the Jews. Henceforth, for three or four centuries, the temporal, kingly type of messianic hope, which had been inspired by the glories of the reign of David, entirely disappeared. It was not revived until the military victories of the Maccabean era had again brought prominently to the front this phase of national glory. As a result of these disappointments Israel's hopes were universalized and spiritualized. Jehovah, instead of a scion of the house of David, was henceforth regarded as the one supreme King of Israel.

Zechariah's Later Exhortations and Predictions In chapters 7 and 8, which conclude the original sermons of Zechariah, the apocalyptic language with which he clothed his earlier predictions regarding the future of the Judean community disappeared, and he spoke as did Amos and Haggai, plainly and directly, regarding the questions that were then stirring the people. When a deputation came from the north to inquire whether or not, now that the temple was being rebuilt, they should continue to observe their fasts in memory of the destruction of Jerusalem and the death of Gedaliah, the prophet raised the searching question of whether their motive in these services was to please Jehovah or to please themselves. He then went on to declare that the only effective way to serve Jehovah was by deeds of justice and kindness, especially to the dependent classes in the community, and that the horrors of the exile had come because their fathers had failed to worship Jehovah by righteous deeds.

The prophet concludes with a brilliant picture of the coming restoration of Jerusalem and of the peace and prosperity that should be the lot of all, because Jehovah was about to gather his scattered people from the east and the west and to establish them in the midst of his sacred city. Other nations should eagerly come to Jerusalem to seek the favor of Jehovah and to ally themselves with his faithful followers, the Jews. In a prophecy, preserved in Micah 4:1–4 and Isaiah 2:1–4 (which probably comes from this period), the same thought is nobly expressed:

It shall come to pass in the latter days,
That the mountain of Jehovah shall be established,

Even the house of our God on the top of the
  mountain,
And it shall be lifted above the hills.
All the nations shall flow to it,
And many peoples shall go and say,
Come, let us go up to Jehovah's mount,
To the house of the God of Jacob,
That he may instruct us in his ways,
And that we may walk in his paths.
For from Zion proceeds instruction,
And Jehovah's word from Jerusalem.

CHAPTER 6

ISRAEL'S TRAINING AND DESTINY

Regarding the seventy years that intervened between the rebuilding of the temple in 516 B.C. and the appearance of Nehemiah in 445 the biblical historians are silent. This silence is probably because there were no important political events in the life of the Judean community to be recorded. During the latter part of his reign Darius bridged the Hellespont and undertook the conquest of the western world. Later, under the reign of his son Xerxes, the mighty hordes of eastern warriors were turned back, and the growing weakness of the great Persian Empire was revealed. In 486 Egypt rebelled, and Persian armies marched along the eastern shore of the Mediterranean, probably levying heavy taxes for their support upon the Jews as well as upon the other peoples of Palestine. The suppression of the rebellion in Egypt illustrated how impossible it was for any of the eastern peoples to withstand even the decadent power of the Persian Empire.

In Palestine the Jews were still the prey of their hostile neighbors. No walls protected the temple and city of Jerusalem. The Jews were probably ground down under their greedy Persian governors. With the disappearance of Zerubbabel the local control fell naturally into the hands of the high priest and his followers, whose civil authority from this time on constantly increased. The words of II Isaiah well describe the lot of the Jews of Palestine during this period:

> *It is a people spoiled and plundered,*
> *They are all snared in holes,*
> *And hidden in prison houses.*
> *They have become a spoil,*
> *With none to rescue,*
> *An object of plunder,*
> *With none to say, Restore.*

Spiritual Forces in Judaism The political horizon furnished little to inspire the disappointed and persecuted Jews. Their eyes were still blinded by the brilliant hopes that had stirred them at the time when the temple was rebuilt. The quenching of these hopes had left them in deeper darkness than before. There seemed no rift in the clouds that overshadowed them. Even their priestly rulers were selfish and inconsiderate. For the faithful few who rose above the discouragements and obstacles that confronted them, however, this period of deepest gloom was lighted by a faith that shines through and glorifies most of the later books of the Old Testament. From the psalms and prophecies of the period it is evident that there were a few who in the midst of these discouraging circumstances found peace and joy. As they meditated upon the experiences of their race, and read and pondered the writings of the earlier prophets, they began to appreciate not only the real significance of their past history but the meaning of the present affliction. The chief spokesman of these immortal heroes of the faith was the prophetic author of Isaiah 40–66.

Evidence That Isaiah 40–66 Were Written in Palestine

Only recently have careful students of Isaiah 40–66 begun to realize that the point of view in all of these chapters is not distant Babylon but Jerusalem. The repeated references in chapter 56 and following to conditions in Jerusalem have led all to recognize their Palestinian origin. The evidence, however, regarding chapters 40–55 is almost equally convincing. The vocabulary and literary figures employed throughout are those peculiar to the agricultural life of Palestine and not to the commercial civilization of Babylon. The problems also are those of the Judean community. The class to whom the prophet addresses his messages is evidently the same as that to which Haggai and Zechariah speak. Jerusalem, not a Jewish colony in Babylon, is the constant object of the prophet's appeal. Babylon is only one of the distant lands of the dispersion. It is from Jerusalem that the prophet ever views the world. Thus in 43:5–6 he declares in the name of Jehovah:

> *Fear not, for I am with thee.*
> *From the east I will bring thine offspring,*
> *And from the west I will gather them;*
> *I will say to the north, Give up!*
> *And to the south, Withhold not!*
> *Bring my sons from afar,*
> *And my daughters from the ends of the earth.*

Interpreted in the light of their true geographical setting, these prophecies gain at once a new and clearer meaning.

Their Probable Date The reference in 43:23–24 to the offerings brought by the people to Jehovah's temple clearly implies that it had already been built. Furthermore, the charges preferred against the Judean community are very similar to those in the book of Malachi, which is generally assigned to the period immediately preceding the arrival of Nehemiah in 445 B.C. From the parallels in chapter 48 and elsewhere it is evident that Jehovah's Messiah in 45:1 is not Cyrus but Israel, the messianic nation, to which Jehovah in earlier days under David and his successors gave repeated victories and far-extended authority. The presence of the name Cyrus seems without reasonable doubt to be due to a later scribe, who thus incorrectly identified the allusion. It is supported by neither the metrical structure nor the context of the passages in which it is found. Furthermore, the ideas in Isaiah 40–55 are almost without exception those that Zechariah had already voiced in germinal form, especially in his latest prophecies preserved in chapters 7 and 8.

They are here more fully and far more gloriously expanded, indicating that their author lived perhaps a generation later than Zechariah. The years between 500 B.C. and 450 B.C. furnish the most satisfactory setting for these prophecies. In a very true sense, however, like many of the psalms, they are timeless. The question of their exact date is comparatively unimportant except as it throws light upon their interpretation.

Their Literary Characteristics The prophecies in Isaiah 40–66 are psalms, sharing the characteristics of all lyric Hebrew poetry. Each is complete in itself and yet closely related to the others both in content and literary form. Their nobility of theme, their breadth of outlook, their wealth of rich and glowing figures, and their finished literary character give them an incontestable place among the greatest writings of the Old Testament. While there is a powerful argument running through them all, the logic is not cumulative but rather moves in a spiral, frequently returning to the same subject but having a gradual onward movement. It is the characteristic Oriental method of thinking, which is the opposite of that of the Western world. These poems are grouped into three cycles that apparently represent the prophet's thinking during succeeding periods. The first cycle is included in 40–48. Chapter 48 is a recapitulation of the thought of the preceding and furnishes a natural conclusion to the first collection. The second group is in 49–55. The note of suffering is here more prominent, and the portrait of the ideal type of servant that Jehovah desires in order to realize his purpose in human history is developed in greater detail. The third group, in 56–66, is by many assigned to another prophet and to a much later period. While the general theme of the group is different and implies a somewhat changed historical background, the characteristic ideas and literary forms of 40–55 also recur here. From the study of Israel's past and future the prophet turns to the closer consideration of the problems in Palestine. The historical allusions are for the most part in accord with the conditions that Nehemiah found in Jerusalem in 445 B.C.

Their Theme and Purpose The poems deal with one theme, the destiny of the chosen people. The prophet first reviews their past history to illustrate Jehovah's purpose, which was being realized through Israel. He notes the different ways in which Jehovah had trained and prepared them for their great task. In the light of the new situation and his enlarged acquaintance with the world the prophet then proceeds to define the task that awaits his people. While he does not break entirely away from the popular expectation that the scattered exiles would yet be restored to Jerusalem to participate in the universal kingdom that was there to be established, he fully appreciates the larger significance of Israel's mission. He recognizes that it is worldwide. He sees that the Jewish race is called not merely to receive honors and material blessings but also to serve suffering and needy mankind. The disappointments and afflictions through which it is passing are but a part of the divine training for that nobler spiritual service. The servant Israel is called to be a witness to all the nations, faithfully to set forth Jehovah's teachings until his law is established in all the earth. Thus the prophet interprets Israel's past, present, and future in its vital relation to the universal life of humanity, and declares that Israel is destined to be a prophet nation and to reveal Jehovah's character to all mankind.

Reasons Why Jehovah Will Restore His People The prophet opens with a declaration that Jerusalem's period of forced service is over, that she has paid double for the sins of the past, and that Jehovah is about to remove all obstacles and restore and exalt his oppressed people. He then gives the reasons for his strong conviction. (1) Jehovah is incomparably superior to the forces of nature, to the nations that hold Israel in bondage, and to the heathen gods whose images are shaped by the hand of man. All the powers of heaven and earth are under his control. He is the creator and supreme ruler of the universe, able to remove all obstacles and to give strength and might to those who put their trust in him. (2) Through his leadership of his people in the past, through their victories over their powerful foes, and in all the experiences of their national life he has shown his power to guide and deliver. (3) Toward Israel, his servant, he stands in a unique relation, for he has chosen and trained his people for a great service in behalf of all the world. Therefore he who is able and eager to deliver will not fail his people in their hour of need. (4) Their present affliction is but a part of the training that is essential before they can perform their task as Jehovah's servant; that task is tenderly to espouse the cause of those who are crushed, to open eyes that are blind, to bring captives out of their confinement, and, as a faithful teacher, to inspire all mankind with love for Israel's God.

The prophet's aim was clearly to encourage his despondent people, to show them the deeper meaning of their present afflictions, to open their eyes to Jehovah's gracious purpose, to give to the entire race a goal for which to live and strive, and, above all, to arouse them to effective action. Doubtless the prophet thought only of the problems of the men of his day, but in his interpretation of Jehovah's worldwide purpose and in the faith and devotion his words inspire he gave to all mankind a universal, undying message.

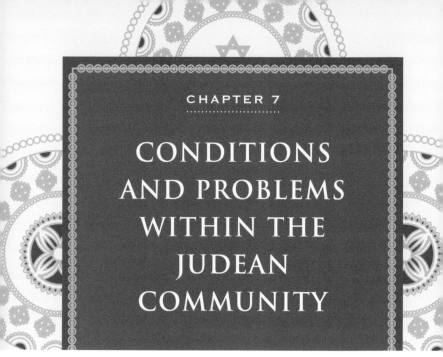

CHAPTER 7

CONDITIONS AND PROBLEMS WITHIN THE JUDEAN COMMUNITY

"Malachi" in the Hebrew means "my messenger," and the word was apparently taken from the opening verse of the third chapter. Like many of the writings of the post-exilic period, the book, therefore, is anonymous. Its date, however, may be determined from its contents. The reference to the desolation of the land of the Edomites suggests that it was written late in the Persian period after the Edomites had been driven out from Mount Seir by the Nabateans and had found a home on the southern borders of Judah. The priests in the Judean community had become corrupt, and the temple service was neglected, indicating that they had lost the early enthusiasm that followed the rebuilding of the sanctuary. The Judean community was discouraged, and a spirit of doubt and questioning prevailed in the minds of those who were faithfully striving to serve Jehovah. The prophecy is an exact picture of conditions as Nehemiah found them, so that the book of Malachi may be dated not far from 445 B.C.

The prophet's method is akin to that of Zechariah. Evidently the early reverence for the word of the prophet has disappeared. Instead of bare assertions, each conclusion is supported by detailed arguments. The author of Malachi is also deeply interested in the ritual and regards the preservation of its purity as essential to the religious life of the Judean community. He charges the priests with failure to observe the ceremonial laws, especially in allowing the people to bring for sacrifice animals that are blind, lame, and sick. These acts are evidence of the religious apathy that had seized even the religious leaders of the people. The prophet declares boldly that under the guise of religion the priests are robbing Jehovah. Above all they are faithless to their responsibilities as the appointed teachers of the people. In 2:5–7 he presents the clearest picture extant of the task of the priest as teacher. His duty was to instruct the people, to help them to overcome temptation, and to make very clear to them the way of duty. This ideal, the prophet declares, was realized by earlier priests, but now those who are the appointed religious guides are misleading the people.

The Need of a Great Moral Awakening The evils the prophet denounced were not confined to the priests. The old Semitic law regarding divorce was exceedingly lax. A husband could lead his wife to the door of his tent and tell her to be gone, thereby severing their marriage relation. The Deuteronomic law sought to relieve this injustice by providing that the husband must place in the hand of his wife, as she departs, a document stating the grounds on which he had divorced her. By the middle of the fifth century B.C. divorce had evidently become exceedingly common in Palestine. The prophet denounced it on the basis of its injustice and cruelty. He also maintained that marriage was a solemn covenant before Jehovah between man and wife, and that he who disregarded it dealt faithlessly and was the especial object of divine displeasure.

Traces of the old heathenism still remained in Judah, and the dependent, oppressed classes received little pity from the selfish, heartless rulers. In the face of these evils the prophet declared that Jehovah would surely send a messenger to punish and to reform priest and people. The prophecy was evidently based on a clear recognition that Jehovah was ever working to train and uplift his people, and that a period of degeneration must surely be followed by a period of reform. In the work of Nehemiah the prophet's hopes were in part fulfilled, but the larger fulfilment of the underlying principle was realized in the thoroughgoing reformatory work of John the Baptist and that of the Great Teacher. In a later appendix to the prophecy of

Malachi this theme is still further developed. The promise is made that another prophet, with the zeal of the great reformer Elijah, would come and prepare the way for a new and nobler era.

The Lot of the Faithful In the prophecy of Malachi are first voiced the despairing cries and doubts of those of the faithful who failed to rise above the effect of the existing social and religious evils. They are the righteous or afflicted who also speak through certain of the earlier psalms of the Psalter (e.g., 10–17, 22). It was a period when the man who did right and was faithful to the demands of the law was thereby condemned to poverty and persecution at the hands of the corrupt priests and rulers. Worse than that, their poverty and wretchedness were interpreted, according to the current belief of the day, as convincing evidence of Jehovah's displeasure because of their sins. It was a time when wickedness triumphed and innocence suffered, and when the question whether or not a righteous God ruled the universe rose persistently in the minds of the faithful. The author of Malachi recognizes and seeks to meet these doubts:

> *Ye have said, It is useless to serve God,*
> *And what gain is it to us to have kept his charge,*
> *And that we have walked in funeral garb before him?*
> *Even now we call the proud happy,*
> *Verily those who work iniquity thrive,*
> *Yea, they tempt God and escape.*

Here the problem is the same as that of the book of Job. To these doubts the prophet could only reply that Jehovah will keep a record of the faithful and in his good time will reward them.

The Problem of Suffering in the Literature of the Period

As was natural, this problem of innocent suffering was prominent in the literature of the period. It became especially insistent at this time, because it had ceased to be the problem of the community and had become that of individuals or of a class. While the nation rested under the shadow of misfortune, a solution of the problem was found in the consciousness of national guilt and in the hope that the affliction would be but temporary. The old dogma that virtue was always rewarded and wickedness punished continued to satisfy Israel's leaders. When, however, a considerable class in the community were conscious that they had committed no crimes worthy of the bitter persecutions and calamities that overtook them, and that it was often just because of their virtue and the steadfastness with which they clung to the nobler ideals of their race that they were thus assailed, the current interpretations of evil were no longer satisfactory. When in time many of them went down to the grave crushed by affliction and the objects of the taunts and revilings of their wicked pursuers, the insufficiency of the current explanation of misfortune was tragically demonstrated. To their minds Sheol or the grave offered no solution, for, as among all early Aryan and

Semitic peoples, it was thought of as the dark, passionless, joyless abode of the shades.

In most of the psalms of this period the poets who speak on behalf of the afflicted class, like the author of Malachi, expressed the hope that Jehovah would speedily come to their deliverance and signally vindicate and reward them. The heroism and fidelity that they represent can be fully appreciated only in the light of this discouraging period when evil was regnant. It was apparently at this time that the great poet, who speaks through the book of Job, presented, with the spirit and method of a modern philosopher, the lot of these innocent sufferers. He also proved for all time that misfortune is not always the evidence of guilt, and that the current doctrine of proportionate rewards and the explanations that were adduced to support it were in certain cases absolutely untenable.

CHAPTER 8

THE PROBLEM AND TEACHINGS OF THE BOOK OF JOB

Like most of the books of the Old Testament, Job is, without reasonable doubt, the work of several different writers. The prose introduction (1–2), with its corresponding conclusion (42:7–17), was probably once an independent story. The words of Jehovah in the epilogue (42:7) clearly implies that, as in chapters 1 and 2, Job had endured the test and had meekly submitted to the afflictions which Satan, with divine approval, had sent upon him, and that on the other hand his friends, like his wife, had urged him to curse God and die. The language and phrases of this prose story are radically different from those in the poem that constitutes the main body of the book. The unique explanation of why Job was afflicted that is given in the opening chapters is also completely ignored in the poetic dialogues (3–31). Likewise the problem of whether or not Job fears God for naught, raised in the prologue, is not taken up again except in the concluding prose epilogue. In the prose story Job's piety conforms to popular standards, while in the poetic sections he is measured by the loftier ethical principles laid down by the pre-exilic prophets (cf. chap. 31). In form, therefore, in aim and in content, the prose story differs fundamentally from the great dramatic poem that constitutes the real book of Job. The main body of the book is found in chapters 3–27, 29–31, 38:1–40:14, and 42:1–6. At a few points the original order has apparently been disarranged and later hands have frequently supplemented the older sections, but the literary unity of the whole is obvious. In three cycles of speeches the problem of innocent suffering is fully developed and the current solutions are presented. In conclusion the voice of Jehovah comes to Job, calling him forth from himself to the contemplation of the larger universe that manifests the divine wisdom and rulership.

The Elihu speeches in 32–37 are evidently from a still later author or authors who wished to rebuke Job's seeming impiety and the failure of his friends to bring forth a satisfactory explanation of the suffering of the innocent. Its independence is shown by the presence of many Aramaic words, by the lack of literary vigor, and by the frequent repetitions, which distinguish it sharply from the writings of the author of the main body of the book. Elihu and his contributions are also completely ignored in the rest of the book and at points where, if they were original, certain references would be almost inevitable. These speeches, in fact, are simply a fuller development of the argument of Eliphaz found in the fifth chapter. They also incorporate many suggestions drawn from the speeches of Jehovah in chapters 38 and 39.

Dates of the Different Parts The classic Hebrew style and the absence of Aramaic words indicate that the prose story is the oldest section of the book. It also reasserts in modified form the dogma current far down into the Persian period, that if the righteous but patiently bear affliction they will surely in the end be richly rewarded. It contains a message well adapted to the needs and beliefs of the Jewish people during the calamities of the Babylonian period. Its conception of Satan as the prosecuting attorney of heaven, and of Jehovah as a transcendental ruler surrounded by a hierarchy of angels, is closely akin to that which first appears in the second chapter of Zechariah. The references to Job in Ezekiel 14:14,20, as one of the three heroes of popular tradition famous for their piety, implies the existence during the exile of a story closely akin to if not identical with the one found in the prologue and epilogue of the book of Job. Such a story was probably current long before the days of Ezekiel, but in its present form it was not committed to writing until the latter part of the Babylonian or the beginning of the Persian period.

The first part of this story was evidently used by the author as an introduction to the great dramatic poem. He thereby deliberately protested against the solution of the problem of innocent suffering suggested by the ancient story. The poem itself cannot be dated earlier than the middle of the Persian period. In it the great ethical and social standards of the pre-exilic prophets are fully accepted. Its marvelous breadth of vision also implies an advanced stage in Israel's thinking. The problem of suffering with which it deals is not merely that of the nation but of the individual or of a class within the Judean community. It is precisely the problem that confronted the author of Malachi and to which he refers in 3:13–16. It is the same problem that bulks largely in the psalms of this period and finds its noblest solution in Isaiah 53. All its affinities, therefore, confirm the conclusion that it comes from the middle of the fifth century B.C. and is probably slightly older than Isaiah 49–55, which presents a more fundamental treatment of the problem of human suffering. The author still holds the old prophetic conception of the universe (38:4–6) and is unaffected by the priestly thought and tendencies that became especially prominent during the closing years of the Persian period.

The Elihu speeches and the supplemental poem in description of wisdom in 28, and of the behemoth and leviathan in 40:15–41:34, probably come from the Greek period.

The Prose Story In the prose story Job is pictured as a man of superlative piety and prosperity. According to the popular standards of the earlier day he lived a blameless life. His afflictions came simply as a means of demonstrating the unselfish character of his piety. In rapid succession he is stripped of all his possessions and afflicted by the vilest of all diseases, apparently the loathsome tubercular leprosy. Even his wife tempts him to curse God and die, but he fully meets the test, and, according to the testimony of the concluding epilogue, receives Jehovah's approval and is restored to the joys of family, reputation, and riches. It is obvious that, as in the stories found in the opening chapters of Genesis, this is a popular narrative freely adjusted to the ends the storyteller wished to attain. The incidents recorded are not in keeping with the ordinary experiences of life, but belong rather to the realm of popular fancy. As a reference in Ezekiel implies, it was probably, like the similar stories regarding Noah and Daniel, a heritage from the common Semitic lore. In fact, a recently discovered Babylonian tablet tells of a famous king of Nippur, Tabi-utul-Bel by name, whose experiences and spirit correspond closely to those of the hero of this prose story.

The message of the prose story of Job, as it was sent out to the Jewish race, was that it was not always possible to understand the reason why the righteous were afflicted, but that if they faithfully met the test, restoration to Jehovah's approval, with the honor and reputation that necessarily follow, were ensured. To the nation such a message was not without its practical application and value, but it failed completely to meet the individual problems that became pathetically insistent during the middle of the fifth century B.C.

The Poem of Job In the later poetic version of the story (which begins with the third chapter) Job himself is the embodiment of the problem of innocent suffering. His friends' suppositions and condemnations add still another burden to his weight of woe. More intolerable, however, than loss of possessions, health, and reputation is his sense of being forsaken and condemned by Jehovah. Job cannot shake himself entirely free from the belief, which had been inculcated in his mind from earliest infancy, that calamity was a sign of divine displeasure, and therefore of sin on the part of the victim. In the series of monologues and dialogues between Job and his friends he voices every phase of the great problem and makes it concrete and objective. With marvelous psychological truth and insight the author has presented the different phases of feeling through which an innocent sufferer in Job's position naturally passes. At times Job is intemperate in his speech and at other times he yields to despondency; again his faith overleaps all obstacles and he holds for the moment a clear belief in the ultimate vindication not only of himself but of Jehovah's justice.

His friends, on the other hand, formulate at length the current explanation of suffering. Job in his sharp retorts makes clear the inapplicability of the arguments and the limitations of the dogmas that they constantly reassert. In the concluding speeches of Jehovah the author with masterly skill takes Job out of his little circle into the larger world of nature, and brings him face to face with the evidences of Jehovah's might, wisdom, and gracious rulership of the great universe and of the complex life of those who inhabit it. Above all, Job learns to know God, not through the testimony of others, but by direct personal experience, and this knowledge begets humility and trust.

Progress in Job's Thought The thought of the book of Job is characteristically Oriental. Instead of moving straight on from premises to conclusion it constantly reverts to the same themes yet advances along independent, parallel lines. Its progress is not objective, as is usually the case in a drama, but almost entirely subjective. There are four parallel lines of progress. First is the conviction, gradually crystallizing into certainty, that the current explanations of suffering are in certain cases inadequate and false. While from one point of view this conclusion is merely negative, it nevertheless opened the eyes of Job and his generation to a larger conception of Jehovah and a far broader interpretation of the universe and of the laws that regulate it. The second is that he is guilty of no crime commensurate with the calamity that had overtaken him. Overwhelmed by misfortune and the reiterated charges of his friends, only through a superhuman struggle did Job ultimately attain the unshaken conviction that he was indeed innocent in the sight of God and man. The third line of progress is that, if not in the present life, in that beyond the grave not only would his reputation be vindicated, but he himself would be fully conscious of that vindication.

As is illustrated by the third chapter, Job in common with his race still shared the belief that for the ordinary individual life beyond the grave was a shadowy existence, far removed from Jehovah's presence. This conception of the life after death was inherited by the Israelites from their Semitic ancestors, and was held in common by most ancient peoples, both of the East and of the West. The Babylonians believed, however, that certain favored mortals—for example, the hero of the flood—were transported to the abode of the gods, there to enjoy blessed individual immortality. The same belief is the foundation of the Hebrew stories regarding Enoch and Elijah. This belief was apparently the germ that in time developed, as in the twelfth chapter of Daniel, into the widespread conviction that the grave would not hold those who had been loyal to Jehovah, but that he would surely raise them again to a glorious life. In the book of Job it is possible to trace the birth pangs of this broader hope. Conscious of his innocence and confronted by the grave, Job repeatedly voices the deep conviction that God, because he is just, will raise his afflicted servant from the grave and accord to him the justice that seems excluded from his present life. This solution of the problem of innocent suffering is not given the central place by the author of the book of Job. It is safe, however, to conjecture that if the appearance of Jehovah had not furnished to the author's mind a more satisfactory conclusion, the vindication after death would have been the solution offered. At several points Job approaches very close to the belief in individual immortality that became a commonly accepted tenet in the trying days of the Maccabean struggle.

The fourth line of progress is that Jehovah, after all, must be just and that he will right the seeming wrongs of life. In his opening speeches Job gives free vent to the anguish and impatience that fills his tortured mind. With a boldness strangely foreign to Hebrew thought, he charges Jehovah with injustice and speaks of him as a cruel monster that watches man, his helpless prey, and takes cruel pleasure in the pain he inflicts. As the discussion progresses Job's mind becomes calmer, and the conviction that God, after all, is just comes more clearly to expression. His strong utterances gradually yield to this quieter mood. Even before he hears the voice of Jehovah, Job has attained an attitude of trust, though he is still groping in darkness. Thus with marvelous fidelity to human nature and experience the author of the book of Job would have made a great contribution to the problem with which he was dealing even had he not added the concluding speeches of Jehovah.

Significance of Speeches of Jehovah To many Western readers the concluding speeches of Jehovah are unsatisfying. They lack the emphasis on Jehovah's love and the divine tenderness in addressing the heroic sufferer that to us would seem to have been a satisfactory conclusion to the great drama. This element is furnished in characteristically concrete form by the epilogue of the book, in which Job's prosperity is restored in double measure and he is personally assured of Jehovah's favor. The severe and realistic author of the great poem, however, knew that in ordinary life such solutions are rare. In the speeches of Jehovah he does not introduce an altogether new element, but emphasizes motifs already developed in the earlier dialogues. The effect of these speeches upon Job are threefold. (1) They rebuke his over-accentuated individualism. (2) They reveal the fundamental contrast between the infinite God and finite man. In the light of this revelation Job plainly recognizes his presumption and folly in attempting, with his limited outlook, to comprehend, much less to criticize, the mighty ruler of all the universe. (3) After Job had thus been led out of himself into personal companionship with God he was content to trust his all-wise guide, even though he recognized his own inability to fathom the mysteries of the universe or to solve the problem of innocent suffering. Thus the great contributions of the book of Job to the problem of suffering are (1) a clear and scientific presentation of the problem, (2) a bold sweeping aside of the insufficient current theological explanations, (3) a vastly enlarged conception of Jehovah's character and rule, and (4) the attitude of faith that comes from a personal experience of God and that trusts unreservedly, even though it cannot see or divine the reason why, and in that trust finds peace and joy.

Although the thought of the book of Job is profound and it deals in a masterly manner with a fundamental human problem, it is more than a mere philosophical discussion. Its primary aim is to set forth the vital truth that God is not to be found through current theological dogmas or intellectual discussions, but through personal experience.

This is the dominant note throughout the book. The greatest calamity that overtakes Job in his hour of deepest distress is the sense of being shut away from God's presence.

> *Oh! that I knew where I might find him,*
> *That I might come even to his throne!*
> *As he looks back fondly to the happy days of old the*
> *   fact that stands forth above all others is that*
> *The Almighty was yet with me.*

Looking forward to a possible vindication after death his hope centers in the belief that

> *Thou wouldst call and I myself would answer thee;*
> *Thou wouldst long for the work of thy hands.*

When at last Jehovah answered Job out of the storm, it was not so much the thought expressed as the fact that God had spoken directly to him that brought penitence and peace:

> *I have heard of thee by the hearing of the ear,*
> *But now mine eye seeth thee.*
> *Therefore I loath my words,*
> *And repent in dust and ashes.*

CHAPTER 9

THE TRAINING AND MISSION OF THE TRUE SERVANT OF JEHOVAH

Isaiah 49–54 contain three distinct portraits of the ideal servant of Jehovah. Each in turn develops characteristics suggested in the preceding. These descriptions are interspersed with exhortations addressed to Jehovah's servant Israel and assurances that God will fully restore Jerusalem and bring back her scattered children. These three portraits of the type of servant that Jehovah required to realize his purpose in human history, together with the earlier portrait in 42:1–7, supplement each other. In the first of these four (42:1–7) the prophetic qualities of the servant are especially emphasized. Like the earlier prophets, he will not fail nor be discouraged until he has established justice on earth. His task is to open blind eyes and to deliver prisoners from the darkness of ignorance and sin in which they were sitting.

In the second picture (49:1–9a) the worldwide mission of the servant is emphasized. He is called not only to gather the outcasts of Israel, but also as an apostle to bring light to all the nations of the earth. In this passage for the first time appears that note of suffering and ignominy which is the lot of the true servant of Jehovah. In the third portrait (50:4–10) the servant is pictured as a disciple, attentively listening to the divine teachings, learning the lessons that will fit him in turn to become a teacher of men. The last and fullest picture (52:13–53:12) describes at length his suffering. A strong contrast is drawn between his present shame and ignominy and the future glory and victory he will achieve through his voluntary and complete self-sacrifice. These pictures embody the prophet's ideal, and they can be fully understood only in the light of their historical background.

The Prophet's Purpose In his earlier poems this great unknown prophet dealt largely with the interpretation of Israel's past history and the proclamation of the coming deliverance (40–48). His chief aims in chapters 49–55 may be briefly epitomized as follows: (1) to interpret the inner meaning of the period of adversity through which the Jewish race was then passing; (2) to make absolutely clear the character and quality of the service that Jehovah required of his chosen people, if they were to realize his purpose in human history; (3) to inspire them all to make the needed sacrifices and thus to prove themselves true servants of Jehovah; and (4) especially to make plain to the innocent and faithful sufferers in the Judean community the real meaning and value of their present shame and suffering, if bravely and voluntarily borne.

Character and Condition of Those to Whom the Prophet Appealed From the allusions in the prophecies themselves it is possible to determine the classes that the prophet had in mind. In 49:2 his address is to the coast lands and the distant peoples who lived at the extremities of Israel's horizon. It is not probable, however, that he anticipated that his message in its present form would go out as it has to all races and nations; rather his attention was fixed on the scattered members of his own race, those who lived in the north and the west and in the distant city of Syene, far up the Nile (49:12). In 49:3 he clearly identifies the nation Israel as Jehovah's servant, whom he makes declare:

> *Jehovah said to me, Thou art my servant,*
> *Israel, in whom I will glorify myself.*

It is evident, however, that the prophet has especially in mind the Judean community amidst which he lived and for which he worked. In 54, as elsewhere, he calls upon this group of discouraged Jews to enlarge their tent, for their period of punishment is over and their foundation and walls are about to be rebuilt. At last they shall cease to tremble at the fury of the oppressor. In 51:18–20 he addresses Jerusalem directly and gives a vivid picture of its condition before the appearance of Nehemiah:

Rouse thee! Rouse thee! stand up, O Jerusalem,
Who hast drunk at Jehovah's hand the cup of his
*   wrath!*
The bowl of reeling thou hast drunken, hast drained!
There is none to guide thee of all the sons whom thou
*   hast borne,*
And none to take thee by the hand of all the sons whom
*   thou hast reared.*
These two things have befallen thee—who can condole
*   with thee?*
Desolation and destruction, famine and the sword—
*   who can comfort thee?*

The Task and Training of Jehovah's Servant The term
"servant" means literally "slave," not in the Western sense,
but in that of the ancient East, where a slave was often a
privileged member of society. In many a Hebrew household
the slaves, next to the children, enjoyed the protection and
consideration of the master of the household. He was under
obligation to guard their welfare and interests. On the other
hand, slaves, like Eleazar in the story of Abraham (Gen. 26),
faithfully cared for the interests of their master and spared no
effort to carry out his commands. Semitic usage had also given
the term "slave" a significant meaning. The faithful officials
of all Oriental kings called themselves his servants or slaves.
It was the common term expressing, on the one hand, confidence and protection, and, on the other, devotion, loyalty,
and service. Most of Israel's patriarchs, kings, and prophets

are spoken of as the servants or slaves of Jehovah. Haggai, in his address to Zerubbabel, called him Jehovah's servant. In Deuteronomy 32:36 the people of Israel are called the servants of Jehovah, and, as has been noted, in the prophecies of the II Isaiah they are frequently referred to as the servant of Jehovah. The term, therefore, was well chosen to express that complete devotion and loyalty to Jehovah that the prophet aimed to evoke from his fellow countrymen. It was also free from the kingly associations and material interpretation that were connected with the word "Messiah."

The prophet's aim was to present so vividly the task and methods of the true servant of Jehovah that all would recognize a personal call to duty. He emphasizes three distinct yet related elements in the mission of the servant. They were (1) to free the prisoners from their captivity, whether imprisoned by walls of stone or brick or under the tyranny of fears and false ideas; (2) to restore the scattered tribes of Israel and thus to lay the foundations for a renewed national life that would furnish concrete evidence to all the world of Jehovah's power to deliver; and (3) to go beyond the narrow bounds of their race and to bring to the nations that were groping in the darkness of heathenism the knowledge and truth that had been imparted to Israel. Thus the unknown prophet laid the foundations for that Kingdom of God, that dominion of God in nature and in the minds of men that was the guide and inspiration of all later prophets and the goal for whose realization the Great Teacher and Prophet of Nazareth labored and died.

The prophet places great emphasis upon the training of Jehovah's servant. He declares that from birth Jehovah formed him to be his servant. In 50:4–7 he is spoken of as a trained disciple attentively listening to the words of his divine teacher, never rebelling at the bitterness of the needful discipline, but ever seeking to prepare himself to give to the fainting a word of help. The steadfastness with which he endures shame and bitter wrongs is the evidence of his ability as a disciple and an essential part in his preparation for his exalted mission.

Methods of Jehovah's Servant In accomplishing his task the servant is to use definite instruction, but his teaching is to be illustrated by his own character and attitude. By the voluntary, uncomplaining endurance of ignominy and suffering he is to do Jehovah's work and win the grateful recognition, not only of his divine Master, but of all succeeding generations. Through a keen analysis of life the prophet had attained to a clear appreciation of the inestimable value of voluntary self-sacrifice. He saw that it was the most effective means of uplifting the race and leading mankind to accept God's mastery over their minds and lives. The truth here presented is illustrated in human experience as clearly today as in the past. The self-denying service of parents is absolutely essential if their children are to attain to the noblest manhood and womanhood. Only through the self-sacrificing labors of those who love their fellow men can social evils be removed and society attain its highest development. The low standards in the business and professional world can be raised only as certain men, with the spirit and courage of the ancient prophets, make their own personal interests and popularity subservient to the rigorous demands of justice. It is the law of life that he who would elevate the standards of his associates and thus lead men to the fullest realization of the divine ideals must ordinarily do it in the face of opposition, ignominy, and seeming failure. It is this quiet, heroic self-sacrifice—the heroism of the commonplace—that the great prophet proclaims is the absolutely essential characteristic of Jehovah's servant. Despised by his contemporaries, the victim of persecution and calamity, he must do his task, leaving the reward and the appreciation to Jehovah and to the enlightened sense of later generations.

Realization of the Ideal of Service The portrait is so concrete that the question naturally arises, who was the servant of whom the prophet was speaking? Undoubtedly the tragic experiences of such prophets as Jeremiah suggested many elements in the picture. For half a century that faithful servant of Jehovah suffered, often shrinkingly, yet voluntarily, a constant martyrdom. Upon him fell the persecutions of his countrymen. Yet in the life of later Judaism those principles for which he lived and died gained acceptance and application. Of him it may be truly said:

> *He was numbered with trangressors,*
> *And himself bore the sins of many,*
> *And interposed for transgressors.*

The unknown author of these immortal poems spoke out of the depth of his own painful experience and doubtless in a large degree realized the ideals of service that he thus effectively set forth. Those of his contemporaries who, amidst persecution and insults, in their lives embodied the ideals of the earlier prophets were crushed like Jeremiah because of the iniquities of others, but by thus pouring out their lifeblood they brought healing to their race. Nehemiah, in responding to the call of service and in turning his back upon the allurements of the Persian court in order to rebuild the city of his fathers, proved himself a faithful servant of Jehovah. With true insight the Christian church has always recognized that in the character and life of Jesus is found the only complete realization of this ancient ideal of service. With the immortal chapters of the II Isaiah he was clearly familiar, and from them he doubtless received many suggestions regarding his divine mission and the methods by which it was to be accomplished. Their author was clearly speaking to his contemporaries, but in portraying the way in which Jehovah's purpose in human history could alone be realized he presented an ideal that has permanent significance in the thought of the human race, Paul rightly recognized that the same responsibility to make this ideal a reality rested upon him, and all who would serve God, when he quoted the words of 49:6 (cf. Acts 13:47):

> *I have set thee for a light of the Gentiles*
> *That thou shouldst be for salvation to the*
> *uttermost parts of the earth.*

CHAPTER 10

NEHEMIAH'S WORK IN REBUILDING THE WALLS OF JERUSALEM

Fortunately the author of the books of Ezra and Nehemiah has quoted at length in the opening chapters of Nehemiah from the personal memoirs of the noble patriot through whose activity the walls of Jerusalem were restored. They are the best historical records in the Old Testament and they shed clear, contemporary light upon this most important period in the evolution of Judaism. The narrative is straightforward and vivid. It lights up the otherwise dark period that precedes Nehemiah and enables the historian to bridge with assurance the century that intervened before the apocryphal book of I Maccabees throws its light upon the course of Israel's troubled history. The detailed description of the rebuilding of the walls in Nehemiah 3 is probably from the Chronicler, but it reveals an intimate acquaintance with the topography and the later history of Judah's capital.

Nehemiah's Response to the Call to Service The presence of a deputation from Jerusalem (including Nehemiah's kinsman Hanani) in the distant Persian capital of Susa was not a mere accident. Nehemiah's response to their appeal and the epoch-making movement he inaugurated reveal the presence of an impelling force. Probably back of all this movement was the work of the great prophet who speaks in Isaiah 40–66. In all that Nehemiah did that influence may be seen. In the fervent and patriotic prayer that he uttered on learning of conditions in Jerusalem he used the term "servant [or servants] of Jehovah" eight times in six short verses. It also echoes the phraseology and thought of the II Isaiah.

The king under whom Nehemiah served was evidently Artaxerxes I. In Nehemiah 12:10–11 the Chronicler states that Eliashib, the high priest in the days of Nehemiah, was the grandson of Joshua, who shared in the rebuilding of the temple in 520 B.C. Eliashib was also the great-grandfather of Jaddua, who was high priest in Jerusalem in 332 B.C., when Alexander conquered Palestine. References in the recently discovered Elephantine letters, as well as in the history of Josephus, confirm the conclusion that Nehemiah set out upon his expedition in the spring of 445 B.C. Like all those who ministered personally to the Persian kings, he was probably a eunuch and still a young man. The true piety that is revealed in his prayer, the courage shown by his daring to appear with sad face in the presence of the absolute tyrant who ruled the Eastern world, and his tact in winning the king's consent to his departure indicate that he was a man of rare energy and ability. Artaxerxes I was famous for his susceptibility to the influence of court favorites. The queen referred to in 1:6 was probably the queen mother Amestris, who exercised commanding authority in the Persian court. Without the royal consent and the resources and authority granted him, Nehemiah could hardly have accomplished the large task he undertook. The arduous journey of fifteen hundred miles over mountains and barren deserts was enough to daunt a man reared in the luxury of an Oriental court, but Nehemiah was inspired by an ideal of service that recognized no obstacles.

Obstacles That Confronted Him The high-priestly rulers do not appear to have welcomed Nehemiah with enthusiasm. Some of them, at least, later sought to undermine his work. It is not difficult to infer the reason for their apathy. People with entrenched wealth and authority are usually conservative, especially if conscious that their position is easily assailable. As the sequel proved, these leaders of the community were simply intent upon self-aggrandizement, even at the expense of the dependent members of the community. A revolutionizing work like that proposed by Nehemiah was certain to affect their vested interests and to reveal their cruel selfishness. Certain of their families had also intermarried with neighboring chieftains, and they were quite content with the existing conditions. A second obstacle was the opposition of the hostile peoples who surrounded the little Judean community. On the east the Ammonites had apparently pressed in and occupied the ancient Hebrew territory as far as the Jordan. Tobiah, the Ammonite, who figures prominently in Nehemiah's narrative, was probably one of their local chiefs. Gashmu, the Arabian, represented the half-civilized Bedouin tribes that had invaded the territory of Judea from the south and east during the period of weakness following the destruction of Jerusalem. Possibly he belonged to the Edomites who then held Hebron and all of the southern part of Judea. Nehemiah also refers to the descendents of Israel's ancient foes, the Philistines, living in the city of Ashdod. On the north the superior resources of Samaria had asserted themselves, and these survivors of the ancient Israelites who lived among the hills of Ephraim had grown into a powerful nation that overshadowed the struggling Judean community. These northerners, however, still worshipped at Jerusalem and were closely allied with the Jews. At their head was Sanballat, the Horonite, who probably came from Bethhoron, in southwestern Samaria. Each of these peoples inherited the feeling of hostility with which their fathers had regarded the people of Judah, and looked with suspicion upon any movement to reestablish Jerusalem's former strength and prestige. Furthermore, the men of the Judean community itself lacked courage and training. With inefficient helpers and with opponents within and without the community, Nehemiah's task seemed well-nigh impossible. That he succeeded in the face of all these obstacles in rebuilding the walls in the incredibly short period of fifty-two days is only explained by his superlative skill, devotion, and energy.

Nehemiah's Plan of Work Fortunately Nehemiah possessed resources as well as tact. He quickly disarmed the opposition and won at least the nominal support of the leaders by entertaining 150 of them as his guests. Thus he was able to place them under personal obligation to him, to keep them under close surveillance, and to command their cooperation. In the second place he appealed to them and to the people by means of eloquent addresses that reveal his enthusiasm and devotion. Furthermore, he did not depend upon the reports of others, but personally studied the situation. His secret midnight ride down through the Valley Gate to the southwest of Jerusalem and thence eastward along the Hinnom Valley to the point where it joins the Kidron, and from there up the valley, gave him most accurate information regarding conditions. In most cases the ancient foundations of the city walls still remained. The first need was to remove the rubbish and to replace stones that had fallen. The towers required certain timbers, which were cut probably from the royal domains to the south of the city. Nehemiah enlisted all members of the community both within and without Jerusalem. He organized them under their local leaders and set each to the task in which he was most interested. Thus the heads of the different villages, the elders of the leading families, the guilds of workmen, and even the priests were all put to work and inspired by the spirit of natural rivalry as well as common loyalty. Nehemiah himself with his immediate followers directed the work, and instituted a strict military rule that secured both efficiency and protection.

The Restored Walls In the light of recent excavations at Jerusalem it is possible to follow Nehemiah's work in detail. In the destruction of the walls by the Chaldeans the city had suffered most on the north, where it was nearly level and protected by no descending valleys. Just north of the temple area a little valley ran up from the Kidron, leaving but a narrow neck of land connected directly with the plateau on the north. Here two great towers were restored that probably occupied the site of the later Roman tower of Antonia. Thence the wall ran westward across the upper Tyropoean Valley, which was here comparatively level. Numerous bands of workmen were assigned to this part of the work. The gate of the old wall was probably identical with the corner gate at the northwestern end of the city. The Ephraim Gate a little farther to the southwest apparently corresponded to the modern Joppa Gate. From this point a broad wall ran to the western side of the city where the hill descended rapidly into the Hinnom Valley, making its defense easy. At the southwestern end of the city stood the Tower of the Furnaces and the Valley Gate, of which the foundations have recently been laid bare. The gate itself was narrow, being only eight feet wide, but the wall was here nine feet thick. The eighteen hundred or two thousand feet of wall along the Hinnom Valley was evidently practically intact, for its repair was entrusted to but one group of workmen. Across the southern end of the Tyropoean Valley the ground was almost level, so that a strong wall was required. Excavations have shown that it was twenty feet thick at its base and supported by six strong buttresses. The Fountain Gate, through which ran the main street down the Tyropoean Valley out into the valley of the Kidron, was the chief southern gate of the city. It was nine feet wide and defended by a tower about forty-five feet square. Portions of this ancient thoroughfare, with its stones worn smooth by the feet of the inhabitants of the ancient city, have been uncovered. Just above the Pool of Siloam, which was within the city walls, was the King's Garden.

Thence the Hill of Ophel ascended rapidly, making necessary the stairs mentioned in Nehemiah 3. The wall on the southeast was readily repaired, for it ran along the sloping western side of the Kidron Valley. The Water Gate probably led down to the Virgin's Fount, and the Horse Gate farther to the north opened directly from the Kidron Valley to the public buildings that occupied the site of Solomon's palace immediately to the south of the temple. It is the space today occupied by the southern end of the temple area, which was thus extended in the days of Herod. Opposite the northeastern end of the temple area the wall curved westward until it reached the great towers that guarded the northern end of the city.

Completion and Dedication of the Walls Under the inspiration of Nehemiah's leadership and as a result of the constant fear of attack, the building of the walls proceeded rapidly and without interruption. To the threats of hostile foes Nehemiah paid little heed. Trained in the Persian court, he saw at once their murderous purpose when they requested a conference in southwestern Samaria on the border of the Plain of Ono. Through the treacherous prophets in the Judean community they sought to play upon his fears and to lead him to compromise himself by taking refuge in the sacred precincts of the temple, but his courage, as well as his high respect for the sanctuary, delivered him from the plot. The cry that he was himself aspiring to the kingship and that his acts were treason against Persia did not daunt him, and when, in response to their malicious reports, the order finally came from the Persian king to cease working, the walls were already rebuilt.

Apparently Nehemiah's original leave of absence was for but a short period. His kinsman Hanani, who had headed the original deputation to Susa, and a certain Hananiah were by him placed in charge of the city. To protect it against sudden attack its gates were closed at night and not opened until the middle of the following forenoon. Effective measures were also instituted to increase its population. When the work of rebuilding the walls was complete, Nehemiah arranged for their public dedication. Starting from the Valley Gate on the southwestern side of the city, one half of the nobles and the people marched along the southern and eastern wall, while Nehemiah with the other half of the people proceeded along the western and northern wall. Finally meeting on the northern side of the temple area, the two companies blended their voices in thanksgiving to Jehovah, who at last had made it possible for them to worship him in his sanctuary secure from attack.

Nehemiah had reorganized the Judean community, rebuilt their walls, and inspired them with a new sense of self-respect, thus he made possible that genuine revival of the Judean state that took place during the succeeding centuries. He, like Ezekiel, Haggai, Zechariah, and the II Isaiah, was indeed one of the makers of Judaism. Ben Sira with true insight declared (49:13):

> *The memorial of Nehemiah is great,*
> *Who raised up for us the walls that were fallen,*
> *And set up the gates and bars,*
> *And raised up our homes again.*

CHAPTER 11

NEHEMIAH'S SOCIAL AND RELIGIOUS REFORMS

The fifty-sixth chapter of Isaiah presents a sharp contrast: on the one hand, a high ideal of justice toward the oppressed and tolerance toward all foreigners who sincerely desired to unite in Jehovah's worship; on the other, the sordid selfishness of the Jewish leaders, who disregarded their responsibilities and thought of religion only as a round of ceremonial observances. The situation is very similar to that in northern Israel in the days of Amos. The II Isaiah stands on the same platform as did his predecessors of the Assyrian period. He strips fearlessly from the rulers of the community the mantle of hypocrisy with which they sought to cover their shame. In clearest terms he declares that their first duty to God is to loose the fetters of injustice and to share their bread with the hungry. This stirring prophetic message is the natural introduction to the reformatory work of Nehemiah.

Nehemiah's Method of Correcting the Social Evils in the Community Nehemiah's address recorded in the fifth chapter of his memoirs completes the picture suggested in Isaiah 56 and 58. The poor had been compelled by their poverty to sell their children into slavery to the rich and ruling class. In order to pay their personal taxes they had also mortgaged their inherited fields, vineyards, and houses. Doubtless much of the tax thus raised went into the pockets of their rulers, who preyed mercilessly upon the helpless and needy. These crimes directly violated the laws of Deuteronomy (cf. Deut. 23:9, 20), as well as those in the older Book of the Covenant (Exod. 21–23). Nehemiah's position, therefore, when he demanded that these evils be righted, was unassailable. In the spirit of and with the methods of the earlier prophets he gathered together the people, probably within the precincts of the temple court, and plainly and unsparingly denounced their acts. There is much in common between this later Jewish layman and the shepherd Amos. Each spoke on the basis of close personal observation and experience, but Nehemiah possessed many advantages over the prophets who had preceded him. His own personal example lent force to his words. Although it was his right as governor, he had exacted no tribute from the Judean community. Even though the opportunity had probably offered itself, he steadily refused to take hereditary land from the poor who applied to him for loans of money or grain. Instead of enslaving his countrymen, he had lost no opportunity to free those who had been forced by misfortune or poverty into slavery. He had also entertained lavishly rich and poor alike, and thus given to all an example of practical charity. His authority as Persian governor doubtless carried great weight with the cringing, greedy leaders at Jerusalem. Above all, the force of his personality was irresistible. It is easy to imagine the powerful impression his words made upon them. The restoration of their lands and the freeing of their children were undoubtedly mighty factors in arousing the men of Jerusalem to those herculean efforts that alone made possible the rebuilding of the walls in the brief period of fifty-two days.

The Historical Value of Nehemiah 13 In his Composition of Ezra-Nehemiah, C. C. Torrey, of Yale, maintains that this chapter is a pure creation of the Chronicler (pp. 44–49). Certainly its phraseology and the subjects with which it deals are characteristic of the Chronicler, but on the whole it is probable that he has here simply recast what was originally an extract from the memoirs of Nehemiah. Some of the phrases peculiar to the Chronicler are loosely connected with the context. The nucleus that remains has the vigorous style of Nehemiah and many of his peculiar idioms. Its courageous, assertive spirit is very different from that of the other writings of the Chronicler. It is also doubtful whether this later writer, with his strong priestly interests, would have made Nehemiah, the layman, a religious reformer and therefore in a sense the rival of Ezra. Above all, the work attributed to Nehemiah in this chapter is in harmony with his spirit and attitude, as revealed in the unquestioned extracts from his memoirs. Already, as stated in 1:20, he had told Sanballat and Tobiah that they should have no portion or memorial in Jerusalem. He had already shown himself keen in righting wrongs within the community. Zeal in preserving the sanctity of the Sabbath and in opposing heathen marriages was characteristic of the Jews of the dispersion rather than of those of Palestine. It is probable, therefore, that this chapter records Nehemiah's work when he revisited Jerusalem some time after 432 B.C., although it must be frankly confessed that the historical evidence is far from conclusive and that the entire account of this second visit, including the chronological data in 5:14 and the reference to the expulsion of Sanballat in 1:20, may possibly be due to the Chronicler's desire to discredit the Samaritans and to enlist the authority of Nehemiah in support of the later priestly laws and customs.

Regulations Regarding the Temple Service The expulsion of Tobiah the Ammonite from the room that had been assigned him in the temple by Eliashib, the high priest, was apparently due to two reasons, first because Tobiah was persona non grata to Nehemiah and had already shown himself to be a dangerous foe to the Jews. The second and chief reason was because the room was needed for storing the offerings that were brought in for the support of the temple officials. These offerings were presented in accordance with the demands of the Deuteronomic regulation, which at this time was the code acknowledged by the Judean community (Deut. 18:4, 14:23, 27, 28). The narrative adds that, with his practical knowledge of affairs, Nehemiah appointed a representative committee consisting of a priest, a scribe, and a Levite, and to them he entrusted the task of receiving and distributing the temple tithes to their kinsmen.

Provisions Regarding Sabbath Observation and Foreign Marriages Far away from the temple, and therefore unable to participate in the distinctive feasts and ceremonials that distinguished the religious life of their race, and confronted by the constant danger of being absorbed by the heathen among whom they found themselves, the Jews of the dispersion placed strong emphasis on two institutions. One was the observation of the Sabbath, and the other was the preservation of the purity of their blood by abstaining from all marriage alliances with their Gentile neighbors. In Palestine, where they were able to revive the ancient feasts in connection with the temple and where the danger of absorption was not so imminent, their practices in these regards appear to have been much more lax. Not only had the priests set the example by contracting foreign marriages, but apparently about this time the author of the beautiful story of Ruth, by citing the tradition regarding the Moabite ancestry of their illustrious King David, voiced the belief of many in the community that such marriages were permissible. Nehemiah, however, rigorously opposed this tendency. He also appreciated the menace to the dignity and character of the temple service, if the commercial pursuits of ordinary days were carried into the Sabbath. His measure, therefore, in closing the gates and thus excluding all traders, was both sane and effective. In setting his face strongly against foreign marriages he was simply enforcing the laws found in Deuteronomy 7:1, 3 and 33:3, which forbade the Hebrews to intermarry with the people of the land.

Significance of Nehemiah's Work In rebuilding the walls of Jerusalem Nehemiah prepared the way for the revival of the Jewish state that characterized the closing years of the Persian period. More important still was his work in reestablishing a close relation between the Jews of the dispersion and those of Palestine. He himself was the connecting link between them, and his activity prepared the minds of the Palestinian Jews for the acceptance of those new principles that were strongly held by leaders like himself. He also enforced the ethical and social ideals of the earlier prophets, and ably advocated the principles that are fundamental in the late priestly laws. Above all, in his own personality as a prophetic layman, he held up before his race an example of patriotism, self-sacrifice, efficiency, and devotion to the service of Jehovah that made a profound and lasting impression upon his own and later generations.

CHAPTER 12

THE TRADITIONAL ACCOUNT OF THE ADOPTION OF THE PRIESTLY LAW

The tradition regarding Ezra and his work presents many difficult problems. Part of it is found in the heart of the book of Nehemiah, while another part is now found in the second half of the book of Ezra. It is not entirely clear whether this dislocation is due to the Chronicler, who desired to give Ezra, the priest and scribe, the precedence before Nehemiah, the layman, or to the mistake of a scribe. Torrey, in Composition of Ezra-Nehemiah, has shown convincingly that the Ezra story in its present form is at least from the school to which the Chronicler belonged, if not from his own pen. Not only does it abound in the characteristic phrases of this voluminous editor, but it also reflects at many points his peculiar conception of the history of this period. Ezra is described as a descendant of Aaron and "a scribe skilled in the law of Moses." His work as inter-preter of the law, which he is represented as bringing in his hand, is typical of the scribes, who were becoming the chief teachers of Judaism in the days of the Chronicler (the Greek period). The decree of Artaxerxes found in the sev-enth chapter of Ezra suggests at every point its late Jewish origin. It confers upon Ezra, the scribe, royal authority far eclipsing that given by Artaxerxes to Nehemiah, his favor-ite. At his summons seventeen hundred priests, Levites, singers, and servants of the temple rally about the standard of the faithful scribe. He is represented as going under the royal protection to Palestine to instruct the Judean com-munity, to reform its abuses, and to institute the rule of the law of Moses that he bore in his hand.

He first holds a great synagogue service in which the law is read to and interpreted for the people. They are then bidden to observe the Feast of Booths or Tabernacles in accordance with its regulations. Later, when he discovers that the people of the land have entered into foreign mar-riages, he tears his clothes and hair and sits for hours over-whelmed by the great crime that rests upon the community. When the people are gathered about him, he upbraids them for their laxness and secures the appointment of a commission with himself at the head to investigate and put an end to these evil practices. When after three months the community has been purified from this foreign element, the people are again assembled to listen to the reading of the law. Then Ezra utters a fervent prayer in which he sets forth Jehovah's leadership of his people in the past and the disasters that have come as a result of their sins. After this public petition for Jehovah's forgiveness, the people through their nobles, Levites, and priests subscribe in writing to the regulations imposed by the lawbook that Ezra had brought. Its more important regulations are also recapitulated. They are to refrain from foreign marriages, to observe strictly the Sabbath laws and also the requirements of the seventh year of release, to bring to the temple the annual tax of one-tenth of a shekel and the other dues required for its support and for the maintenance of the priests and Levites.

The Historical Value of the Ezra Tradition Recognizing that the Ezra tradition comes from the hand of the Chronicler, certain Old Testament scholars are inclined to regard it as entirely unhistorical. It can no longer be regarded as a strictly historical record. Like II Chronicles 31, it is shot through with the ideas current during the Greek period. With no desire to deceive, but with nothing of the modern historical spirit, the Chronicler freely projects the institutions, ideas, and traditions of his own day into these earlier periods. The result is that he has given not an exact or reliable historical record, but his own conception of the way in which the course of history should have unfolded. The Ezra tradition also lacks the support not only of contemporary testimony, but also of all the Jews who wrote during the next few centuries. Ben Sira in his review of Israel's heroes speaks in highest terms of

Nehemiah, but knows nothing of Ezra's work. Even the comparatively late Jewish tradition reflected in the opening chapters of II Maccabees attributes to Nehemiah the reestablishment of the temple service and the collection of the sacred writings of his race. At many points the Ezra tradition is also inconsistent with the straightforward contemporary record contained in Nehemiah's memoirs. The real question is whether or not there is a historical nucleus in the Ezra story, and, if so, what the facts it reflects are.

The Facts Underlying the Ezra Tradition The later records make it clear that during the latter part of the Persian period the attitude of the Jews in Palestine toward their neighbors became more and more exclusive. Nehemiah appears to have given a great impetus to the movement that ultimately resulted in the Samaritan schism and the high wall that henceforth separated Jew and Gentile. The emphasis on the strict observation of the Sabbath grew stronger and stronger, until at the beginning of the Greek period the Jews of Jerusalem preferred to fall before the sword of their foes rather than fight on the Sabbath day. The ritual of the temple became even more elaborate, and its income was greatly increased during the latter part of the Persian period. The extension of the territory of the Judean community implied that its numbers were increased by the return of loyal Jews attracted by the security offered by its walls and by the new spirit that animated the Jews of Palestine. The priestly laws that were formulated to meet the new needs of the Judean community appear to have been written in Palestine and by those closely connected with the temple service, but in the emphasis upon the Sabbath and in their endeavor to prevent marriage with foreigners they suggest the presence and influence of Jews who had returned from the land of the dispersion. It is possible that among those who thus returned was the priest Ezra, and he may have been at the head of one of these groups of returning exiles. In the days of Josiah the code contained in the newly discovered Book of the Covenant was presented to the people in a public assembly and adopted and enforced by the king, who acted as the representative of the people. It is probable that in the small Judean community new regulations gained acceptance in the same way, except that the people were represented by their nobles and priests rather than by a king. The tradition of Ezra, therefore, is typical of the great movement that shaped the life of Judaism in the century immediately following the work of Nehemiah.

Origin and Aims of the Priestly Laws The late priestly laws that molded the life of Judaism are found in the books of Exodus, Leviticus, and Numbers. They do not constitute a unified code, but rather are made up of a series of smaller groups of laws, the older nucleus being the Holiness Code found in chapters 17–26 of Leviticus. In some cases variants of the same law are found in different groups. Certain of these laws simply reiterate in slightly different form those already found in the primitive and Deuteronomic codes, but in general they supplement these earlier codes. The formulation, collection, and codification of these later laws apparently continued until toward the latter part of the Persian period, when the Samaritan schism fixed them in their present form.

To these laws was prefixed, as an introduction, the priestly history that opens with the account of creation in the first chapter of Genesis and briefly traces Israel's history to the settlement in Canaan. The interest of these late priestly historians is, like that of the Chronicler, in the origin of institutions. Thus the object of the first chapter of Genesis is to give the traditional origin and authority of the Sabbath. The account of the flood culminates in a covenant embodying the command that man shall not eat of the blood of sacrificial animals; the priestly stories regarding Abraham aim to give the origin of the rite of circumcision. Israel's early experiences in the wilderness furnish the setting for the giving of the law at Sinai. In this way the late editors of these opening books of the Old Testament connect all of Israel's legislation with Moses and aim to establish its divine authority.

Their Important Regulations The central aim in all these late priestly laws was similar to that of Ezekiel: it was to make Israel a holy people and to prevent them from falling again into the sins to which were attributed the overwhelming disasters that had overtaken them. They sought to accomplish this aim (1) by making the temple and its services the center of the life of the people and through ceremonial barriers and regulations shielding it from everything that might pollute it; (2) by rendering the temple service attractive; (3) by ensuring through rigid ceremonial laws the purity of its priesthood; (4) by preserving the ceremonial cleanliness of the people through strict laws regarding the food they ate and elaborate provisions for their purification in case they were contaminated by contact with what was regarded as unclean; (5) by prohibiting absolutely all marriages with the heathen; and (6) by emphasizing the rigid observation of the Sabbath and other distinctive institutions. In general these late priestly laws represented a return to the older and more primitive conception of religion and defined duty in terms of ceremonial rather than moral acts.

Their Practical Effects Later Judaism represents to a great extent the result of the rigid enforcement of these regulations. Its life was centralized more and more about the temple. In its services the people found their chief interest and joy. The numbers of the priests and Levites were also greatly increased. To the older temple dues many new ones were added. Thus each man brought to the temple the firstborn of his flock. Even his oldest son must be redeemed within a month after his birth by a gift of five shekels. Of every animal slain, the shoulder, two joints, and the stomach went to the priests. Of the vintage and oil and grain they received about one-fiftieth. In addition a tithe was turned over to the Levites. Part of the wool in every sheep shearing, as well as a part of the bread they baked, found its way to the temple. In addition a large income came through the vows made by the people or the conscience money that was paid in either currency or gifts. Although the priests had no temporal authority by which to enforce these laws, it is evident that the people bore their heavy burdens gladly and brought willingly their offerings, that they might thereby win a definite assurance of Jehovah's favor. The law was to them a source of joy rather than a burden. Their love for it steadily grew until two centuries later during the Maccabean persecutions there were many who were ready to lay down their lives for it.

CHAPTER 13

....

THE JEWISH STATE DURING THE LAST CENTURY OF PERSIAN RULE

Behind their restored walls the Jews of Jerusalem enjoyed a sense of security and peace that had not been theirs since the days of Josiah. At last they were free to develop the limited resources of little Judah and gradually to extend their territory northwestward over the fertile plain of Sharon. At the most their numbers and territory were small. The memories of their glorious past and their hopes for the future were their chief inspiration. The belief that in supporting faithfully the service of the temple and in conforming to the definite demands of the ritual they were winning Jehovah's favor was to them an unfailing source of comfort and thankfulness. In the rich services of the temple and in the contemplation of Jehovah's character and deeds they found true joy. These feelings are expressed in certain of the psalms, for example, Psalm 36, which probably comes from this period. In their weakness they looked up in confidence and gratitude to Jehovah who ruled supreme in the heavens and who was able and eager to preserve those who "put their trust in the shadow of his wings." Their one prayer was that his loving-kindness would continue to protect them.

The Growth of the Psalter Nehemiah's work apparently not only gave an impulse to the development of the law and the temple ritual, but also inspired poets to voice their own feelings and those of the community in certain of the psalms now found in the Psalter. It also encouraged them to collect the earlier religious songs of their race. The result of their work is the first edition of the Hebrew Psalter. In its present form the Psalter, like the Pentateuch, is divided into five books with a general introduction consisting of Psalms 1 and 2 and a concluding doxology (Ps. 150). At the end of each of these divisions are shorter doxologies or brief epilogues (e.g., 41:13, 72:19, 89:52, 106:48). The Psalter itself is a library containing a great variety of poems written at different periods, from many different points of view and by many different poets. Like the Priestly Code and the book of Proverbs, it consists of a collection of smaller collections. Thus many psalms in the first half of the Psalter are repeated wholly or in part in later psalms. Psalm 14, for example, is identical to Psalm 73, except that in 14 Jehovah is used as the designation of the Deity and in 73 Elohim (or God).

The problem of determining the dates of the individual psalms and of the different collections is exceedingly difficult, both because the superscriptions were clearly added by later editors who thought thereby to connect the psalm with an earlier writer or historic incident, and because the psalms themselves contain few historical allusions. A great majority of them reflect the teachings of the pre-exilic prophets or, like the book of Proverbs, come from the lips of the sages and deal with universal human problems. Some were written by priests or Levites for use in connection with the song service of the temple. Because of this timeless quality, however, an appreciation of them does not depend upon an exact knowledge of their authorship or historical background. It is possible that a few of the psalms in the first part of the Psalter come from the pre-exilic period, but the great majority reflect the problems, the hopes, the fears, and the trials of the faithful who lived under the shadow of the second temple. While the superscriptions clearly do not come from the original psalmists themselves, they do record the conclusions of the editors who made the earliest collections. The oft-recurring title "Psalm to David" either means that by the editor it was attributed to David as the author, or is a general designation of psalms that were recognized to be comparatively early. The two great Davidic collections, 3–41 and 51–72, were apparently collected not long after the rebuilding of the walls of Jerusalem. They are deeply influenced by the inspiring teachings of the II Isaiah. They are remarkably free from the ceremonialism that became a powerful force in Judaism during the last century of the Persian rule. Psalm 51:16–17, for example, echoes the noble ethical teachings of the great prophets:

> *Thou desirest not sacrifice, else would I give it,*
> *Thou delightest not in burnt offering,*
> *The sacrifice of God is a broken heart,*
> *A broken and a contrite heart, O God, thou wilt*
> *not despise.*

They represent, therefore, the oldest edition of the Psalter and the songs that were probably sung by the temple singers and the people as they went up to the temple on the great feast days during the closing years of the Persian period.

The Prophecy of Joel For a brief moment the clear light of contemporary prophecy is turned upon the Judean community by the little book of Joel. The immediate occasion was the invasion of a great swarm of locusts that swept into Judea either from the desert or from the mountains in the north. It contains in 3:6 the first Old Testament reference to the Greeks. From 3:2 it is evident that the Jewish race has already been widely scattered. In 3:2 the hope is expressed that the time will soon come when strangers shall no longer pass through Jerusalem. The temple, however, and the city walls (2:9) have already been rebuilt, indicating that the prophecy followed the work of Nehemiah. The priests are exceedingly prominent in the life of the community, and Joel, though a prophet, places great emphasis upon the importance of the ritual. When the community is threatened by the swarms of locusts, whose advance he describes with dramatic imagery, he calls upon the people to sanctify a fast and to summon an assembly, and commands the priests to cry aloud to Jehovah for deliverance.

Hopes of the Jews In his prophecy Joel has given a very complete description of the hopes the people entertained regarding the coming day of Jehovah. It is the same day of Jehovah that Zephaniah described, and yet the portrait is very different. A divine judgment is to be pronounced, not upon Jehovah's people, but upon their foes. Here Joel reveals the influence of Ezekiel's graphic descriptions found in the thirty-eighth and thirty-ninth chapters of his prophecy. Vividly he describes the advance of Israel's hereditary foes. With full panoply of war they are pictured as advancing to the Valley of Jehoshaphat, the valley of judgment (popularly identified with the Kidron), where Jehovah is to pass sentence upon them. Then suddenly, as the harvester puts the sickle in the grain, they shall be cut down and utterly destroyed. Also in the prophet's imagination above this carnage rises Jerusalem, an impregnable fortress for the people of Israel, holy and no longer polluted by the presence of heathen invaders. Peace and prosperity shall then be the lot of Jehovah's people. Above all he will pour out his purifying, enlightening spirit upon all classes, so that young and old, slave and free, shall be inspired by the consciousness of his message and presence in their hearts.

Rule of the High Priests The few facts that have been preserved regarding the external history of the Judean community during the last century of the Persian rule are in striking contrast to the inner life and hopes of the people. At their head were the high priests, whose names we know: Eliashib, Johanan, and Jaddua. They constituted a hereditary aristocracy entrenched in the temple, which controlled not only the religious but also the civil life of the Jews. Like all hierarchies it lacked the corrective influence of a superior civil authority. The one safeguard of popular liberties, however, was the written law, which was fast becoming the absolute authority in the life of the community. To it the people could appeal even against the decisions of the priests. It therefore kept alive the inherited democratic spirit that had been the priceless possession of Israel through all its history.

There is every reason for accepting the detailed account that Josephus has given of the quarrel between the high priest Johanan and his brother Joshua, which resulted in the murder of the latter within the sacred temple precincts. Such an opportunity would naturally be improved by the greedy Persian official to impose an onerous tax upon the Jews. The Elephantine letter establishes the fact that Johanan was high priest in 411 B.C. and that Baghohi (of which Bagoses is the Jewish equivalent) was the Persian satrap. It thus directly confirms the testimony of Josephus. References in late Greek writings (Solinus 35:6; Syncellus 1:486) suggest that the Jews about 350 B.C. were involved with the Phoenicians in the rebellion against Persia. These historians state that at this time Jericho was captured and destroyed and that some of the Jewish people were transported to the province of Hyrcania at the south of the Caspian Sea. The rebellion was instigated by Tachos, the ruler of Egypt, who about 362 not only shook off the rule of Persia, but invaded Syria and stirred up the Phoenicians to defy the Persian king. Artaxerxes III, popularly known as Ochus, proved, however, the last ruler who was able to revive the waning power of the Persian Empire. At his accession he slew all the members of the royal family, and throughout his reign (358–337 B.C.) he trusted chiefly to the unsheathed sword to maintain his authority. In 346 B.C. he finally succeeded in collecting a huge army with which he invaded Syria and besieged Sidon. Its king betrayed his city into the hands of the Persians, only to be murdered by the treacherous Ochus. The citizens of Sidon, recognizing that they would receive no mercy from the hands of their conqueror, shut themselves up in their homes and then burned them over their heads. According to the Greek historians forty thousand Phoenicians perished in this revolt.

The Date of the Samaritan Schism Josephus has given an unusually full and detailed account of the final schism between the Jews and Samaritans. He dates it under the high priesthood of Jaddua, who died shortly after the close of the Persian period. He implies, therefore, that the schism took place not long before 332 B.C., when Alexander the Great conquered Palestine. This is also in keeping with the fact that the Elephantine letter written in 411 B.C. knows nothing of a division between Jew and Gentile. The fact that at the time of the division the defecting priests took from Jerusalem the Pentateuch in its final form strongly confirms the conclusion (as Torrey has pointed out in his *Ezra Studies*, pp. 324–330) that the Sanballat who ruled over the Samaritan community was not the contemporary of Nehemiah, but his grandson, who as an old man was ruling in Samaria at the time when Alexander conquered the East.

The Nature and Consequences of the Schism The schism between Jew and Samaritan was but a revival of the ancient rivalry that dated from the days when the Israelites had first settled in Canaan. The destruction of Samaria in 722 and the strong policy of Josiah had apparently led the Samaritans to look to the temple at Jerusalem as the chief sanctuary of the land. Shechem, however, and Mount Gerizim, which rises abruptly on the south, enjoyed traditions that dated from the earliest days of Israel's history. The sacred oak and altar at Shechem figured even in the patriarchal period. At the temple of Baal-berith in Shechem apparently both Canaanites and Israelites worshipped during the days of the settlement. According to the Samaritan version of Deuteronomy 24:4, Mount Gerizim, not Ebal or Jerusalem, was the place where the Israelites, after entering Canaan, were first commanded to raise an altar to Jehovah and to inscribe upon it the laws given to Moses. Even in the Jewish versions of Deuteronomy 11:29 and 27:12

Mount Gerizim is the mountain of blessing. In the light of these passages such commands as, for example, that in Deuteronomy 12:4–5 would naturally be interpreted by the Samaritans as a reference to Gerizim rather than to Jerusalem. The destruction of the Judean capital and temple gave a great incentive to the revival of these Ancient traditions and a new prestige to the northern sanctuary. Until the close of the Persian period, however, the Samaritans evidently regarded Jerusalem as an important shrine and worshipped there side by side with the Jews. The ultimate schism appears to have come as a result of the growing jealousy with which certain of the Jews regarded foreign marriages. The marriage of Manasseh, the brother of Jaddua the high priest, to Nicaso, the daughter of Sanballat II, and his ultimate expulsion by the Jews blew into a flame the smoldering jealousy and opposition that had long existed between the two communities. As Josephus recounts, Sanballat, in order to satisfy his son-in-law, ceded lands and special rights to him and to the other Jerusalem priests, who were attracted by these offers, and ultimately built the famous temple on Mount Gerizim over which Manasseh and his descendants presided. In many ways the temple and service on Mount Gerizim appear to have been duplicates of those at Jerusalem. The same law was recognized by both communities, and they shared together the same traditions and the same ideals, yet their subsequent history illustrates the psychological truth that of all forms of hatred that between brothers is the most venomous and lasting. The bitter rivalry and growing hatred that resulted from this act are reflected even in the wisdom teachings of Ben Sira (B. Sir. 47:21, 24–25). They also fundamentally color the writings of the Chronicler. The strenuous efforts that he made to discountenance the claims of the Samaritans reveals the intensity of the feud even in the Greek period (cf. II Chron. 11:13–16). His zeal in trying to prove that the rebuilders of the Jerusalem temple were of Jewish extraction was doubtless inspired by the Samaritan charge that during the Babylonian and Persian periods they had freely intermarried with the heathen population of the land. He was compelled to admit that even the high priestly families had been guilty of this sin, but asserted that the foreign wives were later divorced or else the offenders were expelled from Jerusalem. In the light of the oldest records it appears that the Samaritans were able to establish almost as pure a lineage as the Jews. Naturally during the succeeding years the ancient breach continued to widen until it was beyond all healing.

SECTION II

THE GREEK AND MACCABEAN AGE

CHAPTER 14

THE JEWS UNDER THEIR GREEK RULERS

The Greek period began with Alexander's conquest of Palestine in 332 and extended to the Maccabean uprising in 168 B.C. For the external history of this period the writings of the historian Josephus are the chief sources. This famous Jewish writer was born in A.D. 37, and apparently lived until about the close of the reign of Domitian in 96. According to his own testimony he was the son of a priest named Mattathiah. Until he was sixteen he studied under the Jewish rabbis. He then spent three years with the Jewish sect known as the Essenes. At the age of nineteen he joined the party of the Pharisees. His point of view in general is that of this dominant popular party. He was able to read Latin, but wrote his histories in Greek. At the age of twenty-six he went to Rome, where he spent three years. Returning to Palestine at the beginning of the great rebellion against Rome, he was appointed revolutionary governor of the important province of Galilee. The appointment was unfortunate, for he proved both incompetent and unreliable. In A.D. 67 he and his followers were shut up by Vespasian in the Galilean city Jotapata. During the siege he vainly tried to desert to the enemy. At the fall of the city he was captured, but his life was spared by Vespasian. In time he ingratiated himself with Titus and also incurred the hostility of his countrymen by trying to persuade them to lay down their arms. He spent the latter part of his life in Rome, devoting himself to study and writing. As a result of his long residence in Rome under the patronage of the Roman emperors, he was powerfully influenced by the Greek and Roman philosophical schools.

Josephus was the great apologist of his race. His chief aims in writing his histories were to excuse his own acts in connection with the great rebellion, to show why the overwhelming calamity had overtaken his race, and to answer the attack of their Gentile foes by tracing the remarkable history of his people and by presenting in attractive form their beliefs, institutions, and laws. Of his two great historical works, the one titled *The Jewish War* was issued probably between A.D. 75 and 79. It opens with the beginnings of the Maccabean struggle and traces the history, with increasing detail, to the destruction of Jerusalem and the suppression of the Jewish revolt at Gyrene, two or three years before the book was written. His second great work was issued in 93 A.D. under the title *The Antiquities of the Jews*. In twenty books it traces

Israel's history from the earliest beginnings to the opening years of the Jewish war (A.D. 68). The first half of this extensive history is based on the author's free paraphrase of the Greek version of the Old Testament. For the latter half he draws largely from the apocryphal book of I Maccabees and from the writings of contemporary Greek and Jewish historians. Chief among these are Polybius, Nicolaus of Damascus, and Strabo. At certain points, where earlier sources fail him, he employs popular romances and late traditions. The result is that the different parts of his history are of widely varying values. All must be carefully tested by the canons of historical criticism. After due allowance has been made for his apologetic purpose and his well-known tendencies, a large and valuable body of historical facts remain with which it is possible at many otherwise obscure points to reconstruct the course of Israel's history.

Alexander's Conquests In many ways Alexander's conquest was the most significant and far-reaching event in the history of Asia. The causes of this great movement were, first, the fact that the limited territory of Greece and Macedonia gave to the powerful Hellenic civilization little opportunity for local expansion. Compelled, therefore, to break these narrow bonds, it naturally spread in the direction of least resistance. Second, the decadent Persian Empire, with its fabulous riches and almost limitless plains, was a lodestone that lured on Greek adventurers to attempt feats that seemed incredible. The third reason was

Alexander's inherited lust for conquest. His father, Philip of Macedon, had long been accumulating the resources that made it possible for his son to realize his ambitious dreams. The fourth reason was Alexander's desire to make the world more glorious by the diffusion of Hellenic culture, ideas, and institutions and by binding all races together into one great, harmonious family. His brilliant conquests are a familiar chapter in the world's history. At Issus, at the northeastern end of the Mediterranean, he won, in 333 B.C., the decisive battle that left him in possession of the western part of the huge Persian Empire. By 332 he was master of Palestine. Tyre, the commercial mistress of the eastern Mediterranean, and Gaza, the key to Egypt, alone offered resistance. The Persian kings by their onerous taxation and cruel policy had completely destroyed the loyalty of their western subjects. In the symbolic pictures of the book of Daniel Alexander is regarded as the "fourth beast, terrible and fearful and exceedingly strong. And it had great iron teeth. It devoured and broke in pieces, and stamped the rest with its feet" (7:17, 23, 8:5–8). Josephus has preserved a popular tradition regarding the meeting between Alexander and the white-robed Jerusalem priests and the homage paid by the conqueror to the God of the Jews. It bears on its face evidence of its unhistorical character. As a matter of fact, the first goal of Alexander's conquest was the rich land of Egypt. Not being possessed of a navy, he entered it through its one vulnerable point, the Wady Tumilat, that ran from the Isthmus of Suez to the Nile delta. By 331 B.C. he was master of the Nile Valley, and thence turned eastward, conquering in succession the different provinces of the great empire, until before his death in 323 B.C. his empire extended from the Mediterranean to the Indus, and in the northeast far up toward Central Asia.

Alexander's conquests were significant because they represented the victory of Greek ideas and culture as well as of arms. In each country conquered he usually succeeded in Hellenizing the native peoples. Greek cities, settled by his veterans and the horde of migratory Greeks that followed in his wake, were founded at strategic points throughout the vast empire. As recent excavations have shown, Greek art and ideas continued to sweep eastward across Asia even after the death of Alexander, until they profoundly influenced the culture and ideas in such distant nations as China and Japan.

Jews in Egypt and Alexandria The crown of Alexander's constructive work was the building of Alexandria in Egypt. Selecting a narrow strip of coast, protected on the south by the low-lying Lake Mareotis and on the north by the Mediterranean, he built there a magnificent Greek city. On the south it was connected by canal with the Canopic arm of the Nile. Alexander thus diverted to this new metropolis the rich trade of the Red Sea and the Nile. A mile distant was the island of Pharos, which was connected with the mainland by a great moll. On either side, protected from the storms, were the eastern and western harbors, large enough to accommodate the merchantmen and navies of the ancient world. On the west was the native Egyptian quarter. In the center, opposite the island of Pharos, was the Greek and official quarter. In the northeastern part of the city was the Jewish quarter. Here the Jews lived together under the rule of their law; they were also represented in the civic council by their own leaders. When Ptolemy, the son of Lagus, became governor of Egypt and, after the death of Alexander, subjected Palestine, he carried back to Alexandria many Jewish captives and attracted others by the special privileges he granted them. In them he recognized valuable allies in developing the commercial resources of Alexandria and in maintaining his rule over the native Egyptians. Here in time the Jews became wealthy and powerful and developed a unique civilization. From the beginning of the Greek period the number of the Jews in Egypt equaled, if it did not surpass, that of the Jews in Palestine. While they maintained close connection with the Jews in Palestine and remained true to their scriptures, they were profoundly influenced by their close contact with the civilization and ideas of the Greek world.

The Rule of the Ptolemies The long-continued rule of the Ptolemies in Egypt is one of the most astonishing phenomena in this remarkable period in human history. Far outnumbered by the native population, involved in almost constant war with their fellow Greeks, they succeeded by sheer audacity and vigilance in maintaining their authority during the many crises through which they passed. Egypt's natural defenses also made its conquest by outside powers exceedingly difficult. Alexandria with its fleet commanded Egypt's one entrance by the sea. In order to protect its eastern gateway, the Isthmus of Suez, it was essential that the Ptolemies should control Palestine. Southern Palestine also commanded the great commercial highway that led southward and eastward to Arabia and Babylonia. Alexandria's ancient rivals, Tyre and Sidon, also lay on the borders of Palestine, and it was essential that they be under the control of Egypt if Alexandria was to remain the mistress of the eastern Mediterranean. Furthermore, Palestine and the Lebanons (known to Josephus as Coele-Syria, that is, Hollow Syria), alone among the countries adjacent to Egypt, possessed the timber required for the building of Alexandria's navies and merchantmen. Hence Ptolemy and his successors spared no effort to maintain their control over the lands lying along the eastern Mediterranean.

In the division of the empire that followed the death of Alexander three rivals struggled in turn for this coveted territory: Ptolemy, in the south; Antigonus, who soon became master of Asia Minor and northern Syria; and Seleucus, to whom fell the Tigris-Euphrates Valley and the more distant eastern provinces. In the decisive battle of Ipsus in 301 B.C. the overshadowing power of Antigonus was broken and the control of southwestern Asia was divided between Seleucus and Ptolemy. By the treaty that was made after the battle, Coele-Syria was given to Ptolemy, but Seleucus and his descendants, who were known as the Seleucids or the Seleucidae, soon attempted to wrest it from Egypt, and during the following century frequently, with varying success, renewed the attempt. In 295 and again in 219 they were for a brief period masters of Palestine, but during most of this period it was held by the Ptolemies.

Fortunes of the Jews of Palestine Josephus's figure of a ship in a storm, smitten by the waves on either side, well describes the lot of the Jews of Palestine during the Greek period. They were in turn victimized and courted by the rival kings of Egypt and Syria. The Jews, on the whole, favored the rule of the Ptolemies, who had made many concessions to their kinsmen in Egypt. The presence of many Jews in Egypt also made this relation more natural. As a rule the Ptolemies during the intervals of peace left the Jews of Palestine largely to themselves, as long as they paid the heavy tribute that was exacted. It was, however, one of the most corrupt periods in human history. The Ptolemaic court was rich, profligate, and constantly degenerating. The popular story of Joseph the tax collector (which Josephus recounts at length), while largely fanciful, vividly reflects the conditions and spirit of the age. Joseph, who evidently belonged to one of the leading families of Jerusalem, by his energy and effrontery secured the valuable right of farming the taxes of Palestine. By the iniquitous methods then in vogue, he succeeded in amassing a great fortune. The splendid ruins of Arak el-Emir on the heights of southern

Gilead, east of the Jordan, represent the huge castle and town built by his son Hyrcanus and testify to the wealth of this Jewish adventurer. The stories that Josephus relates regarding Joseph indicate that the materialism and sensuality that were regnant in Alexandria had penetrated even into the province of Judea.

The one bright spot in the political history of this period is the reign of the high priest Simon, known as the Just. He appears to have devoted himself to developing, so far as was in his power, the interests and resources of the Palestinian Jews and to have lifted the temple service to a state of magnificence that received the unqualified commendation of Jesus, the son of Sirach.

Palestine Conquest by the Seleucids in 311 B.C. Seleucus Nikanor transferred the western capital of his empire, known as Syria (a shortened form of the ancient name Assyria), to Antioch, near the northeastern end of the Mediterranean. This city was situated at the point where the Orontes breaks through the Lebanons and where the great roads from the Euphrates and Coele-Syria converge and run westward to its seaport, Seleucia. It was built in the midst of a fertile valley, partly on an island in the river and partly on its northern bank. Not having natural defenses, the city depended upon its broad, encompassing walls for protection. To this new capital was attracted a diverse native, Greek, and Jewish population. By virtue of its strategic position and its commercial and political importance, it soon became one of the great cities of the eastern Mediterranean. It occupied the natural site on the eastern Mediterranean seaboard for the capital of a great empire. Shut in by the sea on the west and the desert on the east, Syria's natural line of expansion was north and south. Not until 198 B.C., however, under the rule of Antiochus the Great, did it secure permanent control of Palestine. The degenerate house of the Ptolemies made several ineffectual attempts to win back their lost province, but henceforth Palestine remained under the rule of Syria. The personal attractions of Antiochus the Great, the specious promises he made, and disgust because of the corrupt rule of Egypt inclined the Jews of Palestine to welcome this change of rulers. The court at Antioch, however, soon became almost as corrupt as that of Egypt, and the Jews were the victims of the greed and caprice of the Syrian despots. Meantime the insidious Greek culture and vices were influencing and largely undermining the character of the Jewish rulers. Judaism was unconsciously facing a supreme crisis in its history.

CHAPTER 15

THE WISE AND THEIR TEACHINGS

The book of Proverbs is in reality a collection of originally independent groups of proverbs. In its present form it consists of nine general divisions:

1. The preface defining the aims of the book, 1:1–6.
2. A general introduction describing the characteristics and value of the wisdom teaching, 1:7–9:18.
3. A large collection designated as the Proverbs of Solomon, 10:1–22:16. The fact that ten proverbs are repeated in practically the same words indicates that it, like the book of Proverbs as a whole, is made up of smaller collections. In chapters 10–15 the prevailing type of the poetic parallelism is antithetic or contrasting, while in the remainder of the book the synonymous or repeating parallelism prevails.

4. A supplemental collection, 22:17–24:22. This is introduced by the suggestive superscription "Incline your ear and hear the words of the wise."

5. A shorter appendix, 24:23–34, with the superscription "These also are from the wise."

6. The second large collection of proverbs, 25–29. This bears the superscription "These also are the proverbs of Solomon which the men of Hezekiah, king of Judah, transcribed." It contains several proverbs found in the first large collection, and evidently represents later gleanings from the same field.

7. The words of Agur, 30. Of Agur nothing is known beyond his name, which may be simply typical. The latter part of the chapter contains a collection of numerical enigmas that may or may not have been associated at first with the opening section.

8. The words of King Lemuel, 31:1–9.

9. A description of the ideal Hebrew housewife, 31:10–31.

The contents of these collections as well as their superscriptions clearly indicate that these proverbs represent the work of many different wise men, living at different periods and writing from different points of view. Few, if any, can be confidently attributed to Solomon. Even the proverbs in the large collection, 10:1–22:16, which are definitely designated as the Proverbs of Solomon, emphasize monogamy and denounce rulers who oppress their subjects. Many of the proverbs in these larger Solomonic collections give practical advice regarding the bearing of a subject in the presence of the king, and few of them fit in the mouth of the splendor-loving monarch, who by his foreign marriages and grinding taxation exerted a baleful influence upon the political and religious life of Israel. The great majority of the proverbs reflect the noble ethical teachings of the prophets. Clearly the term "Proverbs of Solomon" is simply a late designation of early proverbs the authorship of which, like that of most popular maxims, had long since been forgotten.

Date of the Different Collections The preface and general introduction to the book of Proverbs reflect the immorality and evils that characterized both the Persian and Greek periods. Their background is the corrupt life of the city. The tendency to personify wisdom is also one of the marks of later Jewish thought. It is probable, therefore, that this part of the book of Proverbs was added by a later editor who lived during the Greek period. The oldest collection in the book is clearly to be found in 10:1–22:10. The evils it describes, the oppression of the poor and dependent by the rich and powerful, existed throughout most of Israel's history, but were especially prominent in the days of the divided kingdom immediately before the destruction of Jerusalem. The references to the king imply that the proverb writers had in mind Hebrew rulers. In general their rule is just and they enjoy the respect of their subjects. The prevailing occupation of the people is agriculture. Commerce is just beginning to develop. The exile has not yet cast its shadow over Hebrew life and thought. The majority of these proverbs clearly represent the fruitage of the teachings of the pre-exilic prophets, and many of them come from the days immediately before the final destruction of Jerusalem. From the occasional references to the scoffers, the absence of allusions to idolatry, and the fact that monogamy is here assumed, we may infer that some of them at least come from the Persian or even the Greek periods. It is probable that this large collection was not made until the latter part of the Persian or the early part of the Greek period.

The appendices in 22:17–24:34 contain many repetitions of proverbs found in the larger collection. The prevalence of intemperance, the existence of a merchant class, and the allusions to exiled Jews (e.g., 24:11) point rather clearly to the dissolute Greek period as the age when these small collections were made. The word meaning "transcribe" that is found in the superscription to the second large collection (25–29) is peculiar to the late Hebrew, and implies that this superscription, like those of the Psalms, was added by a late Jewish scribe. The literary form of these proverbs is more complex than those of the other large collection. The kings are feared by their subjects, but figure now as oppressors rather than champions of the people. While this collection may contain a few proverbs coming from the period before the final destruction of Jerusalem, it is probable that, like the smaller appendices to the first large collection, they were not gathered until the early part of the Greek period.

The long appendices in chapters 30–31 are clearly late. The note of doubt in the opening section of 30 is closely akin to that which recurs in the book of Ecclesiastes. It is also based on Isaiah 44:5 and 45:4. Aramaisms and the acrostic form in 31:10–31 imply that the background was the late Persian or early Greek period.

The history of the book of Proverbs is therefore reasonably clear. Its original nucleus was probably a small group of popular proverbs that had been transmitted orally from the days before the final destruction of Jerusalem. These, together with proverbs that first became current during the Persian period, were collected some time in the days following the work of Nehemiah. To these was added in the Greek period the smaller appendices in 22:17–24:34. Possibly the same editor joined to them the large collection found in 25–29. He or some wise man in the Greek period prefixed the elaborate introduction in chapters 1–9. To the whole was added the appendices in chapters 30 and 31. It is probable that by the middle of the Greek period, or at least before 200 B.C., the book of Proverbs was complete in its present form.

The Wise in Israel's Early History Long before 2000 B.C. the scribes of ancient Egypt were busy collecting "the words of counsel of the men of olden time." Many of these ancient maxims still survive. The best-known is that which bears the title "The Wisdom of Ptah-hotep." The desire to preserve and transmit the results of practical experience is the common motive that underlies the work of the wise. It is that which inspires the teachers of all ages. The ancients were keenly alive to the importance of instruction and training. All that is significant in the civilizations of the past is, in a sense, the result of this teaching motif.

In early Israel there were many men and women famous for their ability to give wise counsel. In his stormy career Joab, David's valiant commander, frequently profited by the counsel of certain wise women. David's friend Hushai, by his wily counsel at the time of Absalom's rebellion, saved the king's life. The narrative in II Samuel declares that the counsel of Ahithophel was esteemed almost as highly as the divine oracle. For his keen insight and acute decisions, as well as for his witty utterances, Solomon gained a reputation that made him in the thought of later generations the father of all wisdom literature. In a significant passage found in Jeremiah 18:18 the three classes of Israel's teachers are brought into sharp contrast. In urging that the prophet be put to death his foes declared: "Teaching will not perish from the priest, nor counsel from the wise, nor the word from the prophet." From references in Isaiah and Jeremiah it is evident that before the final destruction of the Hebrew state the counsel of the wise was chiefly political and secular, and often not in accord with the higher ideals of the great pre-exilic prophets.

Their Prominence in the Greek Period The transformation of the wise into religious as well as secular teachers apparently came after the destruction of Jerusalem. It was the result of a variety of forces that have already been studied. The destruction of the Hebrew state and the resulting prominence of the individual led the wise to turn their attention from questions of political to those of personal import. The result is that the word "Israel" is found nowhere in the book of Proverbs. The teachings found there are both individual and universal and apply to Gentile as well as Jew, to the present as well as the past. The gradual disappearance of the prophets during the latter part of the Persian period, and the fact that the priests ever devoted themselves more and more to the ritual and less to teaching, left a great need in the life of Judaism, which called to the front the wise. At the same time the problems of the individual became more and more complex and insistent. This was especially true during the Greek period, when Hellenic civilization, with its corrupting influences, swept over Palestine and the lands of the dispersion. It was a period when the principles enunciated by the earlier prophets had been in general adopted by the Jewish race. The task, however, of interpreting these principles simply and practically into the everyday life of the people was left to these lovers and teachers of men, the wise. The evidence of the voluminous writings of Ben Sira, as well as of the books of Proverbs and Ecclesiastes, makes it quite clear that it was during the Greek period, and possibly in part under the intellectual stimulus of Greek thought, that the wise attained their greatest prominence and influence.

The Aims of the Wise The aims of the wise are in part defined in the remarkable preface to the book of Proverbs, which was intended primarily to describe the purpose of the collection of proverbs that embodies their teachings. Four distinct classes commanded their attention: (1) the ignorant, those who were unacquainted with the moral, religious, and practical heritage received from preceding generations; (2) the inexperienced, those who had not yet learned in the school of life the art of adjusting themselves successfully to their environment; (3) the scoffers, who openly rejected the counsel of the sages; and (4) the disciples, who were eager to learn and profit by the teachings of the wise.

The definite aims of the wise must be inferred from their teachings. They were concerned with the development of the individual, not the nation. Their first aim was to instruct the ignorant in the fundamental moral and religious principles already laid down by earlier priests and prophets. In the words of the preface to the book of Proverbs, they taught

> *That men may learn wisdom and instruction,*
> *May understand intelligent discourses,*
> *May receive instruction in wise dealing,*
> *In justice, judgment, and equity.*

Their second aim was to point out the pitfalls that lay in the path of the inexperienced and to save them from moral wreck by inspiring within them right ideals and ambitions. This aim is also well stated in the preface to the book of Proverbs:

> *That discretion may be given to the inexperienced,*
> *To the youth knowledge and a purpose.*

The third aim of the wise was to educate the receptive and all who came to them in the attitude of disciples. This aim corresponded very closely to that of the modern educator. Again the preface to the book of Proverbs clearly expresses this educational ideal:

> *That the wise man may hear and increase in learning,*
> *And the intelligent man may receive counsel.*
> *That he may understand a proverb and parable,*
> *The words of the wise and their riddles.*

The wise, therefore, sought not merely to instruct, but to educate—that is, to develop sane, happy, and efficient men and women. They sought to train those who would have not only knowledge and experience, but also the ability to apply these successfully in the varied relations of life. Above all, they endeavored to educate not parts of a man, but the whole man. Hence their interest and the subjects that they treat are as broad as human experience.

The wise were keenly alive to the importance of youthful education. The proverb

> *Train up a child in the way in which he should go,*
> *And even when he is old he will not depart from it*

voices the fundamental principle upon which all effective education is based. They recognized that in the plastic days of childhood and youth ideals and character and efficiency could best be developed, and that education was not the work of a moment, but a gradual, progressive development.

Primary education, however, they entrusted to parents, and many proverbs emphasized the responsibility that every parent owed to his child. They also counseled parents regarding the training of their children. The maxims

> *The rod of correction gives wisdom,*
> *But a child left to himself brings disgrace to his mother.*

> *Chastise your son while there is still hope,*
> *And set not your heart on his destruction.*

> *He who spares his rod hates his son,*
> *But he who loves him chastises him.*

express their appreciation of the importance of discipline in the early training of the child. It is not clear at what age the wise took up the instruction of the young. Possibly it was at about the age of twelve, when the individual passed from childhood to adolescence, with its increasing dangers and possibilities. Many of their teachings are especially adapted to the problems of this tempestuous period.

The Methods of the Wise In attaining their aims the wise men of Israel employed a variety of methods. Proverbs such as

> *Every purpose is established by counsel,*
> *And by wise guidance make thou war*

suggest that, as in the days before the exile, they were still active in connection with the civic, social, and national life of the people, and that by influencing public policies they conserved the moral welfare of the individual as well as the state. Many references to "wisdom's voice crying aloud in the public places" suggest that, like the earlier prophets, the wise men at times taught in public, in the marketplaces, in the open spaces within the city gates, or wherever men were gathered together. They appear also to have taught in private, by wise counsel delivering the individual disciple who resorted to them from the perils that beset his path, or aiding him by prudent advice in solving successfully his individual problems.

In 6:32–37 Ben Sira has given a vivid sketch of the schools of the wise, which are clearly the forerunners of the later rabbinical schools:

> *My son, if you wish, you will be instructed,*
> *And if you pay attention, you will become prudent.*
> *If you are willing to hear, you will receive,*
> *And if you listen attentively, you will be wise.*
> *Stand in the assembly of the elders,*
> *And whoever is wise, stick close to him.*
> *Be willing to listen to every discourse,*
> *And let no illuminating proverbs escape you.*
> *If you see a man of insight, hasten to him,*
> *And let your foot wear out his threshold.*
> *Let your mind dwell upon the law of the Most High,*

And meditate continually on his commands.
Thus he will enlighten your mind,
And teach you the wisdom you desire.

It requires little imagination to picture these ancient prototypes of our modern universities. Like all Oriental teachers, the wise doubtless sat cross-legged, with their disciples in a circle about them. They trusted largely to question and answer, and poured out from their own and their inherited experience wise maxims such as would guide the simple and inexperienced and develop efficient manhood.

Their Important Teachings In the opening chapters of Proverbs the wise describe the character and value of the wisdom that represents their teaching as a whole. In chapters 8 and 9 "Wisdom" is personified. Inasmuch as the Hebrew word for "wisdom" is feminine, it is spoken of as a woman. Chapter 9 describes, in a form intended to arrest the attention of the most inattentive, the feast that Wisdom offers to her guests. This is contrasted with Folly's banquet, and the consequences to those who participated in these rival banquets are clearly presented.

In the practical teachings of the wise no question that vitally concerned the individual man was considered beneath their attention. Like the wise modern teacher they made no distinction between the religious and the secular. Everything that influenced man's acts and ideals possessed for them profound religious import. While the proverbial epigrammatic form of their teaching was not conducive to a logical or complete treatment of their theme, yet in a series of concise, dramatic maxims they dealt with almost every phase of man's domestic, economic, legal, and social life. They presented clearly man's duty to animals, to himself, to his fellow men, and to God. If utilitarian motives were urged in the great majority of cases, it is because they sought to reach their pupils on their own level. Although their ideals sometimes fell below those of the great prophets, and especially those of the Great Teacher of Nazareth, the importance of their work in establishing individual standards of right and wrong, in keeping alive in concrete form the principles of the earlier prophets, and in preparing their race for the crises through which it was soon to pass cannot be overestimated. As effective teachers of the individual they have an intensely practical and significant message for all men in the stream of life today as well as in the past.

CHAPTER 16

THE DIFFERENT CURRENTS OF THOUGHT IN JUDAISM DURING THE GREEK PERIOD

Liberty of thought as well as speech was from the first characteristic of Israel's life and thought. It was one of the many valuable heritages that the Hebrews brought with them from the free life of the desert. Their close contact with the outside world, and especially with Hellenic life and thought during the Greek period, increased this sense of freedom. The result is that many different currents of thought are reflected in the Old Testament writings that come from this age. Most familiar and easiest understood is the ritualistic type. It is represented by the Chronicler, who lived and wrote some time between 300 and 250 B.C. For him all life and interest centered about the temple and its services. In general the vision of the ritualists was turned toward the past rather than the present and the future. In the traditions regarding the origin of the temple and its institutions, in keeping the ceremonial law, in participating in the formal ritual, and in joining their songs with those of the temple singers they found an escape from the pettiness of the age and attained the peace and joy that is expressed in many of the psalms of the Psalter.

The Legalists Closely related to the ritualists were those whose interests were all fixed in the study of the law and the teachings of the earlier priests. They regarded the written laws as a complete guide to conduct and the embodiment of Jehovah's supreme message to his race. Psalms like the fragment found in 19:7–14 voice their convictions:

> *The law of Jehovah is perfect, restoring the soul,*
> *The judgments of Jehovah are true and altogether*
> *   just.*
> *By them is thy servant warned; in keeping them*
> *   is great reward.*

They emphasized not merely external acts and words, but inner motives. In character and in conduct they were noble products of the religion that Israel had inherited from the past. By them were probably treasured stories such as are found in the first chapters of the book of Daniel. The detailed references in chapter 2 to the marriage of Antiochus Theos and the daughter of Ptolemy Philadelphus in 248 B.C. and to the murder of Antiochus by his former wife Laodicea, together with the absence of allusions to subsequent events, indicate that these stories were probably committed to writing somewhere between 255 and 245 B.C. Their aim was clearly to emphasize the supreme importance of fulfilling faithfully the demands of the law, even in the face of bitter opposition and persecution, and the certainty that Jehovah would deliver those who were loyal to him. Their teachings were especially adapted to inspire the tried and tempted Jews of the dispersion, who were sorely persecuted by the heathen among whom they lived. The dramatic picture of men who dared face the fiery furnace or the hungry lions rather than depart from the demands of the law undoubtedly proved a great inspiration to the Jews of the Greek period.

The Disciples of the Prophets Throughout the centuries that followed the destruction of Jerusalem the great ethical prophets of the pre-exilic period had never been without spiritual disciples. They faithfully studied and applied in their own lives the principles laid down by their earlier guides. Although the influence of the contemporary prophets constantly waned, the spirit of those earlier champions of the faith yet lived in the hearts of their followers. In many of the psalms of the Psalter, Amos, Isaiah, and Jeremiah speak in terms adapted to the changed problems of the Jews of the Greek period. In Psalm 46 the trust in Jehovah that Isaiah advocated has become a living force in the life of the psalmist and of the class in behalf of which he spoke. In the background one hears the march of the multitude armed by

Alexander for world conquest and the din of conflict as army met army, but over all stands Jehovah, protecting his sanctuary and people, supreme in the lives of men and nations. The narrow, nationalistic, messianic hopes have long since been abandoned, and instead Jehovah is recognized as the one supreme being whose kingdom or dominion includes all the nations of the earth. In imagination these disciples of the prophets saw the time when rich and poor, Jew and Gentile, should bow before Jehovah and be united in loyalty to him. Thus arose that highest conception of the kingdom of God, which is the foundation of Jesus's teaching.

The Date and Character of the Book of Jonah From those who sat at the feet of the earlier prophets came one of the most remarkable books of the Old Testament. In literary form the little book of Jonah is closely akin to the stories in the opening chapters of Genesis and the first half of the book of Daniel. Its many Aramaic words, its quotations from the late book of Joel, its universalism, and its missionary spirit all indicate that it comes either from the closing years of the Persian period or from the earlier part of the Greek period. The story of Jonah, like many similar stories in the Old Testament, was probably known to the Semites centuries before it was employed by the author of the book to point his great prophetic teaching. In the familiar Greek story of Hercules, Hesione, the daughter of the Trojan king, is rescued by the hero from a sea monster that held her in its stomach three days. An old Egyptian tale coming from the third millennium B.C. tells of an Egyptian who was ship-wrecked and after floating three days was swallowed by a great sea monster and thus carried to the land. From India comes the tradition of a man who went to sea contrary to the commands of his mother. While on the way the ship was seized by an unknown power and not allowed to proceed until the offender was three times selected by lot and then cast overboard.

Teachings of the Book of Jonah The value and message of the book of Jonah have in the past been largely overlooked because the true literary character of the book has been misunderstood. It was never intended by its author to be regarded as a historical narrative. Its hero, Jonah, the son of Amittai, according to II Kings 14:25, lived during the reign of Jeroboam II (780–740 B.C.) and predicted the wide exten-sion of the territory of southern Israel, but the Jonah of the story is evidently a Jew of the Persian and Greek periods. By showing the pettiness of his attitude toward the hea-then the author sought to broaden the vision and quicken the conscience of his fellow Jews. The portrait is remark-ably vivid and suggestive. Jonah fled from Jehovah's land and took refuge in the sea, not because he feared the Ninevites, but, as he plainly declares later, because he feared that if he did preach to the Assyrian foes of his race, Jehovah would repent and spare them. In the scene in the midst of the rag-ing tempest the piety of the heathen sailors and their zeal in sparing the guilty Israelite stand forth in favorable contrast to Jonah's action in refusing to carry out Jehovah's command. The Ninevites, clad in sackcloth, repenting for their sins, and craving Jehovah's forgiveness, are far more attractive than the sullen prophet, complaining because Jehovah has spared the heathen foes of his race and later upbraiding Jehovah because of the destruction of the gourd that for a time had protected his head from the burning sun. Jehovah's concluding remonstrance voices the message of the book. Like the New Testament parable of the prodigal son, the story of Jonah presents in graphic form the unbounded love of the heavenly father and contrasts it sharply with the petty jealousies and hatred of his favored people. It was a call to Israel to go forth and become a missionary to all the world and a protest against the nation's failure to perform its God-given task.

The Book of Ecclesiastes Very different is the spirit and purpose of the book of Ecclesiastes. It evidently comes from one of the many wisdom teachers who flourished during the Greek period, and it speaks in the name of Solomon. It is an essay on the value of life. In its original form its thought was so pessimistic that it has been supplemented at many points by later editors. These insertions include proverbs commending wisdom and praising the current wisdom teachings, and the work of a pious scribe, a forerunner of the later Pharisees, who sought to correct the utterances of the original writer (who is commonly designated as Koheleth) and to bring them into accord with current orthodoxy. The language and style of the book are closely akin to those of the Chronicler and the author of the book of Esther. It also contains several Persian words and possibly one Greek word. The book in its earlier form was evidently known to Ben Sira, the author of Ecclesiasticus, who lived about 180 B.C. In 4:13–16 and 10:16–17 there are apparent references to the reign of Ptolemy Epiphanes, who came to the throne of Egypt at the age of five and whose court was famous for its dissoluteness and profligacy. The book, therefore, may be dated with considerable confidence a little before 200 B.C. It was a corrupt, barren period. Crime was rampant in the temple as well as at the court in Alexandria (3:16). The people were crushed by the powerful and were without means of redress (4:1). A despot sat on the throne (10:5–7) and spies lurked everywhere (10:20).

Koheleth's Philosophy of Life The author of the original book of Ecclesiastes is the spokesman of the class in Judaism who were oppressed and crushed by this dreary outlook. He evidently lived in Jerusalem and probably near the temple (5:1, 8:10). From the allusions in 7:26, 28 it is evident that he was unhappily married. From the classic description of old age found in 11:9–12:7 it would appear that when he wrote he was well advanced in years, and spoke out of the depths of his own painful personal experience, having been left without son or close kinsman (4:8). From his teachings it is clear that he had broken away from the orthodox wisdom school. Before his enfeebled vision rose the seamy, dreary side of life, and yet behind the lament of this ancient pessimist is revealed a man of high ideals, impelled by a spirit of scientific thoroughness. Though he was intense and eager in his quest for true happiness and in his analysis of the meaning of life, he found no abiding joy, for his outlook was sadly circumscribed. Life beyond the grave offered to him no hope or compensation. He was, however, by no means an agnostic. He believed in God's rulership of the world, but the God of his faith was inscrutable, far removed from the life of men. Hence, unlike many of his contemporaries, for example, the psalmists, he found little joy or inspiration in his religion. According to the conclusion, which he proclaimed in the beginning of his essay and held consistently throughout, all human striving and ambition, even life itself, are but superlative vanity, nor can man attain any permanent or complete satisfaction. The one positive teaching that Koheleth reiterates is that it is man's highest privilege to extract from passing experiences the small measure of joy and happiness that they offer, and therewith to be content. Compared with many other Old Testament books, the religious value of Ecclesiastes is slight indeed. Its chief value, however, is historical: it presents one phase of thought in the Judaism of this period and shows how sorely the Jewish people needed the spur of a great crisis to rouse them to noble and unselfish action. The book of Ecclesiastes also furnishes the darker background that brings out in clear relief the inspiring messages of the great prophets that had gone before, and of the greater Prophet who was to set before the human race a worthy goal and a fresh and true interpretation of the value of life.

CHAPTER 17

·····························

THE TEACHINGS OF JESUS THE SON OF SIRACH

Out of the large number of anonymous books that come from the Persian and Greek periods one stands forth unique. It is the Wisdom of Ben Sira. With the exception of the Psalter and Isaiah, it is the largest book that has come to us from ancient Israel. Fortunately, its date and authorship may be determined with reasonable certainty. In the prologue to the Greek translation, its translator describes himself as the grandson of Jesus, the son of Sirach, and states that he went to Egypt in 132 B.C. Hence it is probable that his grandfather wrote sometime during the early part of the second century B.C. The appreciative description of Simon the high priest in the fiftieth chapter of Ben Sira indicates that its author was a contemporary as well as an admirer of that famous head of the Judean community. From the references in the rabbinical writings, as well as from the definite statement of Eusebius, it is reasonably certain that this Simon lived between 200 and 175 B.C. Furthermore, the quotations in the writings of Ben Sira from Ecclesiastes in its original form imply that he wrote during the latter part of the Greek period. The complete absence of any reference to the Maccabean struggle also proves beyond question that he lived before 168 B.C. These facts indicate that the date of his writing was somewhere between 190 and 175 B.C.

In the Hebrew version the name of this famous sage appears as Jesus, the son of Eleazar, the son of Sira. In the Greek version, however, he is known simply as Jesus, the son of Sirach. Ben Sira, or Sirach, was apparently his family name, while Jesus is the Greek equivalent of Jeshua or Joshua. From his writings it may be inferred that he belonged to a well-known Jerusalemite family. It is also not improbable that he was connected with the high-priestly line. His references to Simon the high priest reveals his deep sympathies with the ecclesiastical rulers of Jerusalem. The closing words in the Hebrew version of 51:12 are equally significant: "Give thanks to him who chose the sons of Sadok to be priests." In his teachings Ben Sira is in some respects a forerunner of the later Sadducees. Evidently he was a man of influence in the Judean community. His fame as a wise man doubtless attracted many disciples. He was deeply interested in every phase of life. While his point of view was somewhat similar to that of Koheleth, his outlook was thoroughly optimistic. His teachings were positive rather than negative. His faith was that of the fathers, and his purpose constructive. Out of the wealth of teachings inherited from the past, and also out of his own personal experience and observation, he sought to inspire right ideals in the young and to develop them into happy and efficient servants of God and of their fellow men. In this respect he was a worthy representative of the wise who during this period molded the life of Judaism.

His Writings The prologue to the Greek version of the wisdom of Sirach states that he was a devoted student of the earlier scriptures of his race. In 33:16 he acknowledges, in all modesty, his indebtedness to the past:

> *I awakened last of all as one who gathers after the*
> *   great gatherers,*
> *By the blessing of the Lord I profited and filled my*
> *   wine-press as one who gathers grapes.*

It was natural, therefore, that he should write down his teachings in the language of his fathers. Unlike most of his contemporaries, he possessed a classical Hebrew style. Like the wise men whose teachings are preserved in the book of Proverbs, he put his thought into poetic, proverbial form. In his book there is a definite, logical arrangement of ideas. The first part consists of a series of essays on various topics. The same subject is often dealt with in many different settings (e.g., choice of friends, 6:5–17, 7:18, 12:8–12, 37:1–5). These brief essays are grouped together, and each group is provided with a brief introduction, usually in commendation of wisdom. Apparently the first half of the book consists of notes based on Ben Sira's early teachings. Each group of sayings may well represent his teachings on a given occasion. In 31:21–50:24 is found the roll call of Israel's spiritual heroes, beginning with a psalm in praise of Jehovah's majesty and power and concluding with the description of Simon the high priest. This latter part of the book is clearly a pure literary creation, and was probably added by him as a conclusion to the collection of his wisdom teachings.

History of the Book The book containing the writings of Ben Sira was known under a variety of titles. The Latin Church followed the Greek in calling it Ecclesiasticus. This term was applied to those books that were not in the canon, but were held to be edifying and proper for public use in the churches. The Hebrew text of Ben Sira enjoyed wide currency, was frequently quoted by the later rabbis, and was often referred to by later Jewish and Christian writers. It was almost completely supplanted in time, however, by the Greek version. Jerome was acquainted with the Hebrew version, but most of the Church fathers followed the Greek. Ben Sira was apparently quoted by Jesus, by Paul, and by the authors of the Epistle of James and of the Epistle to the Hebrews. Twenty or thirty such references or allusions are found in the New Testament. It was also a great favorite with the church fathers, who quoted from it even more frequently than from the other Old Testament writings. It was adopted in the canon of the Greek and Latin church, but, in common with the other apocryphal books, was given a secondary place by the Protestant reformers. Unfortunately, during the earlier part of the last century it ceased to be printed in the standard editions of the Bible. The modern revival of interest in the apocryphal books, both in Europe and America, is tending to restore this book, in common with I Maccabees, to the position they certainly deserve in the practical working canon of the Old Testament. The discovery in 1896 of a fragment of the original Hebrew manuscript of Ben Sira and the subsequent recovery of many other parts have also tended to arouse wide interest in this hitherto much neglected book. Hebrew portions of thirty-nine out of the fifty-one chapters have thus far been discovered. Most of them come from about the eleventh Christian century and are of widely differing values. By means of these, however, and the quotations by the Jewish rabbis and Christian fathers and in the Greek, Syriac, and Latin versions, it is now possible to restore most of the original Hebrew text, and the resulting translation is far superior to those based on the Greek text.

Its Picture of Jewish Life Ben Sira has given a vivid picture of the domestic, economic, and social life of the Jews of his age. The debased, Oriental conception of marriage had corrupted the atmosphere of the home. Wives were regarded as the possessions of their husbands, and the immoral influence of Hellenism still further undermined the purity and integrity of many a Jewish home. Greek customs and usages were pervading Palestine more and more. Ben Sira refers to banquets with their accompaniments of music and wine. Even these meet with his approval. Agriculture and commerce are the chief occupations of the people. In general Ben Sira voices the wholesome Jewish attitude toward labor:

> *Hate not laborious work;*
> *Neither agriculture that the Most High hath*
> *ordained.*
> *He is especially strong in his commendation of*
> *physicians:*
> *Be a friend to the physician, for one has need of him,*
> *For verily God hath appointed him.*
> *A physician receives his wisdom from God,*
> *And from the king he receives presents.*
> *The knowledge of a physician causes him to lift up his*
> *head,*
> *And before the princes may he enter.*
> *God created medicines out of the earth,*
> *And a prudent man will not be disgusted with them.*

The following proverb has a universal application:

> *He who sins before his maker,*
> *Let him fall into the hands of his physician!*

Rise of the Scribes The writings of Ben Sira reveal the close connection between the earlier wise men and the later

scribes. He lived at the period when the wise man was turning scribe. He himself had a profound respect for the law:

> *A man of understanding will put his trust in the law,*
> *The law is faithful to him as when one asks at the*
> *oracle.*

One of his fundamental teachings is formulated in the
proverb:

> *Fear the Lord and glorify his priests,*
> *And give him his portion even as it is commanded.*

Elsewhere he declares:

> *The leisure of the scribe increases his wisdom,*
> *And he who has no business becomes wise.*

In his famous description of the typical wise man in
39:1–11 may be recognized many of the traits of the later
scribes. As the law and the ritual gained greater prominence
in the life of Judaism, it was inevitable that it should command the attention of the practical teachers of the people.
Thus gradually the wise devoted themselves to its study
and interpretation, ever emphasizing, however, thought
and conduct as well as conformity to the ritual. Scribism
was greatly enriched by its lineal inheritance through the
earlier wise men and long retained the proverbial, epigrammatic form of teaching and the personal attitude toward
the individual and his problems that was one of their greatest sources of strength. The honor the early scribes enjoyed

was well deserved. Their methods were free from the casuistry that characterized many of the later scribes. They not only copied and guarded the law, but were its interpreters, applying it practically to the everyday problems of the people as well as to their duties in connection with the temple service. Their influence upon the Jews in this early period was on the whole exceedingly wholesome, and from their ranks rose the martyrs that a generation later were ready to die for the law.

The Teachings of Ben Sira Ben Sira was acquainted with Greek culture and at several points shows familiarity with Greek ideals and methods of thinking, but his point of view in general was distinctly Jewish. He gathered together all that was best in the earlier teachings of his race. In many ways he represents an advance beyond all that had gone before and a close approximation to the spirit and teachings of Jesus of Nazareth. The God of his faith was omnipotent, majestic, omniscient, just, and merciful. He was the God of all mankind, although it was through Israel that he especially revealed himself. Ben Sira did not, like Ezekiel, think of God as far removed from the life of men and as communicating with them only through angels, but as directly and personally interested in the experiences and life of the individual. In 23:1, 4 he addresses him as "Lord," "Father," and "Master of my life." Thus he employs in the personal sense the term "Father," which was most often on the lips of the Great Teacher of Nazareth. In Ben Sira's stalwart faith and simple trust there is also much that reminds us of the Greater than Solomon. Like the teachers who had preceded him, he had, however, no clear belief in individual immortality (cf. 41:3–4, 38:16, 23) The only reward after death that he could hold up before a good man was his reputation:

> *A good life has its number of days,*
> *But a good name continues forever.*

Consistent with the orthodox wisdom school, he taught that rewards for right living came in this life:

> *Delight not in the delights of the wicked;*
> *Remember they shall not go unpunished to the grave.*

Even though he lacked the inspiration of future hope, Ben Sira taught loyalty to God and fidelity to every duty. Justice toward all, consideration for the needs of the suffering and dependent, and generosity to the poor are constantly urged by this noblest Jew of the age.

CHAPTER 18

THE CAUSES OF THE MACCABEAN STRUGGLE

The first book of Maccabees is in many ways the best history that has come down from ancient Israel. Luther's conclusion that it was more deserving of a place in the Old Testament canon than, for example, the book of Esther is now being widely accepted both in theory and practice. The religious spirit in which it is written, the importance of the events with which it deals, and the faithfulness with which they are recorded all confirm this conclusion. It is the work of a devoted patriot, who appears to have been personally acquainted with the events he records. He was an ardent admirer of Judas Maccabeus and may well have been one of the many valiant Jews who rallied about this sturdy champion. The author was familiar with the early histories of his race, for he has adopted many of the phrases peculiar to the books of Samuel and Kings. His idioms leave no doubt that he wrote in Hebrew, although this version has been lost.

The first book of Maccabees opens with a brief reference to Alexander the Great and to the Greek rulers who succeeded him. The detailed history, however, begins with Antiochus Epiphanes and continues to the death of Simon in 135 B.C. The references in the prologue to the rebuilding of the walls of Jerusalem by Simon's son, John Hyrcanus, between 135 and 125 B.C. and the absence of any allusions to the more important events in the latter part of his reign indicate that his history was probably completed by 125 B.C. It was written, therefore, less than half a century after all the events that it records took place. While the author is a true patriot and keenly interested in the history of his race, he does not allow his patriotism to carry him into exaggeration. He reveals the true historical spirit and a splendid reserve in recounting the epoch-making events he records.

Character and Contents of II Maccabees In marked contrast with I Maccabees is the second book that bears this name. The author states in 2:19–32 that it was based on an earlier five-volume history written by Jason, of Cyrene, in northern Africa. The final epitomizer of this earlier work probably lived not long after 50 B.C. Jason himself appears to have lived somewhere between 160 and 140 B.C. and to have written from northern Syria. The language of the original was evidently Greek. The aim of the author was didactic rather than historical, and he drew freely from popular tradition. In general character it corresponds closely to the work of the Chronicler, who compiled the Old Testament books of Chronicles and Ezra–Nehemiah. The miraculous element is prominent, numbers are frequently enlarged, and Israel's disasters are minimized. Notwithstanding all of its obvious faults, II Maccabees has preserved many important historical facts. Where its testimony differs from that of I Maccabees, the latter in general should be followed, but its account of the events that led to the Maccabean uprising are much more detailed than those of I Maccabees, which it supplements at many important points. With the aid of these two histories it is possible to gain a remarkably vivid and detailed conception of the half century that witnessed the reawakening of Judaism and the birth of a new national spirit.

Aggressive Character of Hellenic Culture Jewish life and religion were at times almost uprooted, but never fundamentally transformed by the Babylonian and Persian conquerors. Alexander, however, and those who followed in his wake introduced an entirely new and aggressive force into the life and thought of Palestine. The centuries that began with 332 B.C. witnessed the most important struggle the world has ever seen. It was fought not on the open battlefield, but wherever in Palestine and the lands of the dispersion the currents of ancient life and commerce met and mingled. It was the age-long conflict between Hellenism and Judaism, those two mighty forces that had long been maturing in the coast lands of the northern and eastern Mediterranean. The outcome of this contest was destined to affect the civilization and faith of all the world throughout the ages.

Judaism represented the life and faith of a peasant people, while Hellenism was born in the city. Wherever Hellenism went, it found expression in civic life. The heathen races of Palestine, the Phoenicians and Philistines on the coast, and the peoples of eastern Jordan readily welcomed the superior civilization of the conquerors. It appealed powerfully to their intellectual, social, and aesthetic sense, and, in the debased form that it assumed in the East, to their passions. Even the Samaritans readily accepted it, and the city of Samaria was settled by a colony of Macedonian soldiers. The ancient cities of Gaza, Askelon, Accho under the name of Ptolemais, Tyre, Sidon, Damascus, Bethshean under its new name Scythopolis, Rabbath-ammon under the name of Philadelphia, and most of the important eastern Jordan cities were soon transformed into active centers of Hellenic culture. Civic pride and patriotism took possession of their inhabitants. Most of the cities had a senate and magistrates elected each year by popular vote. Many of them were adorned by magnificent public buildings, including a forum, theatre, stadium, hippodrome, and gymnasium. Civic patriotism took the place of the old despotism and selfish individualism. Each Hellenic city gave to its citizens new ideals and opportunities. The discussions of the forum, the agora, and the gymnasium inspired them with political, social, and intellectual interests. The plays in the theatres and the races in the hippodrome and stadium amazed and fascinated them. Many of the youths were enlisted in the clubs that were formed in connection with the gymnasium, and all classes participated in the public festivities.

Contrast between Hellenism and Judaism In the broad perspective of history it is clear that both Hellenism and Judaism were essential to the upbuilding and broadening of the human character and ideals. Hellenism in its nobler form brought what Judaism lacked, and Judaism was fitted to correct the evils and fatal weaknesses of Hellenism. Ben Sira vaguely recognized this and sought to reconcile these two types of civilization, but in the second century B.C. men were chiefly aware of the glaring contrasts. Compared with the splendor of the life in the Greek cities that of the orthodox Jews seemed crude and barbarous. The intense horror with which the Jews viewed every form of idolatry led them to reject all forms of art. Their hatred of sensuality and immorality led them to regard with aversion the sports and exercises of the gymnasium and the attendant licentiousness. The practical teachers of Israel looked with suspicion upon the subtleties of the different Greek philosophical schools. On the other hand, the homely, domestic joys of the average Jew and his intense devotion to the service of the temple and to the faith of his fathers seemed contemptible to those familiar with the brilliant, voluptuous life of the Hellenic cities. Hellenism protested against the narrowness, barrenness, and intolerance of Judaism; Judaism protested against the godlessness and immorality of Hellenism. Both were right in their protests, and yet each in a sense needed the other.

Apostasy of the Jews and the Perfidy of the High Priests

At the beginning of the second century B.C. the Judean state was closely encircled by a ring of Hellenic cities and subjected on every side to the seductions of that debased Greek culture that had taken firm root in the soil of Palestine. As was almost inevitable, many of the Jewish youth yielded to its attractions. Distaste for the narrowness and austere customs of their fathers begat in their minds a growing contempt for their race and its religion. Even some of the younger priests forsook the temple for the gymnasium. Unconsciously but surely Judaism was drifting from its old moorings toward Hellenism, until the perfidy of its high priests and the persecutions of Antiochus Epiphanes aroused it to a full realization of its peril. The apostates in Jerusalem found a leader in Jeshua, who had assumed the Greek name of Jason. He was the brother of Onias III, the reigning high priest, and had been sent to represent him at the Syrian court. There he improved the opportunity by promising greater tribute to secure his appointment as high priest. He was soon outbid, however, by a certain renegade named Menelaus, who with the aid of Syrian soldiers drove Jason from Jerusalem and took his place as head of the hellenizing party. The first cause, therefore, of the Maccabean struggle was the apostasy of certain of the Jews themselves. Apparently in large numbers they abandoned the traditions of their race and assumed the Greek garb and customs, thus leading their Syrian rulers to believe that the hellenizing of the entire race would be comparatively easy.

Character of Antiochus Epiphanes The ruler who by his injustice and persecutions fanned the smoldering flame of Jewish patriotism into a mighty conflagration was Antiochus Epiphanes. As a youth he had been educated at Rome with the profligate sons of those who ruled the Imperial City. The Greek and Roman historians, especially Polybius, give vivid portraits of this tyrannical king. In him the prevailing passion for Hellenism found extreme expression. To dazzle his contemporaries by the splendor of his building enterprises and by his dramatic display was his chief ambition. In gratifying thus his selfish ambition he drained the resources of his kingdom and was therefore obliged to resort to extreme measures to replenish his treasury. In 170 B.C. he made a successful campaign into Egypt. Two years later he again invaded the rich land of the Nile, only to find himself confronted by a Roman general, who peremptorily ordered him to retreat. Rome was already the chief power in the eastern Mediterranean, and Antiochus, although in a rage, wisely decided to retire. It was at this inopportune moment that he found Jerusalem in revolt, misled by a false report and by the renegade high priest Jason. Antiochus not only improved this opportunity to loot the temple and slay many of the inhabitants, but from this time on conceived a bitter antipathy to the Jewish race. This antipathy he shared in common with all the Greek world, for already, as a result of the peculiar religion and customs of the Jews and their success in commercial pursuits, what is known today as the anti-Semitic spirit was fully developed. One of Antiochus's chief ambitions was also to hellenize all his subjects, and the Jews alone offered opposition to the realization of this ambition. Hence they could expect no mercy at the hands of this selfish, capricious despot.

Antiochus's Policy toward the Jews The measures Antiochus employed to crush the faith of Judaism were relentlessly thorough. He began with the seizure of Jerusalem, the tearing down of its walls, the fortifying and garrisoning of its citadel with Syrian soldiers and apostate Jews, and the slaughter of all who refused to accede to his demands. Not only was the temple service stopped, but the altar was torn down and desecrated and a heathen altar to Zeus—the abominable desolation of the book of Daniel—was reared in its place. On this swine's flesh was sacrificed, and the presence of harlots in the sacred precincts completed its ceremonial and moral pollution. All the surviving inhabitants of Jerusalem were compelled to sacrifice and pay homage to the heathen gods. Those who retained copies of their laws or persisted in maintaining the customs of their fathers were slain. When many fled to the outlying towns, emissaries of Antiochus pursued them, demanding of each citizen public recognition of the Greek gods. A majority of the Jews apparently yielded to these drastic measures and joined the ranks of the apostates.

Of the many crises through which Israel passed this was in many ways the most severe, but then it gave to the world some of the noblest martyrs. The early Christians who perished for their faith were inspired by the example of their Master and by the hope of blessed, individual immortality. To the Jews of the Greek period, however, the great calamity that overtook them came as a sudden and unexpected blow. No clear hope of immortality at first inspired them, for, like Ben Sira and the earlier teachers of the race, the majority of them probably regarded the life beyond death as a passionless existence in the land of darkness. Even the expectation of family or racial immortality seemed denied by the dark outlook. They died as did Eleazar, the aged scribe, simply because of their devotion to the God and laws of their fathers, and because that loyalty meant more to them than life.

CHAPTER 19

THE EFFECT OF PERSECUTION ON THE JEWS

The persecutions of Antiochus Epiphanes had at last reached the point where patient submission and even martyrdom ceased to be a virtue. His agents had successfully carried the merciless hellenizing campaign throughout practically all the territory of Judea. It was not until they reached its extreme northwestern border that they met the first open opposition. The little town of Modein lay out on the edge of the great plain where the central hills of Palestine break down into low foothills. These are intersected by rushing brooks and crystal clear streams that descend from the heights above. The town lay on a rounded hill about one third of a mile in diameter that rises abruptly in a series of steep terraces. The Wady Malakeh encircled it on the south and west. On the northeastern side, where lies the modern town, was a broad shoulder of land slightly lower and larger than the acropolis. In ancient times it was probably the site of the lower city. Deep, encircling valleys on the north and east completed the natural defenses of this border village that became the altar of Jewish freedom. Today the scattered ruins of the acropolis are covered in springtime with a luxuriant growth of grain and olive trees, making it one of the most picturesque mounds in Palestine. It is surprising that the revolt against the cruel tyranny of Antiochus was led by an aged priest, whose home was outside Jerusalem. He was one of the chief men of Modein, descended from the family of Hasmon. His descendants, the Hasmonians, ultimately became the independent rulers of their race. In Mattathias the long-suppressed, hot indignation of the Jewish race at last found expression. In slaying the apostate Jew and Syrian official, Mattathias evoked that warlike spirit which had in earlier days given Israel a home and a place among the nations. His impulsive act inaugurated a new chapter in Israel's life and thought. In its far-reaching consequences it was comparable only to Moses's impulsive slaying of the Egyptian taskmaster.

Party of the Hasideans or Pious It was fortunate that Mattathias had five able, mature sons to support him. Simon, the eldest, was already famous in council. Judas, who bore the surname Maccabeus (whence came the word "Maccabees"), soon proved himself a great military leader. Jonathan combined the qualities of Simon and Judas with a certain craftiness that makes him the least attractive of the three. Eleazar later proved on the battlefield that he had the qualities that make heroes and martyrs. Among the Judean hills, and especially in the barren, almost inaccessible fastnesses that descend in a series of terraces from the central plateau to the Dead Sea, Mattathias and his followers found refuge. Hither many patriotic Jews had already fled. The Syrian mercenaries, however, led by the relentless apostate Jews, pursued them, and, knowing their scruples, attacked them on the Sabbath day and pitilessly slaughtered them. Learning from this awful example, Mattathias and his sons wisely decided that it was more important to fight for their lives than to die for a mere institution. They soon attracted to their standard all who were still faithful to the law. Chief among these were those known as the Hasideans or Pious. They were the spiritual successors of the pious or afflicted, whose woes are voiced in the earlier psalms of the Psalter. They were also the forerunners of the party of the Pharisees, which was one of the products of the Maccabean struggle. In them faith and patriotism were so blended that, like Cromwell's Ironsides, they were daunted by no odds. At first they depended upon the guerilla type of warfare, to which the hills of Judea were especially adapted. By enforcing the law of circumcision, by punishing the apostates, and by attacking straggling Syrian bands, they encouraged the faltering Jews and intimidated the agents of Antiochus. Mattathias soon died, leaving the leadership to his third son, Judas. The poem recording his dying injunctions voices the inspiration that came at this time to Israel's patriots from their nation's past, and that supreme devotion to the law and dauntless courage that animated the leaders in this great movement.

Date of the Visions in Daniel 7–12 A parallel but different type of character and hope is reflected in the latter part of the book of Daniel. In the form of visions or predictions, these chapters interpret the meaning of the great world movements from the beginning of the Babylonian period to the end of the Greek period. Each vision culminates in a symbolic but detailed description of the rule and persecutions of Antiochus Epiphanes. Several passages describe the destructive policies of this Syrian ruler almost as vividly as the books of Maccabees (Dan. 8:11, 12): "It (Antiochus) magnified itself even to the Prince of the Host (Jehovah), and took away from him the daily sacrifice, and cast down the place of his sanctuary, and set up the sacrilegious thing over the daily sacrifice, and cast down truth to the ground, and did it and prospered."

Daniel 11:20–44 contains a review of the chief events of Antiochus's reign. This description closes with the prediction: "He shall plant his palace between the Mediterranean and the glorious holy mountain; so he shall come to his end and none shall help him." Contemporary records indicate, however, that Antiochus died while engaged in a campaign in distant Persia and not in western Palestine as the author of Daniel anticipated. In the other visions, after the description of Antiochus's persecutions, the details suddenly give way to general predictions, implying that at this point the author turned from the contemplation of past and present events to what was to him future. The great victories of Judas and his followers that led to the restoration of the temple in

165 B.C. are nowhere mentioned. In 11:34 is found an allusion to the Maccabean uprising: "Now when they are falling they shall be helped with a little help; but many shall join themselves to them with false protestations." This movement, clearly, is not regarded by the author as significant. The date of these visions, therefore, may be fixed with great confidence between the years 168 and 166 B.C.

Their Real Character and Aim In interpreting these visions it is important to note that they belong to the so-called apocalyptic type of literature. Already Ezekiel and Zechariah had employed the complex symbolism of the apocalypse to stir the imagination and strengthen the faith of their discouraged countrymen. The aim of the author of the closing chapters of Daniel was primarily to present a religious philosophy of history. Through the rise and fall of nations Jehovah's purpose was slowly but surely being realized. They are the expression of the eternal optimism of the prophets. They voice their deathless hope that "the best is yet to be." They were intended to encourage those in the midst of persecution with the assurance that God was still in his heaven, and that all would yet be right with his world.

The Four Heathen Kingdoms and the Kingdom of God
In the symbolism of the prophet the four beasts of Daniel 7 represented the Chaldean, Medean, Persian, and Greek empires. The fourth beast with iron teeth that devoured and broke in pieces the rest was clearly the empire of Alexander,

and the little horn that sprang up was the little horn which gored and mangled the helpless people of Jehovah. Opposed to the four beasts that represented the angels, or demons, the champions of each of the great heathen kingdoms, was Israel's patron angel Michael. It is this angel who is apparently referred to in 7:13 as coming from heaven, and in appearance like to a son of man. At Jehovah's direction he was to establish a glorious, universal kingdom, the citizens of which were to be the saints, the faithful Jews who remained loyal to Jehovah during the long, cruel persecutions. Not only those who survived but the martyrs sleeping in the dust of the earth were to awake and receive their glorious reward. The apostates were to be sentenced to everlasting shame and contempt. The wise teachers and martyrs who by word and example had striven to keep their race loyal to Jehovah were to be exalted in the coming messianic kingdom. Thus these visions reveal the hopes that inspired certain of the Jewish race in its period of supreme trial: the belief that Jehovah through his angel would speedily overthrow the power of the heathen persecutor, that he would establish a universal kingdom in which his own people should have chief place, and finally that even the bonds of death would not hold those who had died for the law. Thus at last out of this struggle Judaism emerged with a newfound faith in individual immortality. It was still bound up in the belief in the bodily resurrection, but at last the imperishable worth of the individual had become one of the cornerstones of Israel's religion.

CHAPTER 20

THE VICTORIES THAT GAVE THE JEWS RELIGIOUS LIBERTY

Judas Maccabeus was a man of unquestioned courage. In the many battles he fought he was always found at the forefront in the most desperate engagement. More than that he was able to arouse courage in a people that for centuries had learned only to bow unresistingly before their conquerors. All the evidence found in the two books of Maccabees indicates that he was inspired by the noblest patriotism. The motive power in his patriotism was devotion to the law and customs of his race. In this respect he was a leader supremely acceptable to the Hasideans or Pious, who rallied about his standard. In any other age or setting his devotion would have seemed but fanaticism. The situation, however, was extremely critical. Disloyalty to the law and the distinctive rites of Judaism was treason.

If ever in the world's history it was justifiable to meet force with force and to unshield the sword on behalf of religion, this certainly was the occasion. In his military tactics Judas revealed the cunning that characterizes the hunted. He developed great skill in choosing a strategic position and in launching his followers against a vulnerable point in the enemy's line. In this respect he showed himself a disciple of David's able general Joab. They were the same tactics that Napoleon employed so effectively in later days and on larger battlefields. Judas resembled in many ways Israel's first king, Saul. He was impetuous, patriotic, intense, and energetic. He was especially skilled in leading a sudden attack. His task also was strikingly similar to that of Israel's first king, and like Saul in his later days he showed the same inability to organize and hold his followers in a time of comparative peace.

Obstacles against Which Judas Contended When Judas was called to champion the cause of the Jews, they were hated by the rest of the world. It was a disorganized band of fugitives that rallied about him, without homes, resources, or arms. Opposed to him were the large armies of a powerful empire. The Greek mercenaries that fought in the Syrian ranks were armed with coats of mail and the best weapons known to the ancient world. They were also thoroughly trained in the art of war and under the direction of experienced generals. On every battlefield the Syrians outnumbered the Jews almost six to one. Pitted against Judas and his followers were apostates of his own race, who knew the land, were able to spy out the movements of the Jews, and were inspired by the bitterest hatred. The few advantages on the side of Judas were, first, that his followers were aroused to heroic deeds by the peril of the situation. Second, they were inspired by an intense religious zeal. The one force throughout Semitic history that has bound together tribes and nations and made the Semite an almost invincible fighting power has been religion. The familiar illustrations are the Mohammedan conquests that swept victoriously across the Bosporus and conquered Constantinople, also across northern Africa, and surged into southern Europe over the Straits of Gibraltar and threatened for a time completely to engulf Western civilization. Familiar modern illustrations are the Mahdist insurrections that have from time to time taxed the resources of the English in northern Africa. Third, the land of Judea, with its narrow western passes rapidly ascending to the heights above, enabled Judas to choose his battlefield at a point where only a few of the enemy could be brought into action and where a handful of valiant men could keep an army at bay.

Defeat of Apollonius and Seron At first Judas wisely confined himself to guerilla warfare. This enabled him in time to clothe and arm his followers with the garments and weapons taken from the enemy. The most important of these smaller engagements took place north of Jerusalem. As Apollonius, the Syrian governor of Samaria, was advancing into Judea,

Judas suddenly fell upon the Syrians and slew their leader. Henceforth the sword of the Syrian governor was effectively wielded by Judas on behalf of religious liberty.

News of the victory soon brought Seron, the governor of Coele-Syria, with a large army. He advanced from the coast plain by the most direct road to Jerusalem over the famous pass of the Bethhorons. Within a distance of two miles the road ascended nearly fifteen hundred feet. At points it was merely a steep, rocky pass, so that an invading army was forced to march single file and to pull themselves up over the rocks. Here on the heights that looked out toward his home at Modein Judas, appealing to the faith and patriotism of his men, swept down upon the enemy and won his first great victory.

The Battle of Emmaus The first great Jewish victory was a severe blow to the power of Antiochus Epiphanes, for at that time he was confronted by a depleted treasury. He therefore left his kingdom in charge of Lysias, one of his nobles, and set out on a campaign into Persia from which he never returned. Three generals with a large army were sent by Lysias against the Jews. So confident were they of a Syrian victory that a horde of slave merchants accompanied the army that they might purchase the Jewish captives. This time the Syrians avoided the difficult pass of Bethhoron and chose the Wady Ali, along which the modern carriage road winds up from the coast to Jerusalem. The main camp was pitched at Emmaus at the southeastern side of the Plain of Ajalon under the Judean hills. In the meantime, Judas had selected as his headquarters the lofty hill of Mizpah, associated by earlier tradition with Samuel and the scene of the short-lived rule of Gedaliah. It was well chosen, for it commanded a view of the territory to the north, south, and west. While the army of the Syrians, sent by night to surprise Judas, were marching up the northern valley, the Jewish patriots were led westward toward the plain along one of the parallel valleys that penetrated the Judean hills. Having appealed to the patriotic memories and the religious zeal of his followers, Judas led them in a sudden early morning attack against the Syrians encamped near Emmaus. Soon the Syrians were in wild flight across the plain to the Philistine cities, and Judas and his followers were left in possession of the camp and its rich spoils. Panic also seized his pursuers when they saw their camp in possession of the enemy, and Judas was left for the moment undisputed master of the land of his fathers. This victory in the year 166 B.C. was in many ways the most sweeping and significant in early Maccabean history.

The Battle at Bethsura The next year Lysias himself gathered a huge army of sixty thousand infantry and five thousand cavalry and led them against the Jews. This time the Syrians advanced through the broad valley of Elah where David had fought against the Philistine giant. Thence they followed the Wady Sur and turned southward and then eastward, penetrating to the top of the Judean plateau a little north of

Hebron. Approaching from this point the Syrians were protected in their rear by the Idumeans, the descendants of the
Edomites. They succeeded in reaching the point where the
road from the west joins the central highway from Hebron
to Jerusalem. There on a sloping hill crowned with the border town of Bethsura, Judas was able to rally ten thousand
followers to meet the huge Syrian army. From the parallel
account in II Maccabees it is clear that he did not succeed
in winning a decisive victory, but a crisis in Antioch suddenly compelled Lysias to return, leaving the Jews in possession of the battlefield.

Restoration of the Temple Service With mingled sadness and rejoicing Judas proceeded at once to Jerusalem
and with his followers took up the task of restoring the
desecrated temple and its service. The citadel of Acra,
which appears to have been situated on the Hill of Ophel
to the south of the temple, was still strongly garrisoned by
apostate Jews and Syrian soldiers. For nearly a quarter of
a century, until the days of Simon, it continued to be held
by Syrian forces and remained a constant menace to the
peace of Jerusalem. The vivid account of the purification of
the temple reveals the intense devotion of the Jews to this
ancient sanctuary and throws clear light upon the nature of
its service. This epoch-making act is commemorated even
today by the Jews throughout the world and is known as the
Feast of Lights. It is a memorial of that successful struggle
for religious freedom in which principles were established

that have affected the thought and action of all succeeding generations. Through all their many vicissitudes and under their many Gentile rulers, with few exceptions, the Jews have enjoyed uninterruptedly the right of worshipping in accordance with the dictates of their law and the customs of their fathers.

The New Spirit in Judaism Henceforth the law for which their fathers had poured out their lifeblood and for which the Jews had fought so valiantly was regarded with new and deeper veneration and its commands gained a new authority. Again the Jews had enjoyed a taste of freedom and had learned that by united and courageous action they could shake off the hated heathen yoke. This new warlike note is sounded in many of the later psalms of the Psalter. Chapters 9–14, appended to the older books of Zechariah, apparently come from this same period and voice the thought of the conquerors. The words of the ninth chapter express their joy and exultation:

> For I have bent Judah to me, As a bow which
> I have filled with Ephraim; I will urge thy sons
> against the sons of Greece, And I will make thee
> like the sword of a hero. Then Jehovah shall be
> seen above them, And his shaft shall go forth
> like lightning. Jehovah shall blow a blast upon
> a trumpet, And travel on the whirlwinds of the
> south. Jehovah of hosts shall defend them; And

they shall devour and tread down the slingstones,
They shall drink their blood like wine, They shall
be filled with it like the crevices of an altar. And
Jehovah their God shall give them victory in that
day. Like sheep he shall feed them in his land.
Yea, how good and how beautiful shall it be! Corn
shall make the young men flourish, and new wine
the maidens.

The victories of Judas in all probability also inspired
the messianic hope expressed in 9:9–10:

Rejoice greatly, O daughter of Zion. Shout
aloud, O daughter of Jerusalem! Behold thy king
will come to thee; Vindicated and victorious is he,
Humble, and riding upon an ass. Upon the foal
of an ass. He shall cut off chariots from Ephraim,
And horses from Jerusalem; The battle-bow shall
also be cut off, And he shall speak to the nations;
His rule shall be from sea to sea, From the river to
the ends of the earth.

CHAPTER 21

THE LONG CONTEST FOR POLITICAL INDEPENDENCE

The position of the Jewish patriots was both perilous and tragic. A ring of hostile peoples pressed them closely on every side. The Jews were the victims of centuries of wrong and hatred. Those residing in the neighboring lands also suffered from this widespread and bitter hostility. Among all the peoples of southwestern Asia they had no allies except the Nabateans, an Arabian people that had driven the Edomites from their home on Mount Seir. The only bond that bound them to this ambitious heathen race was the common hatred of the Syrians. It was natural, therefore, that Judas a little later should send an embassy with the object of securing the moral support, if not the direct intervention, of the distant Roman power whose influence was beginning to be felt throughout all the Mediterranean coast lands. For the present, however, Judas was dependent simply upon the sword for defense. He also had no time for permanent conquest, for he must prepare himself for the heavier blow that the court of Antioch was preparing to deliver. All that he could do, therefore, was to make sudden attacks upon his foes on every side and rescue the persecuted Jews by bringing them back with him to Judea.

The Jewish Attitude toward the Heathen Reflected in the Book of Esther In these perilous circumstances it is not strange that the Jews gravitated far from the position of broad tolerance advocated by the II Isaiah and the authors of the prophecy of Malachi and in the stories of Ruth and Jonah. In the stress of conflict they completely lost sight of their mission as Jehovah's witnesses to all the world. The destruction of the heathen seemed to them absolutely necessary if Jehovah's justice was to be vindicated. The spirit of this warlike, bloodthirsty age is most clearly formulated in the book of Esther. The presence of Aramaic and Persian words testify to its late date. It is closely allied to the midrashim or didactic stories that were a characteristic literary product of later Judaism. Like the stories of Daniel, the book of Esther contains many historical inconsistencies. For example, Mordecai, carried as a captive to Babylon in 597 B.C., is made Xerxes's prime minister in 474 B.C. Its pictures of Persian customs are also characteristic of popular tradition rather than of contemporary history. Its basis is apparently an old Babylonian tradition of a great victory of the Babylonians over their ancient foes, the Elamites. Mordecai is a modification of the name of the Babylonian god Marduk. Estra, which appears in the Hebrew Esther, was the late Babylonian form of the name of the Semitic goddess Ishtar. Vashti and Hamman, the biblical Haman, were names of Elamite deities. Like the story of creation, this tale has been Hebraized and adapted to the storyteller's purpose. His aim is evidently to trace the origin of the late Jewish feast of Purim. It is probable that this feast was an adaptation of the Babylonian New Year's feast that commemorated the ancient victory. The story in its present form is strongly Jewish. It exalts loyalty to the race, but its morality is far removed from that of Amos and Isaiah. Its exultation over the slaughter of thousands of the heathen is displeasing even in a romance, although it can easily be understood in the light of the Maccabean age in which it was written.

Campaigns against the Neighboring Peoples The first book of Maccabees records in detail the repeated blows that Judas struck against his heathen foes. At Akrabattine, probably identical to the Scorpion Pass at the southwestern end of the Dead Sea, he fought and won a signal victory over his hereditary foes, the Idumeans. His chief enemy on the east was Timotheus, the leader of the Ammonites against whom Judas was successful in the preliminary skirmishes. Angered by these defeats, the heathen east of the Jordan attacked the resident Jews, who fled to one of the towns, where they were besieged. Judas, assembling six thousand of his picked warriors, made a rapid march of three days out into the wilderness. He apparently carried few supplies, but depended rather upon the spoils of the captured towns for support. Bosra, far out on the borders of the desert, was seized and looted. Thence returning westward, he rescued the Jews from the town of Damethah, or, as it appears in the Syriac, Rametha. This is probably identical to the modern town of Remtheh a little south of the Yarmuk on the great pilgrim highway from Damascus to Mecca. After making a detour to the south he crossed the Yarmuk and captured a series of towns lying to the north and northeast of this river. On the return he apparently met his Ammonite foe, who had succeeded in rallying an army, at the point where the pilgrim highway crosses the headwaters of the Yarmuk. Here Judas won a sweeping victory. Then, collecting the many Jews of the dispersion who had settled near these upper waters of the Yarmuk, he returned victoriously to Jerusalem. His brother Simon, who had been despatched on a similar mission to Galilee, likewise came back bringing many fellow Jews and laden with spoils.

Anticipating a renewal of the Syrian attack, Judas next made a rapid campaign into the territory of the Idumeans, capturing the old Hebrew capital of Hebron and carrying his victories as far as Ashdod on the western borders of the Philistine plain. Within a few months he had overrun and partially conquered a territory larger than the kingdom of David. In an incredibly short time this peasant warrior had won more victories against greater odds than any other leader in Israel's history. The results of these victories were necessarily ephemeral. They accomplished, however, three things: (1) Judas intimidated his foes and established his prestige; (2) he was able to rescue thousands of Jews from the hands of the heathen; and (3) by bringing them back to Judea he increased its population and laid the foundations of that kingdom that rose as the result of his patriotic achievements.

The Battle of Beth-zacharias There was still a Syrian outpost in the heart of Judea: it was the citadel at Jerusalem, which looked down upon the temple area. This Judas attempted to capture, but in so doing incited to action the Syrian king, Antiochus Eupator, who had succeeded to the throne after the death of his father Antiochus Epiphanes. Under the direction of his prime minister Lysias he collected a huge army of one hundred thousand infantry and twenty thousand cavalry. To this were added thirty-two elephants with full military equipment—the heavy ordinance used in the warfare of the period. The approach from the plain was along the valley of Elah and up past Bethsura, as in the last Syrian campaign. Judas, who was able at this time to rally an army of ten thousand men, met the Syrian host near the town of Beth-zacharias, a little north of Bethsura on the central highway from Hebron to Jerusalem. This time the natural advantages were with the Syrians, one wing of whose army rested upon a declining hill and the other on the level plain. Thus they were able to utilize their entire fighting force and to launch against the valiant Jews their elephants, against which the heroism of an Eleazar was fruitless. For the first time during this struggle Judas was defeated and fell back upon Jerusalem, where he was closely besieged. Soon the Jews were obliged to surrender, and the Maccabean cause would have been lost had not complications at Antioch compelled the Syrians to retire.

Victories over Nicanor In the treaty that followed the surrender of Jerusalem the religious liberty of the Jews was assured. This concession satisfied the majority of the Hasideans, so that henceforth Judas found himself deserted by a great body of his followers. The apostate high priest who was placed in control of the temple was supported by Syrian soldiery, and Judas was obliged to resort again to outlaw life. He succeeded, however, in winning two signal victories over Nicanor, the Syrian general. The one at Capharsalama was probably fought near the modern town of Kefr Silwan, across the Kidron Valley from the City of David on the southern slope of Jerusalem. In the latter victory Nicanor was slain, and Judas was left for the moment in control of Judea.

The Death of Judas Soon another Syrian army invaded the land. The advance was from the northwest up over the pass of Bethhoron. A little east of the road that ascends from Lower to Upper Bethhoron, near where he won his first great battle and in sight of his home at Modein, the intrepid Jewish champion fought his last battle. Terror at the approach of the enemy had thinned his ranks until he was obliged to meet them with only eight hundred men at his back. Even against these great odds he was on the eve of victory when he was slain. At the sight of their fallen leader his followers fled. This disastrous ending of his career as a warrior obscured to a great extent the character and quality of Judas's services for his people. In brief (1) he taught them to fight for their rights; (2) he helped them to save their law and traditions; (3) he secured for them religious freedom; (4) he restored many of the Jews of the dispersion and thus prepared the way for the consolidated kingdom that later rose with Jerusalem as the center; (5) he inspired his countrymen with ambitions for political independence; and (6) he set them a noble example of courage, patriotism, and practical piety. While measured by the higher standards of a later day Judas is not without his faults, he is unquestionably one of the great heroes of Israel's history and an example to all of unselfish and devoted patriotism.

The Dissensions in the Syrian Court The Jews ultimately attained political independence not primarily through their own efforts, but because the protracted contests between the rival claimants for the Syrian throne gave them opportunities that they quickly improved. In 152 B.C. a youth known as Alexander Balas, who claimed to be a son of Antiochus Epiphanes, raised the standard of revolt against the reigning Syrian king, Demetrius I. The kings of southwestern Asia and Egypt at first lent their support to this impostor. By 150 B.C. he had succeeded in defeating and putting to death Demetrius I. Two years later, however, Demetrius II, the son of the deposed king, appeared with a large body of Cretan mercenaries to contest the throne of his father. Many of the Syrian cities at once espoused his cause. Ptolemy Philometor, of Egypt, finally turned against Alexander Balas, and in 145 B.C. this strange adventurer was slain near Antioch by his own followers. Soon after his death, however, one of his generals, Tryphon, appeared with an infant son of Alexander whom he sought to place on the Syrian throne, thus perpetuating the feud that was constantly undermining the power of the Seleucid kingdom.

Concessions to Jonathan The Jews profited by each turn in these tortuous politics. In 158 B.C., after a period of outlawry in the wilderness east of Judea, Jonathan and his followers were allowed by Demetrius I to settle again within the bounds of Judea. Jonathan established his headquarters at Michmash, the fortress famous for the achievement of Saul's valiant son Jonathan. Here he ruled over the Jews as a vassal of Demetrius, who retained immediate control over the citadel at Jerusalem and the fortified cities that had been built along the borders of Judea. On the appearance of Alexander Balas in 152 B.C. Demetrius I, in order to retain the loyalty of the Jews, permitted Jonathan to maintain a small standing army and to rebuild the fortifications of Jerusalem. To outbid his rival the impostor Alexander Balas conferred upon Jonathan the coveted honor of the high priesthood, thus making him both the civil and religious head of the Jewish state. Disregarding his promises to Demetrius and the contemptible character of Alexander, Jonathan at once proceeded to establish his new authority. He was doubtless more acceptable to the majority of the Jews than the apostate high priests whom he succeeded, but the stricter Hasideans naturally regarded it as a sacrilege that a man whose hands were stained with war and bloodshed should perform the holiest duties in the temple service.

Under Alexander Balas Jonathan's power rapidly increased. He was made governor of Judea, and, under pretense of supporting the waning fortunes of Alexander, he captured in succession the Philistine cities of Joppa, Azotus (Ashdod), Ascalon, and Akron. When Demetrius II became master of Syria, Jonathan succeeded by rich gifts and diplomacy in so far gaining the support of the new king that part of the territory of Samaria was joined to Judea. In return for three hundred talents they were also promised exemption from taxation. Furthermore, membership in one of the royal orders was conferred upon the Maccabean leader. Thus by good fortune and by often questionable diplomacy the Jews finally secured in the days of Jonathan the freedom for which they had fought and that they had partially won under the valiant Judas.

CHAPTER 22

PEACE AND PROSPERITY UNDER SIMON

It was not strange in that corrupt age that Jonathan, who had risen to power largely by intrigue, should himself in the end fall prey to treachery. Tryphon, the general who secretly aspired to the Syrian throne, by lies succeeded in misleading even the wily Jewish leader. His object was to gain possession of southern Palestine, and he evidently believed that by capturing Jonathan he would easily realize his ambition. He overlooked the fact, however, that Simon, next to Judas the ablest of the sons of Mattathias, still remained to rally and lead the Jewish patriots. The natural barriers of Judea again proved insurmountable, for when Tryphon tried repeatedly on the west, south, and east to invade the central uplands, he found the passes guarded by Simon and his experienced warriors. Thus baffled, the treacherous Tryphon vented his disappointment upon Jonathan, whom he slew in Gilead. As the would-be usurper advanced northward, where he ultimately met the fate he richly deserved, Simon and his followers bore the body of Jonathan back to Modein, and there they raised over it the fourth of those tombs that testified to the warlike spirit and devotion of the sons of Mattathias.

Character and Policy of Simon Simon, who was at this crisis called to the leadership of the Jewish race, had been famed from the first for his moderation and wise counsel. In many campaigns he had also shown the military skill and courage that had characterized his younger brothers. In him the noble spirit of Judas lived again. He was devoted to the law, intent upon building up the state, and at the same time deeply and genuinely interested in all members of his race, whether in Judea or in distant nations. Like David and Josiah, he was a true father of his people and set an example that unfortunately his descendants failed to follow. He still recognized the authority of Demetrius II, but the Syrian kingdom was so weak that Simon succeeded in securing a definite promise of the remission of all taxes and ruled practically as an independent sovereign. To strengthen his position he sent an embassy laden with rich gifts to Rome. During a later crisis in his rule its prestige proved of great value, but Simon in following the example of his brothers gave to Rome that claim upon Judea that was destined within less than a century to put an end to Jewish independence. In still further consolidating and developing the resources of his people and in preparing for future expansion, Simon laid the foundations for the later Jewish kingdom. His policy also brought to Palestine that peace and prosperity which made his rule one of the few bright spots in Israel's troubled history.

His Conquests The chief conquest of Simon was the capture of Gazara, the ancient Gezer. This lay on the western side of the Plain of Ajalon. It guarded the approaches to Judea from the west, and above all the highway that ran from Joppa and along which passed the commerce of the Mediterranean. After a stubborn resistance he captured the town, deported part of its heathen population, and settled Jewish colonists in their place. Joppa also was under Simon's control. Thus he also prepared the way for the commercial expansion that was necessary if the Jewish state was to survive in the midst of its many powerful foes. Early in his reign Simon laid siege to the Syrian garrison in Jerusalem and finally, amidst the rejoicing of the people, captured this stronghold and delivered Judea from the presence of the hated foreigners. The temple area was also fortified. Simon's victories, and especially his conquest of the Greek cities on the plain, aroused the Syrian king, Antiochus Sidetes, the son of Demetrius I, to demand heavy indemnity. When Simon refused to pay the tribute a Syrian army was sent to enforce the claim, but they were defeated by a Jewish force under John Hyrcanus. This victory left Simon during the remainder of his reign practically independent of outside authority.

Simon's Authority Simon, with commendable moderation, refrained from attempting to secure for himself the title of king. He did, however, issue coins in his own name, although that right was ordinarily the prerogative only of kings. Upon him was conferred by the grateful people the authority that had first been given Jonathan by the shameless Alexander Balas. In return for Simon's many services and as a tribute to the achievements of his family he was proclaimed by the Jews not only civil governor and military leader, but also high priest. He thus became their rightful leader both in peace and war, and the representative of the nation in the sacred services of the temple. In all but name he was king, and Jewish history would have doubtless flowed in calmer channels had his descendants been contented with these substantial honors.

Completion of the Psalter The reign of Simon probably witnessed the completion of the Psalter. Many of the psalms, especially those in the latter half of the book, bear the unmistakable marks of the Maccabean struggle. In Psalms 74 and 89, for example, there are clear references to the desecration of the temple and the bitter persecutions of Antiochus. They voice the wails of despair that then rose from the lips of many Jews. Many other psalms, for example, Psalm 118, express that intense love and devotion to the law that was from this time on in many ways the most prominent characteristic of Judaism. The prevailingly prominent liturgical element that characterizes the concluding psalms of the Psalter suggest their original adaptation to the song services of the temple. Under the reign of Simon the temple choir was probably extended and greater prominence given to this form of the temple service. The peace and prosperity in the days of Simon gave the opportunity and the incentive to put in final form the earlier collections of psalms and probably to add the introduction found in Psalms 1–2 and the concluding doxology in Psalm 150. The Psalter appears to have been the last to be completed of all the Old Testament books, so that probably before the close of Simon's reign all of the present Old Testament books were written. Discussions regarding the value of such books as Ecclesiastes, Song of Solomon, and Esther continued until nearly the close of the first Christian century, when at last the canon of the Old Testament was completed.

The Religious Life Reflected in the Later Psalms The prevailing note in the psalms found in the latter part of the Psalter is joyous. A deep sense of gratitude to Jehovah for deliverance pervades them. The Jews felt that Jehovah had indeed delivered them "as a bird from the snare of the fowler" (Psalm 124). In the near background were the dark days of persecution. Hostile foes still encircled Israel, but trust in Jehovah's power and willingness to deliver triumphed over all fear.

> *Oh, give thanks to Jehovah for he is good,*
> *For his mercy endureth forever.*

He hath delivered us from our enemies;
Oh, give thanks to the God of heaven,
For his mercy endureth forever.

This was the oft-repeated refrain that was sung in the temple service by the warriors when they returned victorious from battle and by the people as they went about their tasks. The sense of constant danger and of great achievement bound together the Jews of this period as perhaps never before since the days of the exile. The same experiences developed a powerful religious consciousness. Jehovah had repeatedly and signally demonstrated that he was in their midst. Without his strong hand they were helpless against their foes. The apostates had been expelled, and the classes that remained were bound closely together by their desire to preserve their hard-won liberties, by their devotion to the temple and its services, and by a profound respect for the authority of their scriptures. The voice of the living prophet was silent. The priests had ceased to teach and were simply ministers at the altar, and in the turmoil of the Maccabean struggle the teaching of the wise had practically come to an end. Instead the Jews became in every sense the people of the book. It was at this time and as a result of the forces at work in this age that the scribes attained their place as the chief teachers of the people. It was natural that they who copied, edited, and above all interpreted the revered Law and the prophets should have the ear of the masses and should be regarded more and more as the authorized teachers of the Jewish race. Judaism had at last attained its maturity.

CHAPTER 23

THE RULE OF JOHN HYRCANUS AND ARISTOBULUS

E ven his moderation and kindly rule did not deliver Simon from the violent death that overtook all the sons of Mattathias. His murderer was his son-in-law, a certain Ptolemy, who was governor of the Jordan Valley, the resources of which had been developed under Simon. Ptolemy trusted to the support of the Syrian court, but he failed to reckon with two things: (1) the loyalty of the people to their Maccabean leaders, and (2) the ability of Simon's son, John Hyrcanus. Instead of falling a victim to Ptolemy's plot, John at once went to Jerusalem, where he was made the high priest and governor by the people. Ptolemy, who was besieged in the castle of Dok, saved his miserable life only by shameless perfidy.

The Syrian Invasion Antiochus Sidetes proved the ablest Syrian king of this period. Although his first attack had been repelled by Simon, he again attempted, on the accession of Hyrcanus, to reestablish his authority in Palestine. Josephus, in his account, obscures this humiliating chapter in Jewish history. The statement that Hyrcanus took from the tomb of David vast wealth and thus purchased immunity from Syrian attack has all the characteristics of an Oriental tale. Instead, Antiochus Sidetes not only besieged but captured Jerusalem, and doubtless compelled the Jews to pay heavy tribute. Preferring, however, to retain their loyalty rather than to crush them, he left John Hyrcanus in control of Judea, and Jerusalem escaped destruction. In the disastrous campaign against the Parthians in which Antiochus lost his life, John Hyrcanus accompanied him with a following of Jewish soldiers. The death of Antiochus Sidetes in 129 B.C. at last left the Jews free to develop their kingdom without further fear of Syrian interference. This event marks for the Jews the attainment of absolute political freedom—a privilege they continued to enjoy for a little over half a century.

John's Military Policy and Conquests John possessed the characteristic ambitions and energy of his family. In his policy he also seems to have been strongly influenced by the achievements of Israel's early conquering king, David. His aim was to build up a small empire, and by crushing the ancient foes of Israel to secure immunity from further attack. In employing foreign mercenaries he also followed the example of King David. Doubtless he was influenced in doing so by his experiences in the Parthian campaign.

This policy, however, was far removed from the spirit of the early Maccabean leaders who had unsheathed the sword on behalf of their principles. John's first campaign was against the cities to the east of the Jordan and resulted in the conquest of the towns of Medeba and Samaga and the territory subject to them. The conquest of Shechem and southern Samaria was undoubtedly prompted both by hereditary hatred toward the Samaritans and by the desire to provide an outlet for the growing Jewish population. After standing for two centuries, the Samaritan temple on Mount Gerizim was destroyed by the Jews. This sacrilegious act naturally intensified the hatred between Jew and Samaritan that burned so fiercely during the early part of the first Christian century. Marissa and Dora, the chief cities of the Idumeans, were next conquered. With strange inconsistency, John Hyrcanus, whose ancestors had first taken up the sword in defense of religious liberty, compelled the descendants of their old foes, the Edomites, to give up their national religion or else go into exile. This policy was fraught with far-reaching consequences, for among those appointed to rule over the conquered Edomites was Antipater, the ancestor of Herod, who was destined to rule the Jews and to initiate that long series of disasters that culminated in the destruction of the Jewish state. Last of all, John Hyrcanus advanced to the conquest of the Greek city of Samaria. Because of its natural strength and formidable defenses a year was required for the siege, and it was ultimately captured only through famine. The sons of John

Hyrcanus succeeded in holding at bay the Syrian armies that were sent to relieve the besieged. The conquered inhabitants were sold as slaves, and the city was left for a time in complete ruins. The conquest of Scythopolis, the ancient Bethshean, extended the bounds of John's kingdom to the southern hills of Galilee. Thus he became master of a small empire extending out toward the desert on the east, to the South Country on the south, touching the sea at Joppa, and including the entire territory of ancient Samaria on the north. While not as large as the kingdom of David, it was a more perfect political unit and offered superior opportunities for commerce and internal development.

The Break with the Pharisees The successes of John Hyrcanus blinded the majority of the nation to the real issues at stake. But a powerful group, which during the Maccabean period appeared for the first time under the name of Pharisees, began to withdraw their allegiance and silently, at least, to protest against a high priest whose chief ambition was conquest. The story Josephus tells to explain the defection of the Pharisees may be simply a popular tradition, but it is indicative of the division within Judaism that ultimately wrecked the Maccabean state. From the days of John Hyrcanus, the Maccabean rulers, with only one exception, were compelled to meet the silent but strong opposition of the Pharisees. As a result they turned to the rising party of the Sadducees, which henceforth identified itself with the interests of the reigning family. Thus in the year of its greatest triumph the Jewish state became a house divided against itself. Estranged from the better-minded religious leaders of the nation, John Hyrcanus and his successors followed an increasingly secular, selfish policy until they completely forgot the noble ideals for which their fathers had striven.

The Reign of Aristobulus The accession of Aristobulus marks a triumph of that Hellenism against which Judas and Simon had unsheathed the sword. Like many an Oriental monarch, he established his position on the throne by the murder of all members of his family who might contest his power. His inhuman cruelty to his mother and the suspicions that led him to murder his brother reveal a barbarous spirit that can only be explained as a result of the wrong ambitions that had already taken possession of Israel's rulers. Aristobulus's brief reign of one year is marked by two significant acts. The first is the assumption of the title of king. On his own initiative, and apparently without the consent of the people, he placed the diadem upon his head. The other important act was the conquest of part of the territory of Iturea, which was known in later times as Galilee. He found it occupied by a mixed Syrian and Greek population in which were probably a few descendants of the ancient Israelites. Following the policy of his family, he doubtless at once inaugurated a system of colonization that carried to Galilee a strong Jewish population. Henceforth, by virtue of race, language, and religion, Galilee was closely bound to Judea.

CHAPTER 24

THE PHARISEES, SADDUCEES, AND ESSENES

The Maccabean period witnessed the birth of the great parties that henceforth distinguished Judaism. They represented the crystallizing of the different currents of thought that were traceable in the Greek period and even earlier. These diverse points of view were in part the result of the democratic spirit that has always characterized Israel's life. In the striking antithesis between the idealists and the legalists and the practical men of affairs it is also possible to detect the potent influence the prophets had exerted upon the thought of their nation. In the Greek period the Chronicler and certain of the psalmists, with their intense devotion to the temple and its services to the practical exclusion of all other interests, were the forerunners of the later Pharisees. Ben Sira, with his hearty appreciation of the good things of life, with his devotion to the scriptures of his race, with his evident failure to accept the new doctrine of individual immortality, and with his great admiration for the high priests, was an earlier type of the better class of Sadducees. The persecutions of Antiochus Epiphanes developed these parties. As has already been noted, the Hasideans who followed Judas in the struggle to restore the law and the temple service were the immediate predecessors of the early Pharisees. The word "Pharisees" means separatists, and it was used first in the days of Jonathan (Josephus's Antiquities of the Jews III:5:9). In the same connection Josephus refers to the Sadducees. The name of this second party is probably derived not from the Hebrew word sadik, meaning righteous, but from Zadok (later written Sadok or Sadduk), who was placed by Solomon in charge of the Jerusalem temple. It was thus the designation of the aristocratic, high-priestly party. In the Persian and Greek periods the high priests had ruled the Judean state without opposition. It was the rise of the party of the Pharisees that apparently developed that of the Sadducees. This party included the hereditary nobles who supported and sympathized with the Maccabean leaders. The Essenes evidently represent a reaction against the prevailing moral corruption. In many respects they were simply extreme Pharisees. They were zealots in religion, just as the later party of the Zealots were extremists in their hatred of Rome and in the methods they were ready to use in order to attain their ends.

Character and Beliefs of the Pharisees Originally the Pharisees were not a political but a religious party. The opposition of the Sadducees in time led them to enter public life. In politics they were conservatives. They had little sympathy for the popular ambition for political independence and probably regarded with alarm the tendency toward national expansion. Alliances with the heathen nations seemed to them disloyalty to Jehovah. In belief they were progressives. While they stood squarely on the ancient law, they recognized the importance of interpreting it so as to meet the many questions that rose in public and private life. To this great and practically endless task much of their time was devoted. They thus recognized the fact that Israel's law was still in the process of development. To their later interpretations of the law they attributed great authority. One of their maxims was: "It is a worse offense to teach things contrary to the ordinances of the scribes than to teach things contrary to the written law." Naturally their attempt to anticipate by definite regulations each individual problem led them to absurd extremes and in time obscured the real intent of the older laws, but the spirit that actuated it was progressive. They also did not hesitate to accept the growing popular belief in angels and spirits. Like the earlier prophets, they recognized the presence of Jehovah directing the life of the nation and of the individual. They accepted the newborn belief in the immortality of the individual, clinging, however, to the hope of a bodily resurrection. They also held to the popular messianic hopes that became more and more prominent during the Maccabean and Roman periods.

The Pharisees were the most democratic party in Judaism. While for their own members they insisted upon a most rigorous ceremonial regime, they allowed the common people to ally themselves with them as associates. In their acceptance of the popular hopes and in their endeavor to adapt Israel's law to the life of the nation and thus establish a basis for the realization of Israel's hopes they appealed to the masses and exerted over them a powerful influence. Josephus asserts that so great was the influence of the Pharisees with the people that the Sadducees, in order to carry through their policies, were obliged, nominally, at least, to adopt the platform of their rivals. The Pharisees were also zealous in teaching the people and thus kept in close touch with the masses. They, therefore, stood as the true representatives of Judaism. Their principles have survived and are still the foundations of orthodox Judaism.

Character and Beliefs of the Sadducees The Sadducees were few in number compared with the Pharisees. They represented on one side the old priestly aristocracy, and on the other the new nobility that rallied about the Maccabean leaders. They depended for their authority upon their wealth, their inherited prestige, and the support of the throne. They were in reality a political rather than a religious party. In politics they were progressives and opportunists. Any policy that promised to further their individual or class interests was acceptable to them. As is usually the case with parties that represent wealth and hereditary power, they were conservatives in belief. They stood squarely on the earlier scriptures of their race and had no sympathy with the later Pharisaic interpretations and doctrines. Whether or not, as Josephus asserts, they entirely rejected fate—that is, the providential direction of human affairs—is not clear. Probably in this belief they did not depart from the earlier teachings of priests and prophets. Their selfish and often unscrupulous acts suggest a basis for Josephus's claim, even though allowance must be made for his hostile attitude toward them. While they were conservatives in theory, the Sadducees were of all classes in Judaism most open to Greek and heathen influence, for foreign alliances and Hellenic culture offered opportunities for advancement and power.

Character and Beliefs of the Essenes Less important but even more interesting are the Essenes. They were a sect, or monastic order, rather than a political or religious party. Josephus, who asserts that for a time he was associated with them, has given a full account of their peculiar customs. They evidently represented a strong reaction against the prevailing corruption and a return to the simple life. Their spirit of humility, fraternity, and practical charity are in marked contrast to the aims of the Sadducees and the later Maccabean rulers. In their beliefs they were idealists. Their invocation of the sun, their extreme emphasis on ceremonial cleanliness, their tendency toward celibacy, and their distinction between soul and body all suggest the indirect if not the direct influence of the Pythagorean type of philosophy. If the Essenes represented simply an extreme type of Pharisaism, the peculiar form of its development was undoubtedly due to the Greek atmosphere amidst which it flourished. The Essenes do not appear to have had any direct influence in the politics of their day. They were a current apart from the main stream of Judaism, and yet they could not fail to exert an indirect influence. Many of their ideals and doctrines were closely similar to the teachings of John the Baptist and Jesus. Yet there is a fundamental difference between Essenism and primitive Christianity, for one sought to attain perfection apart from life and the other in closest contact with the currents of human thought and activity. While according to Josephus the party of the Essenes at one time numbered four thousand, like all ascetic movements it soon disappeared or else was deflected into the greater stream of monasticism that rose in the early Christian centuries.

CHAPTER 25

THE LIFE AND FAITH OF THE JEWS OF THE DISPERSION

Seleucus Nicanor, who in 311 B.C. founded the city of Antioch, like Alexander granted many privileges to the Jewish colonies whom he thus sought to attract. They not only possessed the rights of citizenship but also lived in their separate quarter. Their synagogue was one of the architectural glories of the city. There they engaged in trade and undoubtedly grew rich, taking on largely the complexion of that opulent Hellenic city. Later the Jewish colony was enlarged by the apostates who fled from Judea when the Maccabean rulers gained the ascendancy. The corrupt and materialistic atmosphere of Antioch doubtless explains why its Jewish citizens apparently contributed little to the development of the thought and faith of later Judaism. Similar colonies were found throughout the great commercial cities of Asia Minor. In many of these cities—for example, Tarsus—they seem to have enjoyed the same privileges as those at Antioch.

The Jews in Egypt The chief intellectual and religious center of the Jews of the dispersion, however, was in Alexandria. It is probable that fully a million Jews were to be found in Egypt during the latter part of the Maccabean period. Industry and commerce had made many of them extremely wealthy and had given them the leisure to study not only their own scriptures but also the literature of the Greeks. The prevailingly friendly way in which the Ptolemaic rulers treated the Jews naturally led them to take a more favorable attitude toward Greek culture. Alexandria itself was the scene of intense intellectual activity. Attracted by the munificence of the Ptolemies and by the opportunities offered by its great library, many of the most famous Greek philosophers and rhetoricians of the age found their home in the Egyptian capital. Public lectures, open discussions, and voluminous literature were only a few of the many forms in which this intellectual life was expressed. Hence it was at Alexandria that Hebrew and Greek thought met on the highest plane and mingled most closely.

The Jewish Temple at Leontopolis After the murder of his father, Onias III, near Antioch, whither he had fled from the persecutions of Antiochus Epiphanes, Onias IV sought refuge in Egypt. Here, as the legitimate head of the Jewish high-priesthood, he was favorably received by Ptolemy and granted territory in the Nile delta to the north of Memphis in which to rear a temple to Jehovah. In the light of discoveries at Elephantine it is evident that this step was not without precedent. Ptolemy's object was to please his Jewish subjects and to attract others to the land of the Nile. Josephus's statement in The Jewish War (VII:10:4) favors the conclusion that the temple was built 243 years (not 343) before its final destruction in A.D. 73, that is, in 170 B.C. In any case it was probably built between 170 and 160 B.C., at the time when the persecutions of Antiochus Epiphanes made pilgrimages to the Jerusalem temple impossible and threatened its continued existence. The plan of the Leontopolis temple indicates that it was not intended to be a rival to the Jerusalem sanctuary, but rather a common place of meeting for the Egyptian Jews and of defense in case of attack. It never seriously rivaled the Jerusalem sanctuary, although in later days it was viewed with jealousy by the Jews of Palestine.

Translation of the Hebrew Scriptures into Greek Far more significant than the building of the Leontopolis temple was the translation of the Hebrew scriptures into Greek. The tradition preserved by Josephus that the translation was made in seventy-two days by seventy-two scholars, sent from Jerusalem by Eleazar the high priest at the request of Ptolemy, is clearly unhistorical. The impossibility of completing so vast a task in this limited time is obvious.

Moreover, the character of the translation indicates that it was the work not of Palestinian but of Alexandrian Jews familiar with the peculiar Greek of Egypt and the lands of the dispersion. It was also the work not of one but of many different groups of translators, as is shown by the variant synonyms employed in different books to translate the same Hebrew words and idioms. In the case of several books the work of two or more distinct translators is readily recognized. The quality of the translation also varies greatly in different books. It is probable that the one historical fact underlying the tradition is that the work of translation was begun in the days of Ptolemy Philadelphus, who may have encouraged his Jewish subjects in their undertaking. From the character of the translations and the nature of the situation it is probable that the first books to be translated were certain historical writings, such as Samuel–Kings and the books of the Law. The remaining books were probably translated by the end of the succeeding century (between 250 and 150 B.C.), for the grandson of Ben Sira implies in his prologue that he was acquainted with the Law, the prophets, and the other writings in their Greek version.

The primary aim of this Greek translation was to put the Hebrew scriptures themselves into the hands of their Greek persecutors as the best possible answer to their false and malicious charges. Evidence of this apologetic purpose is found in the fact that glaring inconsistencies and expressions, where Jehovah is described in the likeness of a human being, were usually left out. Where the Hebrew text was corrupt the translators restored or else freely paraphrased what they thought was the original meaning. In time, however, the translation gained a new importance, for the Jews of Egypt soon began to forget the language of their fathers and so became increasingly dependent for a knowledge of their scriptures upon the Greek translation. In the end it almost completely superseded the original Hebrew version not only in the lands of the dispersion, but even in Palestine itself. A large proportion of the quotations from the Old Testament in the New Testament are from the Greek rather than the Hebrew text. Although it is only a translation, the Greek version, or Septuagint (the Version of the Seventy), as it is popularly known, still possesses a great value for the modern translator, inasmuch as it is based upon Hebrew texts centuries older than any that now exist. At many points, especially in the historical prophetic books, it makes possible the restoration of the original reading where the Hebrew has become corrupt in the long process of transmission.

Apologetic Jewish Writings During the centuries immediately preceding the Christian era the Jews of the dispersion, and especially of Egypt, were the object of constant attack. Manetho, an Egyptian priest, wrote a history purporting to give the origin and the early experiences of the Jews. Portions of this have been preserved and reveal the bitter and unjust spirit with which this race was regarded by the Greek and Egyptian scholars of the day. To defend themselves from these attacks the Jews not only translated their scriptures but employed many different types of writing. A certain Jew by the name of Demetrius about 215 B.C. wrote a commendatory history of the Jewish kings. Aristobulus, the teacher of Ptolemy Philometor, wrote "Explanation of the Mosaic Laws," in which he anticipated, in many ways, the modern interpretation of the early traditions found in the opening books of the Old Testament. Like all Alexandrian scholars, however, he overshot the mark under the influence of the allegorical or symbolic type of interpretation. Other Jewish writers appealed to the older Greek historians and poets. Adopting the unprincipled methods of their persecutors, they expanded the original writings of such historians as Hecataeus, who had spoken in a commendatory way of the Jews. They even went so far as to insert long passages into the writings of the famous Greek poets, such as Orpheus, Hesiod, Aeschylus, Sophocles, and Menander, so as to transform them into ardent champions of the persecuted race. The culmination of this illegitimate form of defense was to insert in the famous Sibylline Books a long passage describing the glories of the Jewish race and voicing the hopes with which they regarded the future. It was in this atmosphere and under the influence of these methods that the anti-Semitic spirit was born in ancient Alexandria. Thence it was transmitted, as a malign heritage, to the Christian church.

The Wisdom of Solomon The noblest literary product of the Jews of the dispersion was the apocryphal book known as the Wisdom of Solomon. It was so called because the author assumed the point of view of Solomon. In so doing he did not intend to deceive his contemporaries, but rather followed the common tendency of his day. Although the book has many characteristic Hebrew idioms, which are due to its Jewish authorship, it was without doubt originally written in Greek. Its author was evidently acquainted with the writings of many of the Greek poets and philosophers. He accepted Plato's doctrine of the preexistence of the soul (8:19–20), of the limitations of the body (9:15), and of the creation of the world out of formless matter (11:17). He was especially influenced by the beliefs of the Epicureans and Stoics. He was acquainted with Hellenic art, astronomy, and science (7:17–29) and throughout shows the influence of Greek methods of thinking. His rejection of the teachings of the book of Ecclesiastes, his wide learning and his conception of immortality indicate that he lived some time after the beginning of the Maccabean struggle. His reference in 3:1–4 is probably to the persecutions through which the Jews of Egypt passed during the reign of Ptolemy Psycon (140–117 B.C.). On the other hand the book clearly antedates the writings of the Jewish philosopher Philo, who lived during the latter part of the first century B.C. The Wisdom of Solomon, therefore, may be dated somewhere between 100 and 50 B.C.

Its Important Teachings The author of the Wisdom of Solomon aimed, first, to commend Israel's faith to the heathen by showing that it was in substantial accord with the noblest doctrines of the Greek philosophers, and, second, to furnish the Jews of the dispersion, who were conversant with Hellenic thought and yet trained in the religion of their race, a working basis for their thought and practice. From the first it appears to have been highly esteemed by the Jews outside Palestine, although it never found a place in the Palestinian canon. Like most wisdom books, it describes at length the beauty and value of wisdom. The figure of Proverbs 8 and 9 is still further developed under the influence of the Greek tendency to personify abstract qualities. In the mind of the author, however, wisdom is simply an attribute of the Deity that he shares in common with men. The book is unique in two respects. First, it contains the earliest references in Jewish literature to a personal devil and identifies him with the serpent that tempted the woman in the garden (2:24, cf. Gen. 3) Elsewhere, however, the author traces sin and evil to men's voluntary acts (e.g., 1:16). Second, it teaches the immortality of righteousness and hence, by implication, the immortality of the individual. "God created man for incorruption," and "the souls of the righteous are in his hand." The doctrine here presented is ethical and spiritual rather than the belief in a bodily resurrection already formulated in the twelfth chapter of Daniel. It also teaches that both the good and bad will be rewarded according to their deeds. Its conceptions of God are exalted. He is the incorruptible spirit in all things, just and yet merciful, the lover of men. The book also places side by side with the Jewish teachings regarding men's duties to God and their fellow men the Greek virtues of moderation, good sense, justice, and courage or fortitude. It also teaches that, like God, each of his children should be a lover of men. Thus the book unites most effectively that which is best in the thought of Judaism and Hellenism and is an earnest of that still nobler union that was later realized in the thought and teachings of Christianity.

CHAPTER 26

THE DECLINE OF THE MACCABEAN KINGDOM

For a picture of the character of Alexander Janneus we are chiefly dependent upon Josephus, and it is not clear how far this late Jewish historian was influenced by the prevailing prejudices against that ruler, who figured as the arch enemy of the Pharisees. The incidents recorded reveal, however, a most sinister character. He was ambitious, but his ambitions were selfish and low. He was energetic and tireless, but his energy was wasted in futile undertakings. Furthermore, he was unscrupulous, vindictive, and merciless. There is not the slightest indication that he was actuated by any worthy ideal of service. To the Jewish state and race it was a great calamity that a man of this type should gain control of the nation at the moment when it had attained its greatest material strength. Under the kindly and wise guidance of Simon the subsequent history of the Jewish state would doubtless have been far different.

Janneus's first aim was to establish his power as an absolute despot. He ardently accepted the ideal of an Oriental ruler that had been imposed upon the Jews during the short reign of his brother Aristobulus. In realizing this ambition he met, as did every other king in Israel's history, the strong opposition of the people and a bold assertion of their inherited liberties. His second aim was to break completely the power of the Pharisees. They were the party of the people and had no sympathy with his policies. In them, therefore, he recognized his chief opponents. His third ambition was to extend the territory of the Jewish state to its farthest natural bounds. Soon after the beginning of his reign he succeeded in arousing the bitter hostility of the Greek cities on his eastern and western borders, of the reigning kings of Egypt, and of the rising Arabian power to the south of the Dead Sea. The objects for which he strove were comparatively petty: possession of the cities of Ptolemais and Gaza and of certain eastern Jordan cities, such as Gadara and Amathus. He was more often defeated than victorious, but his love of struggle and adventure and lust for conquest ever goaded him on. In desperation his subjects even ventured to call in Demetrius, the governor of Damascus, but when Alexander was driven away in defeat the nation's gratitude and loyalty to the Maccabean house reasserted itself and he was recalled. Instead of granting a general armistice and thus conciliating his distracted people, he treacherously used his newly won power to crucify publicly eight hundred of the Pharisees. Horror and fear seized the survivors, so that, according to Josephus, eight thousand of them fled into exile. After six years of civil war and the loss of fifty thousand lives, Alexander Janneus finally realized his first ambition and became absolute master of his kingdom. In achieving his ambitions, however, he well earned the title by which his contemporaries described him, "the Son of a Thracian," that is, Barbarian.

The Effects of His Rule The disastrous effects of the reign of Alexander Janneus may be briefly recapitulated. They were: (1) the destruction of the loyalty of the majority of the Jews to the Maccabean house; (2) the intensifying of the opposition between Pharisees and Sadducees to the point of murderous hate; (3) the extension of the sphere of Jewish influence from the Mediterranean on the west to the desert on the east, and from the Lebanons to the southern desert; and (4) the draining of the lifeblood and energies of the Jewish kingdom, so that it was far weaker and more disorganized than when Janneus came to the throne.

Alexandra's Reign (78–69 B.C.) Alexandra was the second queen who reigned in Israel's history. Her policy, unlike that of Athaliah of old, was on the whole constructive. Although she was the wife of Janneus, she reversed his policy and placed the Pharisees in control. The return of the exiles and the restoration of the prophetic party promised peace and prosperity. The ancient law was expanded and rigorously enforced. According to the Talmud it was during this period that elementary schools were introduced in connection with each synagogue. Their exact nature is not known, but it is probable that law was the subject studied and that the scribes were the teachers. This change of policy was undoubtedly very acceptable to the people, but the Pharisees made the grave mistake of using their new power to take revenge upon the Sadducean nobles who had supported the bloody policy of Alexander Janneus. They soon suffered the evil consequences of attempting to right wrong by wrong. The Sadducees found in Aristobulus, the ambitious and energetic younger son of Janneus, an effective champion. Alexandra, in permitting them to take possession of the many strongholds throughout the land, also committed a fatal error, for it gave them control of the military resources of the kingdom. Aristobulus was not slow in asserting his power, with the result that even before Alexandra died he had seized seventy-two of the fortresses and had aroused a large part of the people to revolt. While her reign was on the whole peaceful, it was but the lull before the great storm that swept over the nation.

Quarrels between Hyrcanus and Aristobulus Unfortunately, Alexandra's older son, Hyrcanus, was indolent and inefficient. He had been appointed high priest and, when Aristobulus assumed the title of king, he compelled Hyrcanus II to be content with this humbler title. Aristobulus's reign might have been comparatively peaceful had not at this time a new and sinister influence appeared in the troubled politics of Palestine. It was one of the results of John Hyrcanus's forcible judaizing of the Idumeans. Antipater, the son of the Idumean whom Alexander Janneus had made governor of Idumea, recognized in the rivalry between Hyrcanus and Aristobulus an opportunity to gain power. He first persuaded Hyrcanus to flee to Petra. Then, with the aid of the Arabian king, Aretas, he finally compelled Aristobulus and his followers to seek refuge on the temple hill in Jerusalem. The picture of the Jews divided into two hostile camps and engaged in bitter civil war in the very precincts of the temple under the leadership of the great-grandsons of the patriotic Simon presents a sad contrast to the noble spirit and valiant achievements of the founders of the Maccabean kingdom who had first taken up the sword in defense of the temple and its service.

Rome's Intervention This situation gave Rome its desired opportunity for intervention. Pompey in 70 B.C. made a successful campaign against Mithridates, king of Pontus, and against Tigranes, king of Armenia. Rome's policy was to conquer all of southwestern Asia as far as the Euphrates. Ignoring the peril of the situation, both Aristobulus and Hyrcanus appealed to Pompey's lieutenant, Scaurus. As a result the Arabians were ordered to withdraw, and Aristobulus for a brief time was left master of the situation. In the spring of 63 B.C., however, when Pompey came to Damascus, there appeared before him three embassies, one representing the cause of Aristobulus, another that of Hyrcanus, and still a third presented the request of the Pharisees that Rome assume political control of Palestine and leave them free to devote themselves to the study and application of the their law. The fall of Aristobulus hastened what was now inevitable. Although he was held a prisoner by Pompey, his followers remained entrenched on the temple hill and were conquered only after a protracted siege and the loss of many lives. Aristobulus and his family were carried off as captives to Rome to grace Pompey's triumph, and the request of the Pharisees was granted: Rome henceforth held Palestine under its direct control. Thus after a little more than a century (165–63 B.C.) the Jews again lost their independence, and the Maccabean kingdom became only a memory, never to be revived save for a brief moment.

Causes of the Fall of the Jewish Kingdom The Jewish kingdom fell as the result of causes that can be clearly recognized. It was primarily because the ideals and ambitions of the Maccabean leaders themselves became material and selfish. They proved unable to resist the temptations of success. Greed for power quenched their early patriotism. The material spirit of their age obscured the nobler ideals of their spiritual teachers. The result was a tyranny and corruption that made the later kings misleaders rather than true leaders of their nation. Parallel to the bitter struggle between the kings and their subjects was the bitter feud between the Sadducees and the Pharisees. Normal party rivalry grew into murderous hatred, and in taking revenge upon each other they brought ruin upon the commonwealth. The final end was hastened by the suicidal feud between the brothers Hyrcanus and

Aristobulus, fomented by the unprincipled machinations of the Idumean Antipater. In the final crisis the Pharisaic policy of submission and of peace at any cost paved the way for the realization of Rome's ambition and made the ultimate conquest of Palestine practically inevitable. Thus the kingdom, founded in the face of almost insuperable obstacles and consecrated with the lifeblood of many heroes, fell ignominiously as the result of the same causes that throughout the ages have proved the ruin of even stronger empires.

Political, Intellectual, and Religious Effects of the Maccabean Struggle This century of valiant achievement, colossal errors, and overwhelming failure left its deep impression upon the Jewish race. It witnessed the return of many Jews of the dispersion to Jerusalem and Judea and the development of a strong sense of racial unity. Henceforth the Jews throughout the world looked to Jerusalem as their true political and religious capital. The events of this period intensified the ancient feud between Jew and Samaritan and gave the latter ample reason for the hostility toward their southern kinsmen that appears in the Gospel narratives. It was during this age that the parties of the Pharisees and Sadducees finally crystallized and formulated the tenets and policies that guided them during the next century. At this time the foundations were laid for the rule of the house of Herod, which exerted such a baleful influence upon the fortunes and destinies of the Jews. It likewise marked the beginning and culmination of Rome's influence over the lands of the eastern Mediterranean and the subjection of the Jews to Gentile rulers that has continued.

The Maccabean period gave to the Jews a greatly enlarged intellectual vision and led them to adopt many of the ideas of their Greek conquerors. In their literature it is easy to recognize the influence of the more logical Greek methods of reasoning and of the scientific attitude toward the universe. It was during this period that the wise were transformed into scribes, and the rule of the scribal method of thinking and interpretation began. The struggles through which the Jews passed intensified their love for the law and the temple services. Duty was more and more defined in the terms of ceremony, and the Pharisees entered upon that vast and impossible task of providing rules for man's every act. Out of the struggles of the Maccabean period came the fusion of Hellenic and Jewish ideas that has become an important factor in all human thought. At last under the influence of the great crises through which they had passed, the belief in individual immortality gained wide acceptance among the Jews. Side by side with this came the belief in a personal devil and a hierarchy of demons opposed to the divine hierarchy at whose head was Jehovah. Last of all the taste of freedom under a Jewish ruler brought again to the front the kingly messianic hopes of the race, and led them to long and struggle for their realization. Thus in this brief century Judaism attained in many ways its final form, and only in the light of this process is it possible fully to understand and appreciate the background of the New Testament history.

THE RULE OF ROME

CHAPTER 27

THE RISE OF THE HERODIAN HOUSE

The first quarter century of Roman rule was in many ways the most complex in Israel's intricate history. There were three chief actors in the drama: (1) Rome, represented first by the leaders of the Republic and later by Pompey, Caesar, and their successors; (2) the popular Jewish party led by Aristobulus and his son Alexander, and Antigonus; and (3) Antipater, supported by his able sons Phasaelus and Herod. Rome's general policy was to allow the Jews as much freedom as possible, but above all to hold Palestine under firm control, for it lay on the eastern border and faced Parthia, the one foe that had successfully defied the powerful mistress of the Mediterranean. The popular Jewish party bitterly resented Rome's interference. True, the Pharisees welcomed the relief from civil war, but they could not hold the majority of the people in leash. The inoffensive

Hyrcanus was left in possession of the high priesthood and from time to time was elevated to positions of nominal civil authority, but he was little more than the plaything of circumstance and party intrigue. The ambitions of Aristobulus and his sons kept Palestine in a state of constant political ferment. Three times in five years they stirred the Jews to rebellion against Rome. The first rebellion was in 57 B.C. and was led by Alexander. He was ultimately driven by the Roman general to Alexandria, the fortress that overlooks the middle Jordan Valley, and was finally forced to surrender. The three great fortresses, Alexandria, Machaerus, and Hyrcanium, were thrown down, and the Jewish state was divided into five districts. Each of these was under a local council consisting of the leading citizens. These reported directly to the Roman proconsul. To neutralize still further the Jewish national spirit, the Hellenic cities in and about Palestine were restored, given a large measure of independence, and placed directly under the control of Rome's representative in the East.

The second rebellion followed quickly and was led by Aristobulus. He was soon obliged, however, to take refuge in the fortress of Machaerus, east of the Dead Sea, where he was captured and sent back again as a captive to Rome. The third rebellion was led by Alexander. It was more formidable, and in the end more disastrous, for the Jews were signally defeated in a battle near Mount Tabor. The only permanent results of these uprisings were the intensifying of Jewish hatred of Roman rule and the increasing of Rome's suspicion of this rebellious people. It was this suspicion that made it possible for the high-priestly party at a later time to force the Roman governor Pilate to put to death one whom he recognized to be an inoffensive Galilean peasant simply because he was accused of having assumed the historic title king of the Jews.

Antipater's Policy Through the troublesome first quarter century of Roman rule Antipater and his family prospered because they were able at every turn in the political fortunes of Syria to make themselves increasingly useful to Rome. At many critical periods he was able to save the Jews from calamity and to secure for them valuable privileges. There is a certain basis for Josephus's overenthusiastic assertion that he was "a man distinguished for his piety, justice, and love of his country" (Josephus's Antiquites of the Jews XIV:11:4c).

Although Hyrcanus was but a tool in Antipater's hands, he never attempted to depose him, and apparently always treated him with respect. To steer successfully through the stormy period during which Rome made the transition from the republican to the monarchical form of government was a difficult task. When Crassus came as the representative of the First Triumvirate, Antipater's gifts and tact were not sufficient to prevent the Roman from plundering the treasures of the temple. Fortunately for the peace of Judea, during the civil war that followed between Pompey and Caesar, the deposed Jewish king Aristobulus and his son Alexander were both put to death. After the decisive battle of Pharsalia in 48 B.C. Antipater quickly espoused the cause of Caesar and performed valuable services for him at a time when the great Roman was threatened by overwhelming forces. By his influence with the people of Syria and Egypt and by his personal acts of bravery he won the favors that Caesar heaped upon him and upon the Jewish people. The old territorial division instituted by Gabinius was abolished, Hyrcanus was confirmed in the high priesthood, and Antipater was made procurator of Judea. Joppa was restored to the Jewish state; the gerusia, the chief assembly of the Jews, was given certain of its old judicial rights; and permission was granted to rebuild the wall of Jerusalem. The Jews were also freed from the duty of supporting Roman soldiers and of serving the Roman legions. The tribute was also in part remitted on the sabbatical year, and the Jews of Palestine and throughout the Roman Empire were confirmed in their religious privileges. Thus Caesar proved himself a friend of the Jews and established precedents to which they frequently appealed in later crises.

Herod's Early Record Among the many rewards conferred upon Antipater was the appointment of his son Phasaelus as governor of Jerusalem and his younger son Herod as governor of Galilee. Thus while still a young man Herod was given an opportunity to demonstrate his ability and energy. He at once took measures to put down the robber bands that infested Galilee and executed their leader, Hezekias. He won thereby the gratitude of the Galileans and the approval of

Rome. Hyrcanus and the Sanhedrin at Jerusalem, however, viewed this assumption of authority with suspicion and alarm. When Herod was summoned before them, he appeared in full military armor and was accompanied by a military following. Provoked by his boldness, the Sanhedrin would have sentenced him to death had not the local Roman governor interfered. The action of the Sanhedrin aroused Herod's spirit of revenge, and before long, gathering his forces, he marched against Jerusalem and would have put to death the Jewish leaders had not his father dissuaded him.

The assassination of Caesar in 44 B.C., followed by the battle of Philippi in 42, changed the political horizon of Palestine. Antipater and his sons, however, following their usual policy, pledged in succession their loyalty to Cassius and Antony, with the result that greater honors were conferred upon them. It was at this crisis that Malichus, a certain Jewish noble, inspired by jealousy and suspicion, treacherously murdered his rival, Antipater. Herod retaliated by instigating the assassination of the murderer, but soon a series of calamities swept over Judea that threatened to obliterate completely the house of Antipater.

The Parthian Conquest During the struggle between Antony and the assassins of Julius Caesar Rome's eastern outposts were left exposed. Their old foes, the Parthians, used this opportunity to seize northern Syria. Encouraged by the presence of the Parthians, Antigonus, the younger son of Aristobulus, in 41 B.C. entered Palestine. With the aid of the Parthians and of the Jews who were opposed to Herod he ultimately succeeded in establishing himself as king. Antipater and Herod's brother Phasaelus became the victims of the Parthian treachery, and Herod after many adventures succeeded in escaping with his family to the strong fortress of Masada at the southwestern end of the Dead Sea. Leaving them under the care of his brother Joseph, Herod after many discouragements and vicissitudes finally found his way to Rome. Unfortunately for the cause of Jewish independence, Antigonus lacked the essential qualities of leadership. Instead of arousing the loyalty of his subjects his chief concern was to take vengeance upon Herod's followers and upon all who had supported the house of Antipater.

Herod Made King of the Jews Herod went to Rome to urge the appointment of Aristobulus III, the grandson of Hyrcanus and the brother of Herod's betrothed wife Mariamne, as king of Judea. Antony and Octavian, to whom he appealed, were rightly suspicious of the survivors of the Maccabean house and appreciative of the services of Herod and his father, Antipater. Therefore, to his complete surprise, they offered him the kingship, and their nomination was speedily confirmed by the senate. History presents no stranger nor more dramatic sight than Herod, the Idumean, accompanied by Antony and Octavian, going to the temple of Jupiter on the Capitoline Hill to offer sacrifices in connection with his assumption of the historic title king of the Jews. At first it was an empty title, but the energy of Herod and the resources of Rome sufficed in time to make it real. In the spring of 39 B.C. Herod landed at Ptolemais and with the apathetic aid of the Roman generals in Palestine began to organize the Jews who rallied about him. Marching down the Mediterranean coast, he succeeded at last in relieving his family, who were besieged at Masada. Idumea and Galilee were then brought into subjection, and after two years of fighting he won an important battle at Isana, a little north of Bethel, which gave him possession of all of Judea except Jerusalem. The final contest for the capital city continued through several months, for Antigonus and his followers realized that they could expect little mercy from Herod and the Romans. Thousands of Jews were slaughtered, but at last the temple itself was captured, and Herod was in fact as well as in name king of the Jews. Antigonus pled in vain for mercy. Departing from their usual policy of clemency toward native rulers, the Romans caused him to be first scourged as a common criminal and then ignominiously beheaded. Thus the Maccabean dynasty, which had risen in glory, went down in shame, a signal illustration of the eternal principle that selfish ambitions and unrestrained passions in an individual or family sooner or later bring disgrace and destruction. While the siege of Jerusalem was still in progress, Herod went north to Samaria and there consummated his long-delayed marriage with Mariamne, the daughter of Hyrcanus, thus in part attracting to himself the loyalty the Jews had bestowed so lavishly and disastrously upon the unworthy sons of Alexander Janneus.

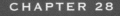
HEROD'S POLICY AND REIGN

The character of Herod is comparatively easy to understand, for it is elemental and one that constantly recurs in history. We in America are familiar with this type, which is represented by our unscrupulous captains of industry or political bosses: energetic, physically strong, shrewd, relentless toward all who threaten to thwart their plans, skillful in organization, not troubled about the rightness of their methods provided they escape the toils of the law, able to command men and successfully to carry through large policies. They are not without their personal attractions, for it is instinctive to admire that which is big and able to achieve. Many of them also make permanent contributions to the upbuilding of the nation. Oriental history is also full of analogies: Nebuchadrezzar, Cyrus, Alexander, and in more recent times Mohammed Ali of Egypt. Herod was largely the product of his inheritance and training. His father, Antipater, had taught him to regard the Jews with secret but well-concealed contempt, and to hate Aristobulus and his ambitious sons. His religion was loyalty to Rome, for this meant wealth and success. He delighted in public approval, and his ambition was to be known as a great builder. As is true with this type of man, he was a natural tyrant. Power was his ruling passion, and he regarded with extreme suspicion any who might take it from him. In this respect the contemporary rulers of the Roman Empire set an example that he was not slow to follow. His Idumean and Arabian blood coursed hot and fierce through his veins. It was an age when moral standards were exceedingly low, and Herod never learned to rule his passions. The Oriental institution of the harem gave him full license, and he lived and loved as he fought and reigned: vehemently. Such a man is especially susceptible to the weaknesses and crimes that come from jealousy, and the influences of his family and court intensified these fatal faults.

Herod is not without his attractive qualities. A man who is able to execute on a large scale and win the title "Great" is never commonplace. In giving Palestine the benefits of a strong and stable government he performed a real service. In his love for Mariamne and for the sons she bore him he was mastered by a passion that for a time ennobled him. Like every man, moreover, who fails to taste the joys of disinterested service for his fellow men, Herod paid the bitter penalty for his own unrestrained selfishness. He awakens pity rather than denunciation. He never found life, because he never learned to lose his life in the service of his people.

His Attitude toward Rome Herod's policy was loyalty at any cost to the man who at the moment ruled Rome. During the first part of his reign Antony's power on the eastern Mediterranean was still in the ascendancy. Notwithstanding the powerful intrigues of Cleopatra, Herod succeeded in retaining the favor of his patron. When the battle of Actium in 32 B.C. revealed Antony's weakness, Herod forthwith cast off his allegiance, and his treachery was one of the chief forces that drove Antony to suicide. Octavian, who henceforth under the title of Augustus attained to the complete control of Rome, recognized in Herod a valuable servant. Herod's title as king of the Jews was confirmed, and Augustus gradually increased his territory until it included practically all of Palestine with the exception of certain Greek cities along the coast and east of the Jordan. Herod's task was to preserve peace in the land thus entrusted to him and to guard the eastern border of the empire against its Parthian foes. This task he faithfully performed.

His Building Activity The spirit and policy of Augustus were clearly reflected in Herod's court and kingdom. When his position was firmly established, Herod devoted himself to magnificent building enterprises. In Antioch, Athens, and Rhodes, he reared great public buildings. Jerusalem, his capital, was provided with a theater, amphitheater, and other buildings that characterize the Greco-Roman cities of the period. The two crowning achievements of Herod's reign were the rebuilding of Samaria and Caesarea as its port on the Mediterranean coast. Both of these cities were renamed in honor of his patron Augustus. On the acropolis of Samaria he built a huge Roman temple, the foundations of which have been uncovered by American excavators. The city itself was encircled by a colonnade, more than a mile long, consisting of pillars sixteen feet in height. Caesarea, like Samaria, was adorned with magnificent public buildings, including a temple, a theater, a palace, and an amphitheater. The great breakwater two hundred feet wide that ran out into the open sea was one of the greatest achievements of that building age. By these acts Herod won still further the favor of Augustus and the admiration of the Eastern world.

His Attitude toward His Subjects The peace Herod brought to Palestine was won at the point of the sword. The fear he felt for his subjects was surpassed only by the fear he inspired in them. He was unscrupulous and merciless in cutting down all possible rivals. The treacherous murder of Aristobulus III, the grandson of Hyrcanus, and the murder of the inoffensive and maimed Hyrcanus are among the darkest deeds in Herod's bloody reign. The power of the Sandhedrin, the Jewish national representative body, was almost completely crushed. Following the policy of Augustus, Herod developed a complex system of spies, or espionage, so that, like an Oriental tyrant, he ruled his subjects by means of two armies: the spies who watched in secret and the soldiers who guarded them openly. His lavish building enterprises led him to load his people with an almost intolerable burden of taxation, and yet for the common people Herod's reign was one of comparative peace and prosperity. At last they were delivered from destructive wars and free to develop the great agricultural and commercial resources of the land. While outside of Judea Herod built heathen temples, he faithfully guarded the temple of Jerusalem and was careful not to override the religious prejudices of his subjects. His measures to relieve their suffering in time of famine reveal a generosity that in a better environment and with better training might have made him a benign ruler.

The Tragedy of His Domestic Life The weakness of Herod's character is most glaringly revealed in his domestic life. Undoubtedly he loved the beautiful Maccabean princess Mariamne, with all the passion of his violent nature. It was a type of love, however, that passes over easily into insensate jealousy. Accordingly, when he left Judea just before the battle of Actium, and later when he went to meet Octavian, he had Mariamne shut up in a strong fortress. Unfortunately Herod, like most despots, was unable to command the services of loyal followers. The discovery of Herod's suspicions toward her aroused the imperious spirit of Mariamne. She was also the victim of the plots of his jealous family. Human history presents no greater tragedy than that of Herod putting to death the one woman whom he truly loved, and later, a victim of his own suspicions and of the intrigues of his son Antipater, finally obtaining royal permission to put to death the two noble sons whom Mariamne had borne to him. It is difficult to find in all history a more pitiable sight than Herod in his old age, hated by most of his subjects, misled by the members of his own family, the murderer of those whom he loved best, finding his sole satisfaction in putting to death his son Antipater, who had betrayed him, and in planning in his last hours how he might by the murder of hundreds of his subjects arouse widespread lamentation.

Effects of Herod's Reign One of the chief results of Herod's policy and reign was the complete extinction of the Maccabean house. Herod's motive and method were thoroughly base, but for the Jewish people the result was beneficial, for it removed one of the most active causes of the suicidal rebellions that had ended disastrously for the Jews and brought them under the suspicion and iron rule of Rome. With his heavy hand Herod also put a stop to the party strife that had undermined the native Jewish kingdom and brought loss and suffering to thousands of Jews. The Pharisees and Sadducees at last were taught the lesson of not resorting to arms, however widely they might differ. By removing the Pharisees from public life Herod directed their energies to developing their ceremonial regulations and to instructing the people. Thus the influence of the Pharisees became paramount with the great majority of the Jews. As Herod extended his rule over all Palestine, he brought into close relations the Jews scattered throughout its territory and so strengthened the bonds of race and religion. In building the temples he also emphasized the ceremonial side of their religious life and centralized it so that even the Jews of the dispersion henceforth paid their yearly temple tax, made frequent pilgrimages to Jerusalem, and regarded themselves as a part of the nation. Furthermore, Herod brought peace and prosperity to his people and gave the Jews an honorable place in the role of nations. Thus, while his career is marked by many unpardonable crimes, he proved on the whole to be an upbuilder and a friend rather than a foe of the Jews.

CHAPTER 29

HEROD'S TEMPLE

It is not difficult to appreciate the reasons that influenced Herod to begin the rebuilding of the temple. Chief among these was doubtless the desire to win still further the approval of his master Augustus. It is also a characteristic of a man of Herod's type to seek to gain popular approval by the munificence of his public gifts. Throughout his reign he was painfully aware of the suspicions of his Jewish subjects. He trusted, and the event proved the wisdom of his judgment, that he might conciliate them by giving them that about which their interest most naturally gathered. The methods he employed in building the temple clearly indicate that this was one of his leading motives. He also gratified the love of construction that had found expression in many of the cities of Palestine and the eastern Mediterranean. He desired to raise a great memorial for himself, and in this hope he was not disappointed, for later generations continued to think of him with gratitude because of the temple that bore his name.

Preparations for the Rebuilding of the Temple Herod's temple was begun in 20 or 19 B.C. and was not entirely completed until a few years before its destruction in A.D. 70. The task in itself was a difficult one, for on the north the city prevented the extension of the temple area, and on the south the hill rapidly descended toward the juncture of the Tyropoean and Kidron valleys. Herod met the difficulty by filling in to the south with vast stone constructions that rose to the height of seventy to ninety feet above the virgin rock. To economize on building materials he built the huge underground vaults and arches known today as Solomon's Stables. Thus with a vast expense of labor and wealth he extended the temple area to the south until it was double that which surrounded Solomon's temple. It was also important to regard in every detail the ceremonial scruples of the Jews. To this end a small army of priests were trained as masons and carpenters in order to do the work in the immediate proximity of the temple. To bring the ancient temple into proportion with the rest of his buildings, a huge porch or façade was reared in front of it on the east, rising, according to Josephus, to the height of 120 feet. For the roof that covered the porches he apparently brought cedar from the distant Lebanons. Only with all the resources of the kingdom at his command was it possible to carry through this vast enterprise.

The Approaches to the Temple The entire temple area was rectangular in form, about twelve hundred feet in length and six hundred feet wide. Its chief approaches were on the south and west. A small gate through which sacrificial animals were introduced immediately into the temple precincts opened from the north. The one gate on the east, which opened into the Kidron Valley, was apparently opposite the eastern entrance to the temple. The two gates on the south opened toward the City of David. The one was a double gate with an incline leading into the temple area, and the other, farther to the east, was a triple gate. The main approaches were from the west. The southern of these was a low viaduct spanning the Kidron Valley and thence by steps or inclined approach ascending to the temple area. Remnants of the arches that spanned the valley at this point and a little farther north are still traceable on the present walls of the temple area far down in the Tyropoean Valley. The third approach, farther to the north, was probably also a viaduct leading directly into the temple area, while the extreme northern approach, according to Josephus, led from the palace of Herod directly to the temple. The entire temple area was encircled by a colonnade. One row of pillars was built into the high wall that surrounded the area. On the south was found the royal porch with its four rows of columns, the first and second about thirty feet apart, the second and third forty-five feet apart, and the third and fourth thirty feet apart. The pillars on the sides were about twenty-seven feet in height, while the two rows in the middle were double that. Each of these colonnades was covered with a richly ornamented cedar roof, thus affording grateful shelter from the sun and storm. The great space at the south of the temple area was the Court of the Gentiles, the common park of the city where all classes of its population freely gathered. The colonnade on the east of the temple area bore the name of Solomon's Porch, and from it the steps led up to the raised platform of native rock twenty or more feet above the Court of the Gentiles. Somewhere to the east of the temple was found the famous Beautiful Gate. The series of steps led into the so-called Court of the Women. West of this was the Court of the Israelites, to which only men were admitted. Thence a broad, high door led to the open space before the temple. Surrounding the altar and cutting off approach to the temple proper was a stone balustrade. The space within this was known as the Court of the Priests. Here no laymen were admitted except as the ritual of private sacrifice required. These inner courts were surrounded by a high wall and adjoining chambers for storage of the paraphernalia used in connection with the sacrifice and for the residence of the priests. On the southern side of the temple was the room where the national council, the Sandhedrin, held its public meetings. Four gates on the north and four gates on the south led from the temple court to the lower Court of the Gentiles.

The Organization of the Temple Service At the head of the temple organization was the high priest. Since the deposition of the ill-fated Hyrcanus the high priests had been appointed by Herod, for to them was entrusted great civil as well as religious authority. The one duty the high priests could not neglect, unless prevented by illness, was to perform the sacrifice on behalf of the people and to enter the Holy of Holies on the day of atonement. Frequently they also offered the sacrifice or presided at the special services on the Sabbath, the new moons, or at the great annual festivals. Otherwise the temple duties were performed by the army of priests and assistants who were associated with the temple. According to Josephus there were twenty thousand priests. They were divided into twenty-four courses. Each course included certain priestly families to which were entrusted for a week the performing of the sacrifices. Corresponding to the twenty-four courses of priests were the courses of the people, who were represented by certain of their number at each of the important services. The priests not only performed the sacrifices but also guarded the temple treasures and the private wealth placed in their keeping. The Levites attended to the more menial duties in connection with the temple service. They aided the priests in preparing the sacrifices and in caring for the utensils that were used in connection with the sacrifice. Some of them were doorkeepers. Probably from the Levites were drafted the temple police at whose head was the captain of the temple. Their task was to preserve order and to prevent Gentiles from entering the sacred precincts of the temple. The singers constituted a third group of Levites.

Two public services were held each day. The first, at sunrise, consisted of the offering of a sacrificial ram with the accompaniment of prayer and song. The same rites were repeated at sunset. After the morning sacrifice the private offerings were presented. On the Sabbaths, new moons, and great festivals, the number of sacrifices was greatly increased and the ritual made more elaborate. Upon the Jews, instructed in the synagogue in the details of the law and taught to regard the temple and its services with deepest reverence, the elaborate ceremonies of this great and magnificent sanctuary must have made a profound impression. As the people streamed up to Jerusalem by thousands at the great feasts, their attention was fixed more and more upon the ritual and the truths it symbolized. Herod's temple also strengthened the authority of the Jewish hierarchy with the people, and gave the scribes and Pharisees the commanding position that they later occupied in the life and thought of Judaism.

CHAPTER 30

THE MESSIANIC HOPES AND THE RELIGIOUS BELIEFS OF JUDAISM

Eternal hopefulness is a marked characteristic of the Hebrew race. Throughout most of their history the greater the calamities that overtook them the greater was their assurance that these were but the prelude to a glorious vindication and deliverance. This hopefulness was not merely the result of their natural optimism, but of the belief, formed by their experiences in many a national crisis, that a God of justice was overruling the events of history, and that he was working not for man's destruction but for his highest happiness and well-being. It was their insight into the divine purpose that led the Hebrew prophets to break away from the popular traditions that projected backward to the beginnings of history the realization of man's fondest hopes. Instead they proclaimed that the golden era lay in the future rather than the past. The hopes of Israel's prophets regarding that future took many different forms. Often the form was determined by the earlier experiences of the nation. At many periods the people looked for a revival of the glories of the days of David. In later days, when they were oppressed by cruel persecutions, they revived in modified form the dreams that had been current in the childhood of the Semitic race, and thought of a supernatural kingdom that was to be inaugurated after Jehovah and his attendant angels, like Marduk in the old Babylonian tradition of the creation had overcome Satan and the fallen angels. Israel's messianic hopes were also shaped and broadened by the teachings of the great ethical prophets. A growing realization of the imperfections of the existing order led them to look ever more expectantly to the time when the prophetic ideals of justice and mercy would be realized in society, as well as in the character of the individual. These different expectations regarding the future are broadly designated as messianic prophecies. The word "messianic," like its counterpart "Messiah" (Greek: "Christ"), comes from the Hebrew word meaning "to smear" or "to anoint." It designated in ancient times the weapons consecrated for battle or the king chosen and thus symbolically set aside to lead the people as Jehovah's representative, or a priest called to represent the people in the ceremonial worship. The common underlying idea in the word is that of consecration to a divine purpose. In its narrower application it describes simply the agent who is to realize God's purpose in history, but in its broader and prevailing usage it designates all prophecies that described the ideal that Jehovah is seeking to perfect in the life of Israel and of humanity, and the agents or agencies, whether individual or national, material or spiritual, natural or supernatural, by which he is to realize that ideal.

The Kingly, Nationalistic Type of Messianic Hope The messianic prophecies of the Old Testament seem only confusing and contradictory until the three distinct types are recognized. These different types of messianic prophecy naturally shade into each other, and yet they are fundamentally distinct and were represented throughout Israel's history by different classes of thinkers. The first is the kingly, nationalistic type of hope. It came into existence as soon as Israel became a nation, and may be traced in the Balaam oracles in Numbers 24:17–19, where the seer is represented as beholding Israel's victorious king smiting its foes, the Moabites and Edomites, and ruling gloriously over a triumphant people. It is echoed in II Samuel 7:10–16 in the promise that the house of David should rule peacefully and uninterruptedly through succeeding generations. Ezekiel, in his picture of the restored nation in 37:21–28, declares in the name of Jehovah that "my servant David shall be king over them and they shall dwell in the land that I have given to my servant Jacob wherein their fathers dwelt, and they shall dwell therein, they and their sons forever, and David my servant shall be their prince forever." In such passages as Isaiah 9 and 11 the Davidic ruler is represented as reigning not despotically or selfishly, but in accordance with the principles of justice and mercy, bringing peace to all his subjects. As has already been noted, in the prophecies of Haggai and Zechariah and in connection with the rebuilding of the second temple Israel's kingly, nationalistic hope reached its culmination, but through the victories of Darius was rudely cast to the ground. For the next three and a half centuries, throughout the Persian and Greek periods, this type of Israel's messianic hope was apparently silenced. The Maccabean struggles and victories, however, and the oppressive rule of Rome stirred this smoldering hope into a flame and gave it wide currency among the people at the beginning of the Christian era. Again the nation came to the forefront. In the beautiful prophecy of Zechariah 9:9–10, which apparently comes from the earlier part of the Maccabean era, is found the noble picture of a peasant king, humble yet victorious, establishing with the sword a worldwide kingdom. Memories of the glorious achievements of the Maccabean leaders kindled the popular imagination. When in 63 B.C. Rome's iron hand closed upon Palestine, the eyes of the Jews looked expectantly for the advent of a champion like David of old, who would crush the heathen, convict the sinful Jews, and gather the faithful people, ruling over them in justice and with tender care. These hopes are most plainly expressed in the Psalms of Solomon, which were written near the beginning of the Roman period. These expectations in their more material form inspired the party of the Zelots during the earlier part of the first Christian century repeatedly to unsheathe the sword in the vain effort to over-throw Rome and to establish at once the rule of the Messiah. It was because this type of hope was so strong in the minds of the common people that the false messiahs who rose from time to time were able to quickly gather thousands about them in the vain expectation that the moment of deliverance had at last arrived.

The Apocalyptic, Catastrophic Type of Messianic Hope

Another class of thinkers in Israel looked not for a tempo-ral but for a supernatural kingdom. It is usually described in the symbolic language of the apocalypse. The inauguration of this kingdom was not dependent upon man's activity but solely upon the will of God. The exact time and manner of its institution was clothed in mystery. Traces of this belief are found in the references in Amos to the popular expecta-tions regarding the day of Jehovah. Evidently the northern Israelites lived in anticipation of a great universal judg-ment day, in which their heathen foes would be suddenly destroyed and they themselves would be exalted. It was a belief that Amos and the ethical prophets who followed him strongly combated, for they were fully aware of the funda-mental weakness in the apocalyptic or catastrophic type of prophecy: it took away from the nation and individual all personal responsibility. Furthermore, its roots went back to the old Semitic mythology. This type of hope, however, was too firmly fixed in the popular mind to be dispelled even by the preaching of Israel's greatest prophets. As a result of the calamities that gathered about the fall of the Hebrew state it was revived. It is found in Ezekiel, Zechariah, and Joel. Each of these prophets looked forward to the time when Jehovah would miraculously overthrow their heathen foes, restore his scattered people, and establish for them a world-wide, eternal kingdom. In the closing chapters of the book of Daniel this form of belief attains its fullest expression in the Old Testament. In the Similitudes of Enoch (37–71), which come either from the latter part of the Maccabean era or else from the days of Herod, these messianic hopes are still further developed. Instead of Israel's guardian angel Michael, represented as coming on the clouds from heaven and in appearance like a son of man, a heavenly Messiah is introduced. He is known by the titles "Messiah," "Elect One," and "Son of Man" (probably taken from the book of Daniel). In Enoch the term "Son of Man" has evidently become, as in IV Esdras, the title of a personal Messiah. He is described as preexistent and gifted with divine authority. When he appears, the dead are to rise, and angels, as well as men, are to be tried before his tribunal. The sinners and the fallen angels he will condemn to eternal punishment. All sin and wrong shall be driven from the earth. Heaven and earth shall be transformed, and an eternal kingdom shall be established in which all the righteous, whether dead or living, shall participate. This was evidently the type of messianic hope held by the Pharisees as well as the Essenes. As a result of the teaching of the Pharisees it was held widely by the Jews of the first Christian century. It was clearly in the minds of Jesus's disciples when he made his last journey to Jerusalem. It was both the background and the barrier to all his work. It is the key to the interpretation of Paul's conception of the Christ, or the Messiah, for he had been educated as a Pharisee. This apocalyptic type of messianic hope powerfully influenced the life and thought of the early Christian Church and even permeated the Gospel narratives. The question of how far Jesus himself was influenced by it is one of the most vital and difficult problems of early Christian history.

The Ethical and Universalistic Type of Messianic Prophecy
Far removed from the kingly, messianic hopes of the people and the supernatural visions of the apocalypses were the plain, direct, practical ideals of Israel's great ethical prophets. Amos, Hosea, Isaiah, and Jeremiah all united in declaring that the realization of Jehovah's purpose in history depended primarily upon the response of his people. They regarded the kingdom of God as a natural growth. It represented the gradual transformation of the characters of men under the influence of God's truth and spirit working in their minds. They hoped and labored to see the nation Israel living in full accord with the demands of justice, mercy, and service. The II Isaiah, under the influences that grew out of the destruction of the temple and closer contact with the heathen world, voiced this type of messianic hope in its broadest and most spiritualized form. He declared that the Israelites had been called and trained for a unique service

and that that service was to be performed by them quietly and unostentatiously, as prophets and teachers of men. He also presented most clearly Israel's missionary ideal, and showed that its task was not to destroy but to bring light to the Gentile world. He and the more enlightened prophets who followed him saw an ever widening kingdom established without the aid of the sword and freed from all racial barriers: the eternal, universal, spiritual kingdom of God on earth. It is evident that in contrast to the other types of messianic prophecy this form was comprehensible, practicable, and alone capable of realization.

The Messianic Hopes of Judaism at the Beginning of the Christian Era Unfortunately, as a result of the varied experiences through which Judaism passed in the centuries immediately preceding the Christian era, its ethical and universal messianic hopes were largely eclipsed. The ideal of the suffering servant appears to have been almost forgotten. As the later Jews read the earlier scriptures of their race in order to determine what the future held in store for them, they fixed their eyes upon the kingly and apocalyptic prophecies. Regarding all scriptures as equally authoritative, they attempted the impossible task of blending these fundamentally different types of prophecy. The result was that their beliefs became, indeed, a complex labyrinth with paths leading in opposite directions. Later events have proved beyond question that these popular types were the dreams of religious enthusiasts rather than true pictures of the way in which the divine purpose was to be perfected in human history, and yet the apocalyptic type of prophecy was not without its significance. It tended to correct the narrow national hopes of the Jews and to lift them to the consideration of that which was spiritual and eternal. It also led them to appreciate the unity of all history, and in times of distress it kept alive their faith in a God who was wisely guiding their destinies. Underlying all these different types of prophecy is the appreciation of the broad truth that God was working out in the lives of men and nations a definite purpose, and that that purpose was good, and that the God behind all history was a God not only of power but also of love. It was inevitable that the ethical and more spiritual expectations of the early Hebrew prophets should find the fullest response in the heart and life of the Great Teacher. In the face of opposition from the leaders of his race, from the multitudes that gathered about him, and even from the disciples who loved and followed him, he proclaimed that the kingdom of God would not come by observation, but that its growth would be natural and gradual like that of the mustard seed, that it was not external but within the hearts of men, that membership in that kingdom depended not upon the arbitrary will of God, but upon men's acting in accord with that will in the everyday relations of life. Thus Jesus prepared the way for the complete fulfillment of all that was noblest and best in Israel's messianic hopes, and in his character and teachings far surpassed the highest expectations of the inspired teachers of his race.

The following essays were delivered in the form of addresses, before the largest associations in the great cities of Germany. Each one is a dear and precious possession to me. As I once more pass them in review, reminiscences fill my mind of solemn occasions and impressive scenes, of excellent men and charming women. I feel as though I were sending the best beloved children of my fancy out into the world, and sadness seizes me when I realize that they no longer belong to me alone, that they have become the property of strangers. The living word falling upon the ear of the listener is one thing; quite another the word staring from the cold, printed page. Will my thoughts be accorded the same friendly welcome that greeted them when first they were uttered?

I venture to hope that they may be kindly received, for these addresses were born of devoted love to Judaism. The consciousness that Israel is charged with a great historical mission, not yet accomplished, ushered them into existence. Truth and sincerity stood sponsor to every word. Is it presumptuous, then, to hope that they may find favor in the New World? Brethren of my faith live there as here; our ancient watchword, "Sh'ma Yisrael," resounds in their synagogues as in ours; the old blood-stained flag, with its sublime inscription, "The Lord is my banner!" floats over them; and Jewish hearts in America are loyal like ours, and sustained by steadfast faith in the Messianic time when our hopes and ideals, our aims and dreams, will be realized. There is but one Judaism the world over, by the Jordan and the Tagus as by the Vistula and the Mississippi. God bless and protect it, and lead it to the goal of its glorious future!

PART II

JEWISH
LITERATURE

CHAPTER 31

A GLANCE AT JEWISH LITERATURE

In a well-known passage of the Romanzero, rebuking Jewish women for their ignorance of the magnificent golden age of their nation's poetry, Heine used unmeasured terms of condemnation. He was too severe, for the sources from which he drew his own information were of a purely scientific character, necessarily unintelligible to the ordinary reader. The first truly popular presentation of the whole of Jewish literature could not have existed in Heine's time, as the most valuable treasures of that literature, a veritable Hebrew Pompeii, have been unearthed from the mold and rubbish of the libraries.

But in the course of this half century, conscientious research has so actively been prosecuted that we can now gain at least a bird's-eye view of the whole course of our literature. Some stretches still lie in shadow, and it is not astonishing that eminent scholars continue to maintain that "there is no such thing as an organic history, a logical development, of the gigantic neo-Hebraic literature," while such as are acquainted with the results of late research at best concede that Hebrew literature has been permitted to garner a "tender aftermath." Both verdicts are untrue and unfair. Jewish literature has developed organically, and in the course of its evolution it has had its spring tide as well as its season of decay, this again followed by vigorous rejuvenescence.

Such opinions are part and parcel of the vicissitudes of our literature, in themselves sufficient matter for an interesting book. Strange it certainly is that a people without a home, without a land, living under repression and persecution, could produce so great a literature; stranger still that it should at first have been preserved and disseminated, then forgotten, or treated with the disdain of prejudice, and finally roused from torpid slumber into robust life by the breath of the modern era. In the neighborhood of twenty-two thousand works are known to us now. Bibliographers were ignorant of the existence of half of these, and in the libraries of Italy, England, and Germany an untold number await resurrection.

In fact, our literature has not yet been given a name that recommends itself to universal acceptance. Some have called it "Rabbinical Literature," because during the Middle Ages every Jew of learning bore the title "Rabbi"; others, "Neo-Hebraic"; and a third party considers it purely theological. These names are all inadequate. Perhaps the only one sufficiently comprehensive is "Jewish Literature." That embraces, as it should, the aggregate of writings produced by Jews from the earliest days of their history up to the present time, regardless of form, of language, and, in the Middle Ages at least, of subject matter.

With this definition in mind, we are able to sketch the whole course of our literature, though in the frame of an essay only in outline. We shall learn, as Leopold Zunz, the Humboldt of Jewish science, well says, that it is

> intimately bound up with the culture of the ancient world, with the origin and development of Christianity, and with the scientific endeavors of the middle ages. Inasmuch as it shares the intellectual aspirations of the past and the present, their conflicts and their reverses, it is supplementary to general literature. Its peculiar features, themselves falling under universal laws, are in turn helpful in the interpretation of general characteristics. If the aggregate results of mankind's intellectual activity can be likened unto a sea, Jewish literature is one of the tributaries that feed it. Like other literatures and like literature in general, it reveals to the student what noble ideals the soul of man has cherished, and striven to realize, and discloses the varied achievements of man's intellectual powers. If we of to-day are the witnesses and the offspring of an eternal,

creative principle, then, in turn, the present is but the beginning of a future, that is, the translation of knowledge into life. Spiritual ideals consciously held by any portion of mankind lend freedom to thought, grace to feeling, and by sailing up this one stream we may reach the fountain-head whence have emanated all spiritual forces, and about which, as a fixed pole, all spiritual currents eddy.

The cornerstone of this Jewish literature is the Bible, or what we call Old Testament literature the oldest and at the same time the most important of Jewish writings. It extends over the period ending with the second century before the common era; it is written, for the most part, in Hebrew; and it is the clearest and the most faithful reflection of the original characteristics of the Jewish people. This biblical literature has engaged the closest attention of all nations and every age. Until the seventeenth century, biblical science was purely dogmatic, and only since Herder pointed the way have its aesthetic elements been dwelt upon along with, often in defiance of, dogmatic considerations. Up to this time, Ernest Meier and Theodor Nöldeke have been the only ones to treat of the Old Testament with reference to its place in the history of literature.

Despite the dogmatic air clinging to the critical introductions to the study of the Old Testament, their authors have not shrunk from treating the book sacred to two religions with childish arbitrariness. Since the days of Spinoza's essay at rationalistic explanation, Bible criticism has been the wrestling ground of the most extravagant exegesis, of bold hypotheses, and hazardous conjectures. No Latin or Greek classic has been so ruthlessly attacked and dissected; no medieval poetry so arbitrarily interpreted. As a natural consequence, the aesthetic elements were more and more pushed into the background. Only recently have we begun to ridicule this craze for hypotheses and returned to more sober methods of inquiry. Bible criticism reached the climax of absurdity, and the scorn was just that greeted one of the most important works of the critical school, Hitzig's "Explanation of the Psalms." A reviewer said: "We may entertain the fond hope that, in a second edition of this clever writer's commentary, he will be in the enviable position to tell us the day and the hour when each psalm was composed."

The reaction began with the recognition of the inadequacy of Astruc's document hypothesis, until then the creed of all Bible critics. Astruc, a celebrated French physician, in 1753 advanced the theory that the Pentateuch—the five books of Moses—consists of two parallel documents, called respectively Yahvistic and Elohistic, from the name applied to God in each. On this basis, German science after him raised a superstructure. No date was deemed too late to be assigned to the composition of the Pentateuch. If the historian Flavius Josephus had not existed, and if Jesus had not spoken of "the Law" and "the prophets," and of the things "which were written in the Law of Moses, and in the Prophets, and in the Psalms," critics would have been disposed to transfer the redaction of the Bible to some period of the Christian era. So wide is the divergence of opinions on the subject that two learned critics, Ewald and Hitzig, differ in the date assigned to a certain biblical passage by no less than a thousand years!

Bible archaeology, Bible exegesis, and discussions of grammatical niceties were confounded with the history of biblical literature, and naturally it was the latter that suffered by the lack of differentiation. Orthodoxy assumed a purely divine origin for the Bible, while skeptics treated the holy book with greater levity than they would dare display in criticizing a modern novel. The one party raised a hue and cry when Moses was spoken of as the first author; the other discovered "obscene, rude, even cannibalistic traits" in the sublime narratives of the Bible. It should be the task of coming generations, successors by one remove of credulous Bible lovers, and immediate heirs of thoroughgoing rationalists, to reconcile and fuse in a higher conception of the Bible the two divergent theories of its purely divine and its purely human origin. Unfortunately, it must be admitted that Meier is right when he says, in his "History of the National Poetry of the Hebrews," that this task wholly belongs to the future; at present it is an unsolved problem.

The æsthetic is the only proper point of view for a full recognition of the value of biblical literature. It certainly does not rob the sacred scriptures, the perennial source of spiritual comfort, of their exalted character and divine worth to assume that legend, myth, and history have combined to produce the perfect harmony that is their imperishable distinction. The peasant dwelling on inaccessible mountain heights, next to the record of Abraham's shepherd life, inscribes the main events of his own career, the anniversary dates sacred to his family. The young count among their first impressions that of "the brown folio," and more vividly than all else remember

> *The maidens fair and true,*
> *The sages and the heroes bold,*
> *Whose tale by seers inspired*
> *In our Book of books is told.*
>
> *The simple life and faith*
> *Of patriarchs of ancient day*
> *Like angels hover near,*
> *And guard, and lead them on the way.*

Above all, a whole nation has for centuries been living with, and only by virtue of, this book. Surely this is abundant testimony to the undying value of the great work, in which the simplest shepherd tales and the naïvest legends, profound moral saws and magnificent images, the ideals of a Messianic future and the purest, the most humane conception of life, alternate with sublime descriptions of nature and the sweet strains of love poems, with national songs breathing hope or trembling with anguish, and with the dull tones of despairing pessimism and the divinely inspired hymns of an exalted theodicy, all blending to form what the reverential love of men has named the Book of books.

It was natural that a book of this kind should become the basis of a great literature. Whatever was produced in later times had to submit to be judged by its exalted standard. It became the rule of conduct, the prophetic mirror reflecting the future work of a nation whose fate was inextricably bound up with its own. It is not known how and when the biblical scriptures were welded into one book, a holy canon, but it is probably correct to assume that it was done by the Soferim, the Scribes, between 200 and 150 B.C. At all events, it is certain that the three divisions of the Bible—the Pentateuch, the Prophets, and the miscellaneous writings—were contained in the Greek version, the Septuagint, so called from the seventy or seventy-two Alexandrians supposed to have done the work of translation under Ptolemy Philadelphus.

The Greek translation of the Bible marks the beginning of the second period of Jewish literature, the Judeo-Hellenic. Hebrew ceased to be the language of the people; it was thenceforth used only by scholars and in divine worship. Jews for the first time met Greek intellect. Shem and Japheth embraced fraternally. "But even while the teachings of Hellas were pushing their way into subjugated Palestine, seducing Jewish philosophy to apostasy, and seeking, by main force, to introduce paganism, the Greek philosophers themselves stood awed by the majesty and power of the Jewish prophets. Swords and words entered the lists as champions of Judaism.

The vernacular Aramaean, having suffered the Greek to put its impress upon many of its substantives, refused to yield to the influence of the Greek verb, and, in the end, Hebrew truth, in the guise of the teachings of Jesus, undermined the proud structure of the heathen." This is a most excellent characterization of that literary period, which lasted about three centuries, ending between 100 and 150 CE. Its influence upon Jewish literature can scarcely be said to have been enduring. To it belong all the apocryphal writings originally composed in the Greek language that were for that reason not incorporated into the Holy Canon. The center of intellectual life was no longer in Palestine, but at Alexandria in Egypt, where three hundred thousand Jews were then living, and thus this literature came to be called Judeo-Alexandrian. It includes among its writers the last of the Neoplatonists, particularly Philo, the originator of the allegorical interpretation of the Bible and of a Jewish philosophy of religion; Aristeas; and pseudo-Phokylides. There were also Jewish littérateurs: the dramatist Ezekielos; Jason; Philo the Elder; Aristobulus, the popularizer of the Aristotelian philosophy; Eupolemos, the historian; and probably the Jewish Sybil, who had to have recourse to the oracular manner of the pagans to proclaim the truths of Judaism, and to Greek figures of speech for her apocalyptic visions, which foretold, in biblical phrase and with prophetic ardor, the future of Israel and of the nations in contact with it.

Meanwhile the word of the Bible was steadily gaining importance in Palestine. To search into and expound the sacred text had become the inheritance of the congregation of Jacob, of those who had not lent ear to the siren notes of Hellenism. Midrash, as the investigations of the commentators were called, by and by divided into two streams—Halacha, which establishes and systematizes the statutes of the Law, and Haggada, which uses the sacred texts for homiletic, historical, ethical, and pedagogic discussions. The latter is the poetic and the former is the legislative element in the Talmudic writings, whose composition, extending over a thousand years, constitutes the third, the most momentous, period of Jewish literature. Of course, none of these periods can be so sharply defined as a rapid survey might lead one to suppose. For instance, on the threshold of this third epoch stands the figure of Flavius Josephus, the famous Jewish historian, who, at once an enthusiastic Jew and a friend of the Romans, writes the story of his nation in the Greek language—a character as peculiar as his age, which, listening to the mocking laughter of a Lucian, saw Olympus overthrown and its gods dethroned, the temple at Jerusalem pass away in flame and smoke, and the new doctrine of the son of the carpenter at Nazareth begin its victorious course.

By the side of this Janus-faced historian, the heroes of the Talmud stand enveloped in glory. We meet with men like Hillel and Shammaï, Jochanan ben Zakkaï, Gamaliel, Joshua ben Chananya, the famous Akiba, and later on Yehuda the Prince, friend of the imperial philosopher Marcus Aurelius and compiler of the Mishna, the authoritative code of laws superseding all other collections. Then there are the fabulist

Meïr; Simon ben Yochaï, falsely accused of the authorship of the mystical Kabbala; Chiya; Rab; Samuel, equally famous as a physician and a rabbi; Jochanan, the supposed compiler of the Jerusalem Talmud; and Ashi and Abina, the former probably the arranger of the Babylonian Talmud. This latter Talmud, the one invested with authority among Jews, by reason of its varying fortunes, is the most marvelous literary monument extant. Never has a book been so hated and so persecuted, so misjudged and so despised, so prized and so honored, and, above all, so imperfectly understood, as this very Talmud.

For the Jews and their literature it has had untold significance. That the Talmud has been the conservator of Judaism is an irrefutable statement. It is true that the study of the Talmud unduly absorbed the great intellectual force of its adherents, and brought about a somewhat one-sided mental development in the Jews, but it also is true, as a writer says, that

> whenever in troublous times scientific inquiry was laid low; whenever, for any reason, the Jew was excluded from participation in public life, the study of the Talmud maintained the elasticity and the vigor of the Jewish mind, and rescued the Jew from sterile mysticism and spiritual apathy. The Talmud, as a rule, has been inimical to mysticism, and the most brilliant Talmudists, in propitious days, have achieved distinguished success in secular science.

The Jew survived ages of bitterness, all the while clinging loyally to his faith in the midst of hostility, and the first ray of light that penetrated the walls of the Ghetto found him ready to take part in the intellectual work of his time. This admirable elasticity of mind he owes, first and foremost, to the study of the Talmud.

From this much abused Talmud, as from its contemporary the Midrash in the restricted sense, sprouted forth the blossoms of the Haggada—that Haggada

> *Where the beauteous, ancient sagas,*
> *Angel legends fraught with meaning,*
> *Martyrs' silent sacrifices,*
> *Festal songs and wisdom's sayings,*
> *Trope and allegoric fancies—*
> *All, howe'er by faith's triumphant*
> *Glow pervaded—where they gleaming,*
> *Glist'ning, well in strength exhaustless.*
>
> *And the boyish heart responsive*
> *Drinks the wild, fantastic sweetness,*
> *Greets the woful, wondrous anguish,*
> *Yields to grewsome charm of myst'ry,*
>
> *Hid in blessed worlds of fable.*
> *Overawed it hearkens solemn*
> *To that sacred revelation*
> *Mortal man hath poetry called."*

A story from the Midrash charmingly characterizes the relation between Halacha and Haggada. Two rabbis, Chiya bar Abba, a Halachist, and Abbahu, a Haggadist, happened to be lecturing in the same town. Abbahu, the Haggadist, was always listened to by great crowds, while Chiya, with his Halacha, stood practically deserted. The Haggadist comforted the disappointed teacher with a parable. "Let us suppose two merchants," he said, "to come to town, and offer wares for sale. The one has pearls and precious gems to display, the other, cheap finery, gilt chains, rings, and gaudy ribbons. About whose booth, think you, does the crowd press?—Formerly, when the struggle for existence was not fierce and inevitable, men had leisure and desire for the profound teachings of the Law; now they need the cheering words of consolation and hope."

For more than a thousand years this nameless spirit of national poesy was abroad and produced manifold works, which, in the course of time, were gathered together into comprehensive collections, variously named Midrash Rabba, Pesikta, Tanchuma, and so on. Their compilation was begun in about 700 CE, that is, soon after the close of the Talmud, in the transition period from the third epoch of Jewish literature to the fourth, the golden age, which lasted from the ninth to the fifteenth century, and, according to the law of human products, shows a season of growth, blossom, and decay.

The scene of action during this period was western Asia, northern Africa, sometimes Italy and France, but chiefly Spain, where Arabic culture, destined to influence

Jewish thought to an incalculable degree, was at that time at its zenith.

> A second time the Jews were drawn into the vortex of a foreign civilization, and two hundred years after Mohammed, Jews in Kairwan and Bagdad were speaking the same language, Arabic. A language once again became the mediatrix between Jewish and general literature, and the best minds of the two races, by means of the language, reciprocally influenced each other. Jews, as they once had written Greek for their brethren, now wrote Arabic; and, as in Hellenistic times, the civilization of the dominant race, both in its original features and in its adaptations from foreign sources, was reflected in that of the Jews.

It would be interesting to analyze this important process of assimilation, but we can concern ourselves only with the works of the Jewish intellect. Again we meet, at the threshold of the period, a characteristic figure, the thinker Sa adia, ranking high as author and religious philosopher, known also as a grammarian and a poet. He is followed by Sherira, to whom we owe the beginnings of a history of Talmudic literature, and his son Haï Gaon, a strictly orthodox teacher of the Law. In their wake come troops of physicians, theologians, lexicographers, Talmudists, and grammarians. Great is the circle of our national literature: it embraces theology, philosophy, exegesis, grammar, poetry, and jurisprudence, even astronomy and chronology, mathematics and medicine. But these widely varying subjects constitute only one class, inasmuch as they all are infused with the spirit of Judaism, and subordinate themselves to its demands. A mention of the prominent actors would turn this whole essay into a dry list of names. Therefore it is better for us merely to sketch the period in outline, dwelling only on its greatest poets and philosophers, the molders of its character.

The opinion is current that the Semitic race lacks the philosophic faculty. Yet it cannot be denied that Jews were the first to carry Greek philosophy to Europe, teaching and developing it there before its dissemination by celebrated Arabs. In their zeal to harmonize philosophy with their religion, and in the lesser endeavor to defend traditional Judaism against the polemic attacks of a new sect, the Karaites, they invested the Aristotelian system with peculiar features, making it, as it were, their national philosophy. At all events, it must be universally accepted that the Jews share with the Arabs the merit "of having cherished the study of philosophy during centuries of barbarism, and of having for a long time exerted a civilizing influence upon Europe."

The meager achievements of the Jews in the departments of history and history of literature do not justify the conclusion that they are wanting in historic perception. The lack of writings on these subjects is traceable to the sufferings and persecutions that have marked their pathway. Before their chroniclers had time to record past afflictions, new sorrows and troubles broke in upon them. In the Middle Ages, the history of Jewish literature is the entire history of the Jewish people, its course outlined by blood and watered by rivers of tears, at whose source the genius of Jewish poetry sits lamenting. "The Orient dwells an exile in the Occident," Franz Delitzsch, the first alien to give loving study to this literature, poetically says, "and its tears of longing for home are the fountain-head of Jewish poetry."

That poetry reached its perfection in the works of the celebrated trio, Solomon Gabirol, Yehuda Halevi, and Moses ben Ezra. Their dazzling triumphs had been heralded by the more modest achievements of Abitur, writing Hebrew, and Adia and the poetess Xemona (Kasmune) using Arabic, to sing the praise of God and lament the woes of Israel.

The predominant, but not exclusive, characteristic of Jewish poetry is its religious strain. Great thinkers, men equipped with philosophic training and at the same time endowed with poetic gifts, have contributed to the huge volume of synagogue poetry, whose subjects are praise of the Lord and regret for Zion. The sorrow for our lost fatherland has never taken on more glowing colors, never been expressed in fuller tones than in this poetry. As ancient Hebrew poetry flowed in the two streams of prophecy and psalmody, so the Jewish poetry of the Middle Ages was divided into Piut and Selicha. Songs of hope and despair, cries of revenge, exhortations to peace among men, elegies on every single persecution, and laments for Zion, follow each other in kaleidoscopic succession. Unfortunately, there never was lack of historic matter for this poetry to elaborate. To furnish that was the well-accomplished task of rulers and priests in the Middle Ages, alike "in the realm of the Islamic king of kings and in that of the apostolic servant of servants." So fate made this poetry classical and eminently national. Those characteristics which, in general literature, earn for a work the description "Homeric," in Jewish literature make a liturgical poem "Kaliric," so called from the poet Eliezer Kalir, the subject of many mythical tales, and the first of a long line of poets, Spanish, French, and German, extending to the sixteenth or seventeenth century. The literary history of this epoch has been written by Leopold Zunz with warmth of feeling and stupendous learning. He closes his work with the hope that mankind, at some future day, will adopt Israel's religious poetry as its own, transforming the elegiac Selicha into a joyous psalm of universal peace and goodwill.

Side by side with religious poetry flourishes secular poetry, clothing itself in rhyme and meter, adopting every current form of poesy, and treating every appropriate subject. Its first votary was Solomon Gabirol, that

> *Human nightingale that warbled*
> *Forth her songs of tender love,*
> *In the darkness of the sombre,*
> *Gothic mediæval night.*
>
> *She, that nightingale, sang only,*
> *Sobbing forth her adoration,*

To her Lord, her God, in heaven,
Whom her songs of praise extolled.

Solomon Gabirol may be said to have been the first poet thrilled by Weltschmerz. "He produced hymns and songs, penitential prayers, psalms, and threnodies, filled with hope and longing for a blessed future. They are marked throughout by austere earnestness, brushing away, in its rigor, the color and bloom of life; but side by side with it, surging forth from the deepest recesses of a human soul, is humble adoration of God."

Gabirol was a distinguished philosopher besides. In 1150, his chief work, "The Fount of Life," was translated into Latin by Archdeacon Dominicus Gundisalvi, with the help of Johannes Avendeath, an apostate Jew, the author's name being corrupted into Avencebrol, later becoming Avicebron. The work was made a textbook of scholastic philosophy, but neither Scotists nor Thomists, neither adherents nor detractors, suspected that a heretical Jew was slumbering under the name Avicebron. It remained for an inquirer, Solomon Munk, to reveal the face of Gabirol under the mask of a garbled name. Amazed, we behold that the pessimistic philosopher of today can as little as the schoolmen of the Middle Ages shake himself free from the despised Jew. Schopenhauer may object as he will, it is certain that Gabirol was his predecessor by more than eight hundred years!

Charisi, whom we shall presently meet, has expressed the verdict on his poetry, which still holds good:

Solomon Gabirol pleases to call himself the small
yet before him all the great must dwindle and fall.
Who can like him with mighty speech appall?
Compared with him the poets of his time are without
    power
he, the small, alone is a tower.
The highest round of poetry's ladder has he won.
Wisdom fondled him, eloquence hath called him son
and clothing him with purple, said: "Lo!
my first-born son, go forth, to conquest go!"
His predecessors' songs are naught with his compared
nor have his many followers better fared.
The later singers by him were taught
the heirs they are of his poetic thought.
But still he's king, to him all praise belongs
for Solomon's is the Song of Songs.

By Gabirol's side stands Yehuda Halevi, probably the only Jewish poet known to the reader of general literature, to whom his name, life, and fate have become familiar through Heinrich Heine's *Romanzero*. His magnificent descriptions of nature "reflect southern skies, verdant meadows, deep blue rivers, and the stormy sea," and his erotic lyrics are chaste and tender. He sounds the praise of wine, youth, and happiness, and extols the charms of his lady love, but above and beyond all he devotes his song to Zion and his people.

"In the whole compass of religious poetry, Milton's and Klopstock's not excepted, nothing can be found to surpass the elegy of Zion," says a modern writer, a non-Jew. This

soul-stirring "Lay of Zion," better than any number of critical dissertations, will give the reader a clear insight into the
character and spirit of Jewish poetry in general.

We have loitered long with Yehuda Halevi, and still not
long enough, for we have not yet spoken of his claims to
the title philosopher, won for him by his book *Al-Chazari.*
But now we must hurry on to Moses ben Ezra, the last and
most worldly of the three great poets. He devotes his genius
to his patrons, to wine, to his faithless mistress, and to "bac-
chanalian feasts under leafy canopies, with merry minstrelsy
of birds." He laments over separation from friends and kin,
weeps over the shortness of life and the rapid approach of
hoary age—all in polished language, sometimes, however,
lacking euphony. Even when he strikes his lyre in praise
and honor of his people Israel, he fails to rise to the lofty
heights attained by his mates in song.

With Yehuda Charisi, at the beginning of the thirteenth
century, the period of the epigones sets in for Spanish-
Jewish literature. In Charisi's *Tachkemoni,* an imitation of
the poetry of the Arab Hariri, jest and serious criticism,
joy and grief, the sublime and the trivial, follow each other
like tints in a parti-colored skein. His distinction is the ease
with which he plays upon the Hebrew language, not the
most pliable of instruments. In general, Jewish poets and
philosophers have manipulated that language with surprising dexterity. Songs, hymns, elegies, penitential prayers,
exhortations, and religious meditations, generation after
generation, were couched in the idiom of the psalmist, yet

the structure of the language underwent no change. "The development of the neo-Hebraic idiom from the ancient Hebrew," a distinguished modern ethnographer justly says, "confirms, by linguistic evidence, the plasticity, the logical acumen, the comprehensive and at the same time versatile intellectuality of the Jewish race. By the ingenious compounding of words, by investing old expressions with new meanings, and adapting the material offered by alien or related languages to its own purposes, it has increased and enriched a comparatively meagre treasury of words."

Side by side with this cosmopolitanism, illustrated in the Haggada, whose pages prove that nothing human is strange to the Jewish race, it reveals, in its literary development, as notably in the Halacha, a sharply defined subjectivity. Jellinek says: "Not losing itself in the contemplation of the phenomena of life, not devoting itself to any subject unless it be with an ulterior purpose, but seeing all things in their relation to itself, and subordinating them to its own boldly asserted *ego,* the Jewish race is not inclined to apply its powers to the solution of intricate philosophic problems, or to abstruse metaphysical speculations. It is, therefore, not a philosophic race, and its participation in the philosophic work of the world dates only from its contact with the Greeks." The same author, on the other hand, emphasizes the liberality, the broad sympathies, of the Jewish race, in his statement that the Jewish mind, at its first meeting with Arabic philosophy, absorbed it as a leaven into its intellectual life. The product of the assimilation was—as early as the twelfth century, mind you—a philosophic conception of life, whose broad liberality culminates in the sentiment expressed by two most eminent thinkers: Christianity and Islam are the precursors of a world religion, the preliminary conditions for the great religious system satisfying all men. Yehuda Halevi and Moses Maimonides were the philosophers bold enough to utter this thought of far-reaching significance.

The second efflorescence of Jewish poetry brings forth exotic romances, satires, verbose hymns, and humorous narrative poems. Such productions certainly do not justify the application of the epithet "theological" to Jewish literature. Solomon ben Sakbel composes a satiric romance in the Makamat form, describing the varied adventures of Asher ben Yehuda, another Don Quixote; Berachya Hanakdan puts into Hebrew the fables of Aesop and Lokman, furnishing La Fontaine with some of his material; Abraham ibn Sahl receives from the Arabs, certainly not noted for liberality, ten gold pieces for each of his love-songs; Santob de Carrion is a beloved Spanish bard, bold enough to tell unpleasant truths unto a king; Joseph ibn Sabara writes a humorous romance; Yehuda Sabbataï, epic satires, *The War of Wealth and Wisdom,* and *A Gift from a Misogynist*; and unnamed authors, *Truth's Campaign,* and *Praise of Women.*

A satirist of more than ordinary gifts was the Italian Kalonymos, whose *Touchstone,* like Ibn Chasdaï's Makamat *The Prince and the Dervish,* has been translated into German. Contemporaneous with them was Süsskind von Trimberg, the Suabian minnesinger, and Samson Pnie, of Strasbourg, who helped the German poets continue *Parzival,* while later on, in Italy, Moses Rieti composed "The Paradise" in Hebrew *terza-rima.*

In the decadence of Jewish literature, the most prominent figure is Immanuel ben Solomon, or Manoello, as the Italians call him. Critics think him the precursor of Boccaccio, and history knows him as the friend of Dante, whose *Divina Commedia* he travestied in Hebrew. The author of the first Hebrew sonnet and of the first Hebrew novel, he was a talented writer, but as frivolous as talented.

This is the development of Jewish poetry during its great period. In other departments of literature, in philosophy, in theology, in ethics, in Bible exegesis, the race is equally prolific in minds of the first order. Glancing back for a moment, our eye is arrested by Moses Maimonides, the great systematizer of the Jewish Law, and the connecting link between scholasticism and the Greek-Arabic development of the Aristotelian system. Before his time Bechaï ibn Pakuda and Joseph ibn Zadik had entered upon theosophic speculations with the object of harmonizing Arabic and Greek philosophy, and in the age immediately preceding that of Maimonides, Abraham ibn Daud, a writer of surprisingly liberal views, had undertaken, in "The Highest Faith," the task of reconciling faith with philosophy. At the same time rationalistic Bible exegesis was begun by Abraham ibn Ezra, an acute but reckless controversialist. Orthodox interpretations of the Bible had, before him, been taught in France by Rashi (Solomon Yitschaki) and Samuel ben Meïr, and continued by German rabbis, who, at the same time, were preachers of morality, a noteworthy phenomenon in a persecuted tribe.

How pure and strong its ethical principles were is shown by its religious poetry as well as by its practical Law. What pervades the poetry as a high ideal, in the application of the Law becomes demonstrable reality. The wrapt enthusiasm in the hymns of Samuel the Pious and other poets is embodied, lives, in the rulings of Yehuda Hakohen, Solomon Yitschaki, and Jacob ben Meïr; in the legal opinions of Isaac ben Abraham, Eliezer ha-Levi, Isaac ben Moses, Meïr ben Baruch, and their successors, and in the codices of Eliezer of Metz and Moses de Coucy. A German professor of a hundred years ago, after glancing through some few Jewish writings, exclaimed, in a tone of condescending approval: Christians of that time could scarcely have been expected to enjoin such high moral principles as this Jew wrote down and bequeathed to his brethren in faith!

Jewish literature in this and the next period consists largely of theological discussions and of commentaries on the Talmud produced by the hundred. It would be idle to name even the most prominent authors; their works belong to the history of theologic science and rarely had a determining influence upon the development of genuine literature.

We must also pass over in silence the numerous Jewish physicians and medical writers, but it must be remembered that they, too, belong to Jewish literature. The most marvelous characteristic of this literature is that in it the Jewish race has registered each step of its development. "All things learned, gathered, obtained, on its journeyings hither and thither—Greek philosophy and Arabic, as well as Latin scholasticism—all deposited themselves in layers about the Bible, so stamping later Jewish literature with an individuality that gave it an unique place among the literatures of the world."

The travelers, however, must be mentioned by name. Their itineraries were wholly dedicated to the interests of their coreligionists. The first of the line is Eldad, the narrator of a sort of Hebrew *Odyssey.* Benjamin of Tudela and Petachya of Ratisbon are deserving of more confidence as veracious chroniclers, and their descriptions, together with Charisi's, complete the Jewish library of travels of those early days, unless, with Steinschneider, we consider, as we truly may, the majority of Jewish authors under this head. For Jewish writers a hard, necessitous lot has ever been a storm wind, tossing them hither and thither, and blowing the seeds of knowledge over all lands. Learning proved an enveloping, protecting cloak to these mendicant and pilgrim authors. The dispersion of the Jews, their international commerce, and the desire to maintain their academies stimulated a love for travel, made frequent journeyings a necessity, indeed. In this way only can we account for the extraordinarily rapid spread of Jewish literature in the Middle Ages. The student of those times often chances across a rabbi, who this day teaches, lectures, writes in Candia, tomorrow in Rome, next year in Prague or Cracow, and so Jewish literature is the "wandering Jew" among the world's literatures.

The fourth period, the Augustan age of our literature, closes with a jarring discord—the expulsion of the Jews from Spain, their second home, in which they had seen ministers, princes, professors, and poets rise from their ranks. The scene of literary activity changes: France, Italy, but chiefly the Slavonic East, are pushed into the foreground. It is not a salutary change; it ushers in three centuries of decay and stagnation in literary endeavor. The sum of the efforts is indicated by the name of the period, the Rabbinical, for its chief work was the development and fixation of Rabbinism.

Decadence did not set in immediately. Certain beneficent forces, either continuing in action from the former period, or arising out of the new concatenation of circumstances, were in operation: Jewish exiles from Spain carried their culture to the asylums hospitably offered them in the Orient and a few of the European countries, notably Holland; the art of printing was spreading, the first presses in Italy bringing out Jewish works; and the sun of humanism and of the Reformation was rising and shedding solitary rays of its effulgence on the Jewish minds then at work.

Among the noteworthy authors standing between the two periods and belonging to both, the most prominent is Nachmanides, a pious and learned Bible scholar. With logical force and critical candor he entered into the great conflict between science and faith, then dividing the Jewish world into two camps, with Maimonides's works as their shibboleth. The Aristotelian philosophy was no longer satisfying. Minds and hearts were yearning for a new revelation, and in default thereof steeping themselves in mystical speculations. A voluminous theosophic literature sprang up. The Zohar, the Bible of mysticism, was circulated, its authorship being fastened upon a rabbi of olden days. It is altogether probable that the real author was living at the time; many think that it was Moses de Leon. The liberal party counted in its ranks the two distinguished families of Tibbon and Kimchi, the former famed as successful translators, the latter as grammarians. Their best-known representatives were Judah ibn Tibbon and David Kimchi. Curiously enough, the will of the former contains, in unmistakable terms, the opinion that "Property is theft," anticipating Proudhon, who, had he known it, would have seen in its early enunciation additional testimony to its truth. The liberal faction was also supported by Jacob ben Abba-Mari, a friend of Frederick II and Michael Scotus. Abba-Mari lived at the German emperor's court at Naples and quoted him in his commentary upon the Bible as an exegete. Besides there were among the Maimunists, or rationalists, Levi ben Abraham, an extraordinarily liberal man; Shemtob Palquera, one of the most learned Jews of his century; and Yedaya Penini, a philosopher and pessimistic poet, whose "Contemplation of the World" was translated by Mendelssohn and praised by Lessing and Goethe. Despite this array of talent, the opponents were stronger, the most representative partisan being the Talmudist Solomon ben Aderet.

At the same time disputations about the Talmud, ending with its public burning at Paris, were carried on with the Christian clergy. The other literary current of the age is designated by the word "Kabbala," which held many of the finest and noblest minds captive to its witchery. The Kabbala is unquestionably a continuation of earlier theosophic inquiries. Its chief doctrines have been stated by a thorough student of our literature as: All that exists originates in God, the source of light eternal. He Himself can be known only through His manifestations. He is without beginning, and veiled in mystery, or, He is nothing, because the whole of creation has developed from nothing. This nothing is one, indivisible, and limitless—*En-Sof*. God fills space, He is space itself. In order to manifest Himself, in order to create, that is, disclose Himself by means of emanations, He contracts, thus producing vacant space. The *En-Sof* first manifested itself in the prototype of the whole of creation, in the macrocosm called the "son of God," the first man, as he appears upon the chariot of Ezekiel. From this primitive man the whole created world emanates in four stages: *Azila, Beria, Yezira, Asiya*. The *Azila* emanation represents the active qualities of primitive man. They are forces or intelligences flowing from him, at once his essential qualities and the faculties by which he acts. There are ten of these forces, forming the ten sacred *Sefiroth,* a word that first meant "number" but came to stand for "sphere." The first three *Sefiroth* are intelligences, the seven others, attributes. They are supposed to follow each other in this order: (1) *Kether* (crown); (2) *Chochma* (wisdom); (3) *Beena* (understanding); (4) *Chesed* (grace), or *Ghedulla* (greatness); (5) *Ghevoora* (dignity); (6) *Tifereth* (splendor); (7) *Nezach* (victory); (8) *Hod* (majesty); (9) *Yesod* (principle); (10) *Malchuth* (kingdom). From this first world of the *Azila* emanate the three other worlds, *Asiya* being the lowest stage. Man has part in these three worlds; a microcosm, he realizes in his actual being what is foreshadowed by the ideal, primitive man. He holds to the *Asiya* by his vital part (*Nefesh*), to the *Yezira* by his intellect (*Ruach*), to the *Beria* by his soul (*Neshama*). The last is his immortal part, a spark of divinity.

Speculations like these, followed to their logical issue, are bound to lead the investigator out of Judaism into Trinitarianism or Pantheism. Kabbalists, of course only in rare cases, realized the danger. The sad conditions prevailing in the era after the expulsion from Spain, a third exile, were in all respects calculated to promote the development of mysticism, and it did flourish luxuriantly.

Some few philosophers, the last of a long line, still await mention: Levi ben Gerson, Joseph Kaspi, Moses of Narbonne in southern France, long a seat of Jewish learning; then, Isaac ben Sheshet, Chasdaï Crescas, whose "Light of God" exercised deep influence upon Spinoza and his philosophy; the Duran family, particularly Profiat Duran, successful defender of Judaism against the attacks of apostates and Christians; and Joseph Albo, who in his principal philosophic work, *Ikkarim*, shows Judaism to be based upon three fundamental doctrines: the belief in the existence of God, Revelation, and the belief in future reward and punishment. These writers are the last to reflect the glories of the golden age.

At the entrance to the next period we again meet a man of extraordinary ability, Isaac Abrabanel, one of the most eminent and esteemed of Bible commentators, in early life minister to a Catholic king, later a pilgrim scholar wandering about exiled with his sons, one of whom, Yehuda, has fame as the author of the *Dialoghi di Amore*. In the train of exiles passing from Portugal to the Orient are Abraham Zacuto, an eminent historian of Jewish literature and sometime professor of astronomy at the University of Salamanca; Joseph ibn Verga, the historian of his nation; Amatus Lusitanus, who came close upon the discovery of the circulation of the blood; Israel Nagara, the most gifted poet of the century, whose hymns brought him popular favor; later, Joseph Karo, "the most influential personage of the sixteenth century," his claims upon recognition resting on the *Shulchan Aruch,* an exhaustive codex of Jewish customs and laws; and many others. In Salonica, the exiles soon formed a prosperous community, where flourished Jacob ibn Chabib, the first compiler of the Haggadistic tales of the Talmud, and afterward David Conforte, a reputable historian. In Jerusalem, Obadiah Bertinoro was engaged on his celebrated Mishna commentary, in the midst of a large circle of Kabbalists, of whom Solomon Alkabez is the best known on account of his famous Sabbath song, *Lecho Dodi*. Once again Jerusalem was the objective point of many pilgrims, lured thither by the prevalent Kabbalistic and Messianic vagaries. True literature gained little from such extremists. The only work produced by them that can be admitted to have literary qualities is Isaiah Hurwitz's "The Two Tables of the Testimony." It is a sort of cyclopedia of Jewish learning, compiled and expounded from a mystic's point of view.

The condition of the Jews in Italy was favorable, and their literary products derive grace from their good fortune. The Renaissance had a benign effect upon them, and the revival of classical studies influenced their intellectual work. Greek thought met Jewish a third time. Learning was enjoying its resurrection, and whenever their wretched political and social condition was not a hindrance, the Jews joined in the general delight. Their misery, however, was an undiminishing burden, yea, even in the days in which, according to Erasmus, it was joy to live. In fact, it was growing heavier. All the more noteworthy is it that Hebrew studies engaged the research of scholars, albeit they showed care for the word of God, and not for His people. Pico della Mirandola studies the Kabbala; the Jewish grammarian Elias Levita is the teacher of Cardinal Egidio de Viterbo, and later of Paul Fagius and Sebastian Münster, the latter translating his teacher's works into Latin; popes and sultans prefer Jews as their physicians in ordinary, who, as a rule, are men of literary distinction; the Jews translate philosophic writings from Hebrew and Arabic into Latin; Elias del Medigo is summoned as arbiter in the scholastic conflict at the University of Padua, all to no avail; ruin is not averted. Reuchlin may protest as he will, the Jew is exiled, the Talmud burnt.

In such dreary days the Portuguese Samuel Usque writes his work *Consolaçam as Tribulações de Ysrael*, and Joseph Cohen, his chronicle "The Vale of Weeping," the most important history produced since the day of Flavius Josephus—additional proofs that the race possesses native buoyancy, and undaunted heroism in enduring suffering. Women, too, in increasing number, participate in the spiritual work of their nation, among them Deborah Ascarelli and Sara Copia Sullam, the most distinguished of a long array of names.

The keen critic and scholar Azariah de Rossi is one of the literary giants of his period. His researches in the history of Jewish literature are the basis upon which subsequent work in this department rests, and many of his conclusions still stand unassailable. About him are grouped Abraham de Portaleone, an excellent archaeologist, who established that Jews had been the first to observe the medicinal uses of gold; David de Pomis, the author of a famous defense of Jewish physicians; and Leo de Modena, the rabbi of Venice, "unstable as water," wavering between faith and unbelief, and, Kabbalist and rabbi though he was, writing works against the Kabbala on the one hand and against rabbinical tradition on the other. Similar to him in character is Joseph del Medigo, an itinerant author who sometimes reviles and sometimes extols the Kabbala.

There are men of higher calibre, as, for instance, Isaac Aboab, whose *Nomologia* undertakes to defend Jewish tradition against every sort of assailant; Samuel Aboab, a great Bible scholar; Azariah Figo, a famous preacher; and, above all, Moses Chayyim Luzzatto, the first Jewish dramatist, the dramas preceding his having interest only as attempts. He, too, is caught in the meshes of the Kabbala, and falls a victim to its powers of darkness. His dramas testify to poetic gifts and to extraordinary mastery of the Hebrew language, the faithful companion of the Jewish nation in all its journeyings. To complete this sketch of the Italian Jews of that period, it should be added that while in intellect and attainments they stand above their brethren in faith of other countries, in character and purity of morals they are their inferiors.

Thereafter literary interest centers in Poland, where rabbinical literature found its most zealous and most learned exponents. Throughout the land schools were established, in which the Talmud was taught by the *Pilpul*, an ingenious, quibbling method of Talmudic reasoning and discussion, said to have originated with Jacob Pollak. Again we have a long succession of distinguished names. There are Solomon Luria, Moses Isserles, Joel Sirkes, David ben Levi, Sabbataï Kohen, and Elias Wilna. Sabbataï Kohen, from whom, were pride of ancestry permissible in the republic of letters, the present writer would boast descent, was not only a Talmudic writer; he also left historical and poetical works. Elias Wilna, the last in the list, had a subtle, delicately poised mind, and deserves special mention for his determined opposition to the Kabbala and its offspring Chassidism, hostile and ruinous to Judaism and Jewish learning.

A gleam of true pleasure can be obtained from the history of the Dutch Jews. In Holland the Jews united secular culture with religious devotion, and the professors of other faiths met them with tolerance and friendliness. Sunshine falls upon the Jewish schools, and right into the heart of a youth who straightway abandons the Talmud folios and goes out into the world to proclaim to wondering mankind the evangel of a new philosophy. The youth is Baruch Spinoza!

There are many left to expound Judaism: Manasseh ben Israel, writing both Hebrew and Latin books to plead the cause of the emancipation of his people and of its literary preeminence; David Neto, a student of philosophy; Benjamin Mussafia; Orobio de Castro; David Abenator Melo, the Spanish translator of the Psalms; and Daniel de Barrios, poet and critic—all using their rapidly acquired fluency in the Dutch language to champion the cause of their people.

In Germany, a mixture of German and Hebrew had come into use among the Jews as the medium of daily intercourse. In this peculiar patois, called *Judendeutsch*, a large literature had developed. Before Luther's time, it possessed two fine translations of the Bible, besides numerous writings of an ethical, poetical, and historical character, among which particular mention should be made of those on the German legend-cycles of the Middle Ages. At the same time, the Talmud receives its due of time, effort, and talent. New life comes only with the era of emancipation and enlightenment.

Only a few names shall be mentioned; the rest would be bound soon to escape the memory of the casual reader: there is a historian, David Gans; a bibliographer, Sabbataï Bassista; and the Talmudists Abigedor Kara, Jacob Joshua, Jacob Emden, Jonathan Eibeschütz, and Ezekiel Landau. It is delight to be able once again to chronicle the interest taken in long neglected Jewish literature by such Christian scholars as the two Buxtorfs, Bartolocci, Wolff, Surrenhuys, and De Rossi. Unfortunately, the interest dies out with them, and it is significant that to this day most eminent theologians, decidedly to their own disadvantage, content themselves with unreliable secondary sources, instead of drinking from the fountain itself.

We have arrived at the sixth and last period, our own, not yet completed, whose fruits will be judged by a future generation. It is the period of the rejuvenescence of Jewish literature. Changes in character, tenor, form, and language take place. Germany for the first time is in the van, and Mendelssohn, its most attractive figure, stands at the beginning of the period, surrounded by his disciples Wessely, Homberg, Euchel, Friedländer, and others, in conjunction with whom he gives Jews a new, pure German Bible translation. Poetry and philology are zealously pursued, and soon Jewish science, through its votaries Leopold Zunz and S. J. Rappaport, celebrates a brilliant renascence, such as the poet describes: "In the distant East the dawn is breaking," The olden times are growing young again.

Die Gottesdienstlichen Vorträge der Juden, by Zunz, published in 1832, was the pioneer work of the new Jewish science, whose present development, despite its wide range, has not yet exhausted the suggestions made by the author. Other equally important works from the same pen followed, and then came the researches of Rappaport, Z. Frankel, I. M. Jost, M. Sachs, S. D. Luzzatto, S. Munk, A. Geiger, L. Herzfeld, H. Graetz, J. Fürst, L. Dukes, M. Steinschneider, D. Cassel, S. Holdheim, and a host of minor investigators and teachers. Their loving devotion roused Jewish science and literature from their secular sleep to vigorous, intellectual life, reacting beneficently on the spiritual development of Judaism itself. The molders of the new literature are such men as the celebrated preachers Adolf Jellinek, Salomon, Kley, and Mannheimer; the able thinkers Steinheim, Hirsch, and Krochmal; the illustrious scholars M. Lazarus and H. Steinthal; and the versatile journalists G. Riesser and L. Philipson.

Poetry has not been neglected in the general revival. The first Jewish poet to write in German was M. E. Kuh, whose tragic fate has been pathetically told by Berthold Auerbach in his *Dichter und Kaufmann.* The burden of this modern

Jewish poetry is, of course, the glorification of the loyalty and fortitude that preserved the race during a calamitous past. Such poets as Steinheim, Wihl, L. A. Frankl, M. Beer, K. Beck, Th. Creizenach, M. Hartmann, S. H. Mosenthal, Henriette Ottenheimer, Moritz Rappaport, and L. Stein sing the songs of Zion in the tongue of the German. And can Heine be forgotten, he who in his *Romanzero* has so melodiously, yet so touchingly, given word to the hoary sorrow of the Jew?

In an essay of this scope no more can be done than give the barest outline of the modern movement. A detailed description of the work of German-Jewish lyrists belongs to the history of German literature, and, in fact, on its pages can be found a due appreciation of their worth by unprejudiced critics, who give particularly high praise to the new species of tales, the Jewish village, or Ghetto, tales, with which Jewish and German literatures have latterly been enriched. Their object is to depict the religious customs in vogue among Jews of past generations, their home life, and the conflicts that arose when the old Judaism came into contact with modern views of life. The master in the art of telling these Ghetto tales is Leopold Kompert. Of his disciples for all coming after him may be considered such A. Bernstein described the Jews of Posen; K. E. Franzos and L. Herzberg-Fränkel, those of Poland; E. Kulke, the Moravian Jews; M. Goldschmied, the Dutch; S. H. Mosenthal, the Hessian; and M. Lehmann, the southern German. To Berthold Auerbach's pioneer work this whole class of literature owes its existence, and Heinrich Heine's fragment, *Rabbi von Bacharach*, a model of its kind, puts him into this category of writers, too.

And so Judaism and Jewish literature are stepping into a new arena, on which potent forces that may radically affect both are struggling with each other. Is Jewish poetry on the point of dying out, or is it destined to enjoy a resurrection? Who would be rash enough to prophesy aught of a race whose entire past is a riddle, whose literature is a question mark? Of a race which for more than a thousand years has, like its progenitor, been wrestling victoriously with gods and men?

To recapitulate: We have followed out the course of a literary development, beginning in grey antiquity with biblical narratives, assimilating Persian doctrines, Greek wisdom, and Roman law; later, Arabic poetry and philosophy; and, finally, the whole of European science in all its ramifications. The literature we have described has contributed its share to every spiritual result achieved by humanity, and is a still unexplored treasury of poetry and philosophy, of experience and knowledge.

"All the rivers run into the sea; yet the sea is never full," saith the Preacher; so all spiritual currents flow together into the vast ocean of a world literature, never full, never complete, rejoicing in every accession, reaching the climax of its might and majesty on that day when, according to the prophet, "the earth shall be full of the knowledge of the Lord, as the waters cover the sea."

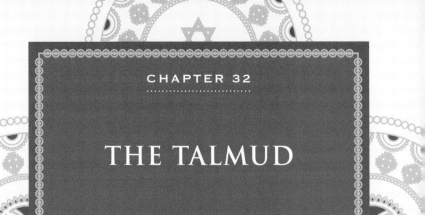

CHAPTER 32

THE TALMUD

In the whole range of the world's literatures there are few books with so checkered a career, so curious a fate, as the Talmud has had. The name is simple enough, it glides glibly from the tongue, yet how difficult to explain its import to the uninitiated! From the Dominican Henricus Seynensis, who took "Talmud" to be the name of a rabbi— he introduces a quotation with *Ut narrat rabbinus Talmud*, "As Rabbi Talmud Relates"—down to the church historians and university professors of our day, the oddest misconceptions on the nature of the Talmud have prevailed even among learned men. It is not astonishing, then, that the general reader has no notion of what it is.

Only within recent years the Talmud has been made the subject of scientific study, and now it is consulted by philologists, cited by jurists, and drawn upon by historians; the general public is beginning to be interested in it; and of late the old Talmud has repeatedly been summoned to appear in courts of law to give evidence. Under these circumstances it is natural to ask, what is the Talmud? It is futile to seek an answer by comparing this gigantic monument of the human intellect with any other book; it is *sui generis*. In the form in which it issued from the Jewish academies of Babylonia and Palestine, it is a great national work, a scientific document of first importance, the archives of ten centuries, in which are preserved the thoughts and opinions, the views and verdicts, the errors, transgressions, hopes, disappointments, customs, ideals, convictions, and sorrows of Israel—a work produced by the zeal and patience of thirty generations, laboring with a self-denial unparalleled in the history of literature. A work of this character assuredly deserves to be known. Unfortunately, the path to its understanding is blocked by peculiar linguistic and historical difficulties. Above all, explanations by comparison must be avoided. It has been likened to a legal code, to a journal, to the transactions of learned bodies, but these comparisons are both inadequate and misleading. To make it approximately clear a lengthy explanation must be entered upon, for, in truth, the Talmud, like the Bible, is a world in miniature, embracing every possible phase of life.

The origin of the Talmud was simultaneous with Israel's return from the Babylonian exile, during which a wonderful change had taken place in the captive people. An idolatrous, rebellious nation had turned into a pious congregation of the Lord, possessed with zeal for the study of the Law. By degrees there grew up out of this study a science of wide scope, whose beginnings are hidden in the last book of the Bible, in the word *Midrash*, translated by "story" in the authorized version. Its true meaning is indicated by that of its root, *darash*, "to study, to expound." Four different methods of explaining the sacred scriptures were current: the first aimed to reach the simple understanding of words as they stood; the second availed itself of suggestions offered by apparently superfluous letters and signs in the text to arrive at its meaning; the third was "a homiletic application of that which had been to that which was and would be, of prophetical and historical dicta to the actual condition of things"; and the fourth devoted itself to theosophic mysteries—but all led to a common goal.

In the course of the centuries the development of the Midrash, or study of the Law, lay along the two strongly marked lines of Halacha, the explanation and formulating of laws, and Haggada, their poetical illustration and ethical application. These are the two spheres within which the intellectual life of Judaism revolved, and these two elements, the legal and the aesthetic, make up the Talmud.

The two Midrashic systems emphasize respectively the rule of law and the sway of liberty: Halacha is law incarnate; Haggada, liberty regulated by law and bearing the impress of morality. Halacha stands for the rigid authority of the Law, for the absolute importance of theory—the law and theory the Haggada illustrates by public opinion and the dicta of commonsense morality. The Halacha embraces the statutes enjoined by oral tradition, which was the unwritten commentary of the ages on the written Law, along with the discussions of the academies of Palestine and Babylonia, resulting in the final formulating of the Halachic ordinances. The Haggada, while also starting from the word of the Bible, only plays with it, explaining it by sagas and legends, by tales and poems, allegories, ethical reflections, and historical reminiscences. For it, the Bible was not only the supreme law, from whose behests there was no appeal, but also "a golden nail upon which" the Haggada "hung its gorgeous tapestries," so that the Bible word was the introduction, refrain, text, and subject of the poetical glosses of the Talmud. It was the province of the Halacha to build, upon the foundation of biblical law, a legal superstructure capable of resisting the ravages of time, and, unmindful of contemporaneous distress and hardship, to trace out, for future generations, the extreme logical consequences of the Law in its application. To the Haggada belonged the high, ethical mission of consoling, edifying, exhorting, and teaching a nation suffering the pangs, and threatened with the spiritual stagnation, of exile; of proclaiming that the glories of the past prefigured a future of equal brilliancy and that the very wretchedness of the present was part of the divine plan outlined in the Bible. If the simile is accurate that likens the Halacha to the ramparts about Israel's sanctuary, which every Jew was ready to defend with his last drop of blood, then the Haggada must seem "flowery mazes, of exotic colors and bewildering fragrance," within the shelter of the Temple walls.

The complete work of expounding, developing, and finally establishing the Law represents the labor of many generations, the method of procedure varying from time to time. In the long interval between the close of the Holy Canon and the completion of the Talmud can be distinguished three historical strata deposited by three different classes of teachers. The first set, the Scribes—*Soferim*—flourished in the period beginning with the return from Babylonian captivity and ending with the Syrian persecutions (220 B.C.), and their work was the preservation of the text of the Holy Writings and the simple expounding of biblical ordinances. They were followed by the Learners—*Tanaïm*—whose activity extended until A.D. 220. Great historical events occurred in that period: the campaigns of the Maccabean heroes, the birth of Jesus, the destruction of the Temple by the Romans, the rebellion under Bar-Kochba, and the final complete dispersion of the Jews. Amid all these storms the *Tanaïm* did not for a moment relinquish their diligent research in the Law. The Talmud tells the story of a celebrated rabbi, than which nothing can better characterize the age and its scholars. Night was falling. A funeral cortege was moving through the streets of old Jerusalem. It was said that disciples were bearing a well-beloved teacher to the grave. Reverentially the way was cleared, not even the Roman guard at the gate hindered the procession. Beyond the city walls it halted, the bier was set down, the lid of the coffin opened, and out of it arose the venerable form of Rabbi Jochanan ben Zakkaï, who, to reach the Roman camp unmolested, had feigned death. He went before Vespasian, and, impressed by the noble figure of the hoary rabbi, the general promised him the fulfilment of any wish he might express. What was his petition? Not for his nation, not for the preservation of the Holy City, not even for the Temple. His request was simple: "Permit me to open a school at Jabneh." The proud Roman smilingly gave consent. He had no conception of the significance of this prayer and of the prophetic wisdom of the petitioner, who, standing on the ruins of his nation's independence, thought only of rescuing the Law. Rome, the empire of the "iron legs," was doomed to be crushed, nation after nation to be swallowed in the vortex of time, but Israel lives by the Law, the very law snatched from the smoldering ruins of Jerusalem, the beloved alike of crazy zealots and despairing peace advocates, and carried to the tiny seaport of Jabneh. There Jochanan ben Zakkaï opened his academy, the gathering place of the dispersed of his disciples and his people, and thence, gifted with a prophet's keen vision, he proclaimed Israel's mission to be, not the offering of sacrifices, but the accomplishment of works of peace.

The *Tanaïm* may be considered the most original expounders of the science of Judaism, which they fostered at their academies. In the course of centuries their intellectual labor amassed an abundant store of scientific material, together with so vast a number of injunctions, prohibitions, and laws that it became almost impossible to master the subject. The task of scholars now was to arrange the accumulation of material and reduce it to a system. Rabbi after rabbi undertook the task, but only the fourth attempt at codification, that made by Yehuda the Prince, was successful. His compilation, classifying the subject matter under six heads, subdivided into sixty-three tractates, containing 524 chapters, was called Mishna, and came to be the authority appealed to on points of law.

Having assumed fixity as a code, the Mishna in turn became what the Bible had been for centuries—a text, the basis of all legal development and scientific discussion. So it was used by the epigones, the *Amoraïm*, or Speakers, the expounders of the third period. For generations commenting on the Mishna was the sum total of literary endeavor. Traditions unheeded before sprang to light. New methods asserted themselves. To the older generation of Halachists succeeded a set of men headed by Akiba ben Joseph, who, ignoring practical issues, evolved laws from the Bible text or from traditions held to be divine. A spiritual, truly religious conception of Judaism was supplanted by legal quibbling and subtle methods of interpretation. Like the sophists of Rome and Alexandria at that time, the most celebrated teachers in the academies of Babylonia and Palestine for centuries gave themselves up to casuistry. This is the history of the development of the Talmud, or more correctly of the two Talmuds, the one finished in A.D. 390 being the expression of what was taught at the Palestinian academies, and the other, more important one, completed in A.D. 500 of what was taught in Babylonia.

The Babylonian, the one regarded as authoritative, is about four times as large as the Jerusalem Talmud. Its thirty-six treatises (*Massichtoth*), in our present edition, cover upward of three thousand folio pages, bound in twelve huge volumes. To speak of a completed Talmud is as incorrect as to speak of a biblical canon. No religious body, no solemn resolution of a synod, ever declared either the Talmud or the Bible a completed whole. Canonizing of any kind is distinctly opposed to the spirit of Judaism. The fact is that the tide of traditional lore has never ceased to flow.

We now have before us a faint outline sketch of the growth of the Talmud. To portray the busy world fitting into this frame is another and more difficult matter. A catalogue of its contents may be made. It may be said that it is a book containing laws and discussions, philosophic, theologic, and juridic dicta, historical notes and national reminiscences, injunctions and prohibitions controlling all the positions and relations of life, curious, quaint tales, ideal maxims and proverbs, uplifting legends, charming lyrical outbursts, and attractive enigmas side by side with misanthropic utterances, bewildering medical prescriptions, superstitious practices, expressions of deep agony, peculiar astrological charms, and rambling digressions on law, zoology, and botany, and when all this has been said, not half its contents have been told. It is a luxuriant jungle, which must be explored by him who would gain an adequate idea of its features and products.

The Ghemara, that is, the whole body of discussions recorded in the two Talmuds, primarily forms a running commentary on the text of the Mishna. At the same time, it is the arena for the debating and investigating of subjects growing out of the Mishna, or suggested by a literature developed along with the Talmudic literature. These discussions, debates, and investigations are the opinions and arguments of the different schools, holding opposite views, developed with rare acumen and scholastic subtlety, and finally harmonized in the solution reached. The one firm and impregnable rock supporting the gigantic structure of the Talmud is the word of the Bible, held sacred and inviolable.

The best translations—single treatises have been put into modern languages—fail to convey an adequate idea of the discussions and method that evolved the Halacha. It is easier to give an approximately true presentation of the rabbinical system of practical morality as gleaned from the Haggada. It must, of course, be borne in mind that Halacha and Haggada are not separate works; they are two fibers of the same thread. "The whole of the Haggadistic literature—the hitherto unappreciated archives of language, history, archaeology, religion, poetry, and science—with but slight reservations may be called a national literature, containing as it does the aggregate of the views and opinions of thousands of thinkers belonging to widely separated generations. Largely, of course, these views and opinions are peculiar to the individuals holding them or to their time"; still, every Haggadistic expression, in a general way, illustrates some fundamental, national law, based upon the national religion and the national history. Through the Haggada we are vouchsafed a glance into a mysterious world, which mayhap has hitherto repelled us as strange and gruesome. Its poesy reveals vistas of gleaming beauty and light, luxuriant growth and exuberant life, while familiar melodies caress our ears.

The Haggada conveys its poetic message in the garb of allegory song, and chiefly epigrammatic saying. Form is disregarded; the spirit is all-important, and suffices to cover up every fault of form. The Talmud, of course, does not yield a complete system of ethics, but its practical philosophy consists of doctrines that underlie a moral life. The injustice of the abuse heaped upon it would become apparent to its harshest critics from a few of its maxims and rules of conduct, such as the following:

> Be of them that are persecuted, not of the persecutors.

> Be the cursed, not he that curses.

> They that are persecuted, and do not persecute, that are vilified and do not retort, that act in love, and are cheerful even in suffering, they are the lovers of God.

> Bless God for the good as well as the evil. When thou hearest of a death, say, "Blessed be the righteous Judge."

> Life is like unto a fleeting shadow. Is it the shadow of a tower or of a bird? It is the shadow of a bird

in its flight. Away flies the bird, and neither bird nor shadow remains behind.

Repentance and good works are the aim of all earthly wisdom.

Even the just will not have so high a place in heaven as the truly repentant.

He whose learning surpasses his good works is like a tree with many branches and few roots, which a windstorm uproots and casts to the ground. But he whose good works surpass his learning is like a tree with few branches and many roots; all the winds of heaven cannot move it from its place.

There are three crowns: the crown of the Law, the crown of the priesthood, the crown of kingship. But greater than all is the crown of a good name.

Four there are that cannot enter Paradise: the scoffer, the liar, the hypocrite, and the backbiter.

Beat the gods, and the priests will tremble.

Contrition is better than many flagellations.

When the pitcher falls upon the stone, woe unto the pitcher; when the stone falls upon the pitcher, woe unto the pitcher; whatever betides, woe unto the pitcher.

The place does not honor the man, the man honors the place.

He who humbles himself will be exalted; he who exalts himself will be humbled.

Whosoever pursues greatness, from him will greatness flee; whosoever flees from greatness, him will greatness pursue.

Charity is as important as all other virtues combined.

Be tender and yielding like a reed, not hard and proud like a cedar.

The hypocrite will not see God.

It is not sufficient to be innocent before God; we must show our innocence to the world.

The works encouraged by a good man are better than those he executes.

Woe unto him that practices usury, he shall not live; whithersoever he goes, he carries injustice and death.

The same Talmud that fills chapter after chapter with minute legal details and hairsplitting debates outlines with a few strokes the most ideal conception of life, worth more than theories and systems of religious philosophy. A Haggada passage says 613 injunctions were given by Moses to the people of Israel. David reduced them to eleven; the prophet Isaiah classified these under six heads; Micah enumerated only three: "What doth the Lord require of thee, but to do justly, and to love mercy, and to walk humbly with thy God." Another prophet limited them to two: "Keep ye judgment, and do righteousness." Amos put all the commandments under one: "Seek ye me, and ye shall live"; and Habakkuk said: "The just shall live by his faith." This is the ethics of the Talmud.

Another characteristic manifestation of the idealism of the Talmud is its delicate feeling for women and children. Almost extravagant affection is displayed for the little ones. All the verses of scripture that speak of flowers and gardens are applied in the Talmud to children and schools. Their breath sustains the moral order of the universe: "Out of the mouth of babes and sucklings has God founded His might." They are called flowers, stars, the anointed of God. When God was about to give the Law, He demanded of the Israelites pledges to assure Him that they would keep His commandments holy. They offered the patriarchs, but each one of them had committed some sin. They named Moses as their surety; not even he was guiltless. Then they said: "Let our children be our hostages." The Lord accepted them.

Similarly, there are many expressions to show that woman was held in high esteem by the rabbis of the Talmud:

Love thy wife as thyself; honor her more than thyself.

In choosing a wife, descend a step.

If thy wife is small, bend and whisper into her ear.

God's altar weeps for him that forsakes the love of his youth.

He who sees his wife die before him has, as it were, been present at the destruction of the sanctuary itself; around him the world grows dark.

It is woman alone through whom God's blessings are vouchsafed to a house.

The children of him that marries for money shall be a curse unto him.

this latter a warning singularly applicable to the circumstances of our own times.

The peculiar charm of the Haggada is best revealed in its legends and tales, its fables and myths, its apologues and allegories, its riddles and songs. The starting point of the Haggada usually is some memory of the great past. It entwines and enmeshes in a magic network the lives of the patriarchs, prophets, and martyrs, and clothes with fresh, luxuriant green the old ideals and figures, giving them new life for a remote generation. The teachers of the Haggada allow no opportunity, sad or merry, to pass without utilizing it in the guise of an apologue or parable. Alike for wedding feasts and funerals, for banquets and days of fasting, the garden of the Haggada is rifled of its fragrant blossoms and luscious fruits. Simplicity, grace, and childlike merriment pervade its fables, yet they are profound, even sublime, in their truth. "Their chief and enduring charm

is their fathomless depth, their unassuming loveliness."
Poems constructed with great artistic skill do not occur.
Here and there a modest bud of lyric poesy shyly raises its
head, like the following couplet, describing a celebrated but
ill-favored rabbi:

> *Without charm of form and face.*
> *But a mind of rarest grace."*

Poets naturally have not been slow to avail themselves
of the material stored in the Haggada. Many of its treasures, tricked out in modern verse, have been given to the
world. The following is a sample:

BIRTH AND DEATH

> *His hands fast clenched, his fingers firmly clasped,*
> *So man this life begins.*
> *He claims earth's wealth, and constitutes himself*
> *The heir of all her gifts.*
> *He thinks his hand may snatch and hold*
> *Whatever life doth yield.*

That is a glimpse of the world of the Haggada—a
wonderful, fantastic world, a kaleidoscopic panorama of
enchanting views.

Well can we understand the distress of
mind in a mediaeval divine, or even in a modern savant, who, bent upon following the most

subtle windings of some scientific debate in
the Talmudical pages—geometrical, botanical,
financial, or otherwise—as it revolves round the
Sabbath journey, the raising of seeds, the com-
putation of tithes and taxes—feels, as it were,
the ground suddenly give way. The loud voices
grow thin, the doors and walls of the school-
room vanish before his eyes, and in their place
uprises Rome the Great, the Urbs et Orbis and
her million-voiced life. Or the blooming vineyards round that other City of Hills, Jerusalem
the Golden herself, are seen, and white-clad
virgins move dreamily among them. Snatches of
their songs are heard, the rhythm of their choric
dances rises and falls: it is the most dread Day
of Atonement itself, which, in poetical contrast,
was chosen by the "Rose of Sharon" as a day of
rejoicing to walk among those waving lily-fields
and vine-clad slopes. Or the clarion of rebellion
rings high and shrill through the complicated
debate, and Belshazzar, the story of whose ghastly
banquet is told with all the additions of madden-
ing horror, is doing service for Nero the bloody;
or Nebuchadnezzar, the Babylonian tyrant, and
all his hosts, are cursed with a yelling curse—à
propos of some utterly inappropriate legal point,
while to the initiated he stands for Titus the "at
last exploded" "Delight of Humanity." . . . Often,

far too often for the interests of study and the glory of the human race, does the steady tramp of the Roman cohort, the password of the revolution, the shriek and clangor of the bloody field, interrupt these debates, and the arguing masters and disciples don their arms, and, with the cry, "Jerusalem and Liberty," rush to the fray.

Such is the world of the Talmud.

INDEX

A

Acrostic form, 19, 20, 151
Afterlife, 80–81, 88–89, 92, 191,
    222, 233, 242
Alexander the Great, 130, 139–141,
    143–144, 163, 190–191
Alexandra, Queen, 237–238
Amos, 41, 46, 66, 111, 269, 271, 329
Antigonus, 143, 249–250, 251
Antiochus, Epiphanes, 146, 182,
    183–185, 186–187, 189, 195, 227
Antipater, 217, 245, 247–250, 252
Antony, 249, 250, 254
Aristobulus, 219, 238–239, 240,
    246, 247
Augustus, 254, 255, 259

B

Babylon, 30–38, 39–41, 47–48,
    49–51, 54–56
Balas, Alexander, 206–207, 208
Ben Sira, 109, 157, 166, 168–176,
    220

C

Christianity, 47, 100, 225, 270–271,
    272–273, 281
Chronicles, 36, 52, 53, 54, 118, 179
Cyrus, King, 48–51, 54, 56–57, 71

D

Daniel, Book of, 161, 163, 184,
    189–190, 233, 268, 270
Darius, 56–57, 59, 65, 68

E

Ecclesiastes, Book of, 151, 165–166,
    167, 169, 171, 232
Education, 155–156, 183, 237,
    311–312, 322
Egypt
    Jewish literature in, 39, 287
    Jewish temple in, 59
    Jews in, 23–25, 27–29, 141–142,
        144, 227–230, 287
        power struggle in, 142–144
        wise men of, 151
Elephantine, 25–29, 59
Essenes, 137, 221, 224–225, 270
Esther, Book of, 166, 177, 201–202
Ezekiel, 21, 22, 24, 30–38, 41
Ezra, 52, 54–55, 58, 112, 116–118,
    120

F

Feast of Lights, 197

G

Gedaliah, 18, 23, 66, 196
God. *See* Jehovah

H

Hellenism, 139–141, 153, 160, 172,
    179–185, 224, 286
Herod, 248–258, 259–264
Holiness Code, 42–45, 120
Hyrcanus, John, 178, 211, 215–219,
    238–240, 246–251

I

Isaiah
    addressing Jerusalem, 69, 70–71
    Babylon and, 49
    predicting national destruction,
        41
    psalms of, 72–74
    reforms and, 110, 111, 271
    serving Jehovah and, 93, 100, 162

social principles and, 46
Talmud and, 328
Israel. *See* Jerusalem/Palestine/Israel

J
Janneus, Alexander, 235–237
Jehoiachin, 20, 45–46
Jehovah
destroying enemies, 35, 128
displeased with Jews, 57, 79
Job and, 82–92
kingdom of, 190–191
protecting Jews, 62–63, 81, 163
restoring homeland, 34–36
restoring temple, 57–58
serving, 93–100, 162
training Jews, 73–75, 78, 96–98
Zechariah's impression of, 60–61
Jeremiah, 19–21, 25, 34, 41, 49,
99–100, 152
Jerusalem/Palestine/Israel
apocalyptic messianic hope of,
269–271
defeating Samarit Príbor ans, 217
destruction of, 17
Essenes in. *See* Essenes
ethical messianic hope of,
271–272
exiles returning to, 51, 54–55
Herod and, 248–258, 259–264
Hyrcanus leading, 215–219
Jewish life in, 172–173
legalists in, 161–162
nationalistic messianic hope of,
267–269
Nehemiah rebuilding walls of,
101–109, 115
peace in, 124–125
politics in, 238. *See also* Pharisees;
Sadducees
priests ruling, 69
ritualists in, 160–161
Roman rule of, 239–241,

245–247, 248, 249
Syria ruling, 145–146
Jesus, 47, 100, 163, 225, 271, 273,
321
Job, 63, 80, 81, 82–92
Joel, 127–128, 163, 270
John the Baptist, 78, 225
Jonah, Book of, 163–165
Josephus
Antiquities of the Jews and, 221,
247
Greek translations and, 224, 228
history of, 137–139
Pharisees/Sadducees and, 218,
221, 223
temple and, 260, 263
wealth of, 144–145
Josephus, Flavius, 283, 288, 310
Joshua, 62–64, 129, 169, 288, 313

K
Koheleth, 165, 166–167

L
Lamentations, Book of, 18–21
Law, Jewish
authority of, 129
effects of, 122–123
Holiness Code and, 42–43
Midrash and, 288, 290–291, 319
origin of, 120–121
Pharisees interpreting, 222
purpose of, 121–122
violations of, 111
Literature, Jewish. *See also* Talmud
in Babylon, 39–41
Europe and, 293, 304, 311–314
exile/journey stories in, 303–304
Greek translations of, 228–230,
286–287
Haggada/Halacha in, 288,
290–291, 299, 319–320, 325
on history, 293–294

Italy influencing, 309–310
Judeo-Alexandrian, 287
Kabbala and, 211, 306–307
mysticism and, 305
Pentateuch and, 283
philosophy and, 293, 307–308
poetry in, 294–302, 314–315. *See also* Psalter
scholars of, 283–284, 307–309, 310–315

M

Maccabean revolt, 177–185, 187, 188, 192–206, 207–215, 241–242, 257
Malachi, 71, 76–77, 79, 81, 85, 201
Mattathias, 187–188, 209, 210, 215
Messiah, 64, 65, 71, 97, 265, 269–271
Messianic prophecies, 266–267

N

Nebuchadrezzar, 25, 31, 45, 57, 252, 332
Nehemiah, 52, 101–109, 110–112, 113, 114–115

P

Palestine. *See* Jerusalem/Palestine/Israel
Pharisees, 218, 220–223, 236–237, 238, 240, 257, 270
Priests, 37, 42, 76–77, 79, 116–117, 129–130, 263
Proverbs, Book of, 147–159
Psalter, 125–127, 162, 198, 212–213. *See also* Literature, Jewish, poetry in
Ptolemies, 142–144, 146, 227, 228

S

Sadducees, 221, 223–224, 238, 240, 257

Samaritans, 53, 55, 119, 121, 130–133, 217
Samuel, 40, 45, 53, 152, 177, 229
Satan, 63, 82, 84, 266
Septuagint, 228–230, 286
Sibylline Books, 231
Solomon, 28, 147–149, 152, 165, 231–232, 260

T

Talmud. *See also* Literature, Jewish
  Amoraïm and, 323
  Babylonian, 289, 324
  benefits of, 289–290
  contents of, 324–325
  Haggada/Halacha in, 319–320, 325–328, 330–333
  Midrash and, 319–320
  origin of, 318
  Soferim and, 286, 321–323
  Tanaïm and, 321–322
  time span of, 288
  women/children in-, 329–330
Temple
  in Egypt, 228
  Herod rebuilding, 259–264
  Jehovah and, 57–59
  Maccabeus restoring, 197
  offerings at, 22–23, 51, 113–114
  problems for, 61–62
  restoration of the, 36–38, 52–59

Y

Yahu Temple, 27–29

Z

Zechariah, 54, 55, 58, 60–67, 84, 190, 268
Zerubbabel, 51, 58, 62, 63–64, 65, 69, 97